Bedtime Meditation for Kids

This Book Includes: Bedtime Stories for Kids, Kids Sleep Meditation, Mindfulness Meditation for Kids.

LILLY ANDERSEN

Bedtime Stories for Kids

A Complete Collection of Meditation Stories, Fables and Fairy Tales to Help Children and Toddlers Fall Asleep Fast and Have a Peaceful Sleeping.

Kids Sleep Meditation

A Complete Collection of Stories to Help Children Reduce Stress and Anxiety, Learn Mindfulness Meditation and Go to Sleep Feeling Calm, Happy and Confident.

Mindfulness Meditation for Kids

A Complete Guide for Kids, with Daily Exercises to Relieve Stress, Anxiety, Build Responsibility and Promote Peacefulness and Positive Thinking.

Bedtime Stories for Kids

A Complete Collection of Meditation Stories, Fables and Fairy Tales to Help Children and Toddlers Fall Asleep Fast and Have a Peaceful Sleeping.

LILLY ANDERSEN

© **Copyright 2020 - All rights reserved.**

The content contained within this book may not be reproduced, duplicated or transmitted without direct written permission from the author or the publisher.

Under no circumstances will any blame or legal responsibility be held against the publisher, or author, for any damages, reparation, or monetary loss due to the information contained within this book. Either directly or indirectly.

Legal Notice:

This book is copyright protected. This book is only for personal use. You cannot amend, distribute, sell, use, quote or paraphrase any part, or the content within this book, without the consent of the author or publisher.

Disclaimer Notice:

Please note the information contained within this document is for educational and entertainment purposes only. All effort has been executed to present accurate, up to date, and reliable, complete information. No warranties of any kind are declared or implied. Readers acknowledge that the author is not engaging in the rendering of legal, financial, medical or professional advice. The content within this book has been derived from various sources. Please consult a licensed professional before attempting any techniques outlined in this book.

By reading this document, the reader agrees that under no circumstances is the author responsible for any losses, direct or indirect, which are incurred as a result of the use of information contained within this document, including, but not limited to, — errors, omissions, or inaccuracies.

Tables of Contents

Introduction.. 7

The Princess in The Flammenburg 10

Crime Fighters 14

Oscar Has Tea 20

The Long Neck who Told Tall Tales 29

Baggi's Unwanted Slide 61

The Night I Met a Ghost 69

Rexy and Friends 75

Scott and Nancy Learn to Get Along................. 110

Magic at the Magic Show................................. 127

Finishing the Witch's Brew............................... 134

Mouse of Doom 141

Neck Made for Dance 151

Grandpa Heinz and the mermaid...................... 161

Noah Rides an Airplane **171**

Conclusion **180**

Introduction

By reading to your child, you are creating memories that they will carry with them always. Stories like these may be used to enforce morality and enable that creativity that seems to come naturally to all children. Allow your children to explore the magic of other destinations from the comfort of your own home. In this book, we will be going inside the Fun mazing Circus to learn about many new friends.

These stories are centered on teaching strategies for problem solving and relaxation. Each chapter is an introduction to a character that includes a clear moral message or is designed to assist your child in falling asleep. Each tale will stress the importance of positive thinking, meditation, or breathe control. These narratives that you will spin to your little ones before they sleep, will provide a strong and lasting sense of value. Reading to your children can also serve to kick-start their imagination in a way that other electronic media will never be able to do. So, thank you again for taking a chance on us and using this book to shepherd your children toward making decisions that benefit both themselves and others.

While each story is unique, the underlying purpose of each remains the same—to confer to readers some degree of insight into moral behavior and proper conduct. Through the careful application of allegory, the stories contained herein are intended not only to engage and captivate but serve as thought-provoking tools by which your children might avail themselves of one of man mankind's most powerful attributes—thoughtfulness and self-reflection.

In addition, each story uses colorful and imaginative characters, settings and situations to create an environment which will not only help children to become interested in the story itself, but also serve as a vehicle to convey a moral teaching and lesson. Plus, the stories in this book seek to create traditions and memories which will create everlasting moments that your will children will treasure for the rest of their lives. These are the kinds of moments that your children will surely love to live with their children someday, too.

These stories can be read in any order you like, so please do feel free to skip around and choose which stories you think your child will like best for each night. Your child will be invited to kickstart the power of their imagination with a prompt to get into each meditation, and this will help to build a great foundation for a lifetime practice of meditation. The benefits of learning and using mindfulness meditation and relaxation techniques for everyone cannot be overstated. The following chart is just a few of the many behavioral, emotional, and physical benefits of employing mindfulness meditation and relaxation techniques.

The Princess in The Flammenburg

Once upon a time there was a poor man who had had as many children as holes in a sieve and all the people in his village as godparents. When he was again born a son, he sat down on the road to ask the first best to be godfather. Then an old man in a  gray cloak came to meet him, he asked, and he agreed and went to the baptism. As a baptismal gift, the old man gave the father a cow with a calf. That was born the same day as the boy and had a golden star on his forehead. The boy grew older and bigger and the calf also grew, became a big bull and the boy led him every day to the mountain meadow. But the bull was able to speak, and when they were on the top of the mountain, the bull spoke: "Stay here and sleep, I want to find my own willow!" As soon as the boy fell asleep, the bull ran like lightning on the big one Sky meadow and eats golden star flowers. When the sun went down, he hurried back, woke the boy, and then they went home. So, it happened every day until the boy was twenty years old. One day the bull spoke to him: "Now sit between my horns, I carry you to the king. Demand from him a seven-meter-long iron sword and tell him that you want to save his daughter. " Soon they arrived at the castle. The boy dismounted, went to the king and said why he had come. He gladly gave the shepherd boy the required sword. But he had no hope of ever seeing his daughter again. Already many brave youths had tried in vain to rescue them, because a twelve-headed dragon had kidnapped them, and this lived far away, where nobody could get to. First, there was a high, insurmountable mountain on the way there, secondly, a wide and stormy sea, and third, the dragon lived in a castle of flame. If anyone had succeeded in crossing the mountains and the sea, he would not have been able to penetrate through the mighty flames, and if he had succeeded, the dragon would have killed him. When the boy had the sword, he sat down between the horns of the bull, and in no time, they were before the great mountain. "Now we have to turn back," he said to the bull, for it seemed impossible for him to get across. But the bull said: "Wait a minute!", Put the boy on the ground, and as soon as that happened, he took a start and pushed with his huge horns the whole mountain on the side. Now the bull again put the boy between the horns. They moved on and came to the sea. "Now we have to turn back!" Said the boy, "because no one can go over there!" "Wait a minute," said the bull, "and hold on to my horns." He bent his head to the water and soffit and soothed the whole sea, so that they moved on dry feet as in a meadow. Now they were soon at the Flammenburg. From afar, they were met with such a glow that the boy could not stand it anymore. "Stop!" He shouted to the bull, "no farther, or we'll have to burn." The bull, however, ran very close and poured the sea he had drunk into the flames, so that they soon extinguished and a more powerful one Smoke arose that darkened the whole sky. Then the twelve-headed dragon rushed out of the black clouds angrily. "Now it's up to you!" Cried the bull to the boy, "make sure you knock all the heads off the monster!" He took all his strength, grasping the mighty sword in both hands, and giving the dragon one like that quick blow that blew all heads off. But now the monster struck and curled on the earth, causing her to tremble. The bull took the dragon's trunk on its horns and hurled it so high up to the clouds, until no trace of it was to be seen. Then he spoke to the boy: "My service is now over. Now go to the castle, there you will find the princess and lead her home to her father! "With that he ran away to the sky meadow, and the boy did not see him again. He found the princess, and she was very glad that she was redeemed from the terrible dragon. They drove to their father, held a wedding, and it was a great joy throughout the kingdom.

Crime Fighters

Have you ever thought it would be cool to be a crime fighter? You know, to be a real-life hero? What if I told you that you could see what it was like to be a crime fighter right now, without having to move a single muscle? You really can- In your mind! Your mind  is capable of doing many incredible things, including something called Visualization.

To begin your visualization practice, close your eyes. Really, close your eyes (unless you are the one reading this, of course!) To build a very strong visualization, it is usually helpful to first center yourself and be sure you are giving your brain the very best tools it needs to work with. In this case, that means oxygen, and oxygen means taking some good, deep breaths.

You are going to take some slow, deep breaths now, following along with my instruction: Breathe in very slowly, 1 – 2 – 3 – 4. Now breathe out, very slowly, 1 – 2 – 3 – 4. Excellent. Now again very slowly, 1 – 2 – 3 – 4 and breathe back out very slowly, 1 – 2 – 3 – 4 very nice. Once more, very slowly in 1 – 2 – 3 – 4 and back out very slowly, 1 – 2 – 3 – 4. Great!

Take a moment to review how you feel. Are you comfy and feeling good? Okay, great.

Picture yourself, in your mind's eye, standing in a park. You are on a sidewalk beside a pond. It is early morning, and the wildlife here in the park is just waking up. You take a long, deep breath in and enjoy the fresh air as you watch as a mama duck leads her baby ducklings along behind her. They are waddling along the path on the opposite side of the pond as you watch as the little fluffy ducklings try and keep up with mama duck.

Suddenly a stiff breeze comes whistling through the trees, blowing the crisp fall leaves through the air. You pull your sweater tighter around yourself as you can feel that the fall weather is getting colder and colder, and it likely won't be too much longer before there is the first snowfall of winter.

You continue to stroll along the sidewalk, and you watch as the parks and recreation employees spread pine needles out around the smaller trees and shrubbery to keep their roots warm for the cold weather to come. You notice that one of the workers is mixing pine needles and hay into a wooden crate that is turned on its side. You wonder what it is for, so you head over to him and ask. He tells you that it will be a winter home for the mama duck and her baby ducklings and that they will place it over by the pond for them to have a place to warm up as it gets cold.

You love this, and you continue on your walk around the park, thinking how nice it will be for the mama duck and the baby ducklings to have a warm place for the winter. You listen to the songs of the last of the birds in the trees before they fly south for winter, and you enjoy the way the steady breeze blows the colorful autumn leaves through the air.

The park is beautiful this time of the year with the golden yellows and fiery reds of the falling trees dancing in the breeze, and you finally make your way back over to the opposite side of the pond and you see where the workers placed the crate for the mama duck and her baby ducklings. You smile again at the thought of the duck family having a nice place to keep warm this winter. You hear a scraping noise that you can't quite place and then you see something strange that stops you in your tracks. The crate is moving... by itself! You cautiously step towards it, trying to figure out how it is moving by itself! The ducks are swimming around in the pond, clueless that their winter home is being tampered with. You look around for the workers, but they have already finished and left. It is just you here.

Well, you will not let the ducks' winter home be taken by whoever is inside of that crate. That would be a crime! You are now finally close enough that you can peer inside the crate, and now you see a furry little black, white, and gray face peering back out of you. It's a raccoon!

What on earth is this raccoon trying to do? It looks like it is trying to push the crate into the forest, maybe as a home for itself? Well, that certainly will not do. A raccoon is perfectly capable of finding its own winter shelter, but this duck family is not. You grab a stick that is laying nearby and begin tapping loudly on the top of the crate to spook the raccoon- it works!

The raccoon scampers out quickly, looking back at you and chittering angrily before running back into the forest. That raccoon can be just as mad as it wants to be, but you are a crime fighter today! You will not let a critter's home be stolen out here on your watch.

You look around to see if there's any way to help keep the ducks home safe from this happening again and that is when you see it; there is a small boulder nearby that is just large enough to keep the crate from being moved by another animal like the raccoon was able to do, but small enough to still provide plenty of room for the duck family. In fact, the boulder will probably even help keep the crate even more snuggly warm because it will help block some of the winter wind.

You step back and admire your work and hear a "quack quack" from behind you. You turn around and see the mama duck leading her baby ducklings towards the crate, so you step out of the way and watch as they file into the crate and settle in.

It may not seem like much, but you are grateful that you were able to stop an active crime in progress and be a hero for this duck family. You are glad you were here to be a crime fighter!

You do not have to leave your duckling friends just yet if you don't want to. You can spend as long as you want here and you can come back anytime you'd like.

You can create anything you want in your mind. Imagine where you want to go and build the picture in your mind. Be sure to imagine how you want it to smell, taste, hear, and feel. The more detailed you can make your mental picture, the more you will enjoy being there.

It is all up to you. Perhaps as you drift off to sleep, you may find yourself back here in the park, fighting crime wherever you see it.

Oscar Has Tea

Oscar was a full four years older than his little sister Minnie. Ever since she was born, Oscar was always helping Minnie out. When she was a baby, he would help by getting her fresh 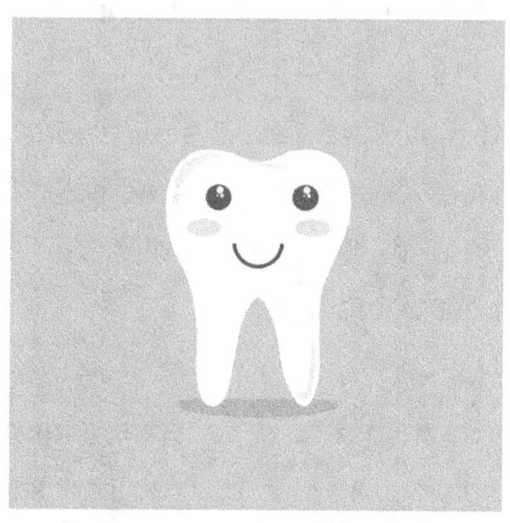 diapers so his mom and dad could change her soiled diapers. He would also help get her bottle and her pacifier, and her favorite elephant blanket to help keep her calm. Every night when she went to bed, Oscar would kiss her forehead and say goodnight before his mom rocked Minnie to sleep and then laid her in her crib. When Minnie started crawling, Oscar showed her how to get around. Then, he showed her how to walk and how to talk. Oscar even showed Minnie how to run, jump, hop, and skip. He was always showing Minnie cool tricks and helping her learn how to do fun things with him. When it was bath time, Oscar would make sure Minnie had her favorite toys, and he would help bring her a dry towel when it was time to get out. Then, he would sit by quietly as his dad read Minnie a bedtime story after her bath to help her relax while his mom took a small break to have a tea. As Minnie and Oscar got older, Oscar found himself wanting more alone time. While he loved his little sister Minnie very much, he sometimes wanted to just play by himself. When he wanted alone time, Oscar would go to his room, close the door, and play with his blocks and his racecars by himself. Usually, Minnie would stay out of his room and play with her own toys in her own room. Sometimes, Oscar could hear Minnie crying from the other room when she wanted something, but his mom said no. Usually, though, Minnie was pretty calm and always played nicely. She was a very good baby, their parents said. One day, Minnie kept crying, and Oscar did not understand why. At first, he thought maybe she had wanted something to eat or wanted a toy that his mom said no to. But the crying kept happening, and it did not seem to stop. Oscar waited in his room, wondering if Minnie would be okay or if she was in trouble. When the crying did not stop, Oscar went to check on his sister. "What is wrong?" Oscar asked when he got into the living room. Oscar's mom was rocking Minnie back and forth in the rocking chair, and Oscar's dad was in the kitchen, preparing something for Minnie. "Minnie has a fever." Oscar's mom said, cuddling Minnie close. "A fever?" Oscar asked. "Yes, Minnie is not feeling well." Oscar's dad said, coming into the room with a small cup of medicine for Minnie. "Why is she not feeling well?" Oscar asked. "Minnie is getting her molars now."

Oscar's mom smiled, holding Minnie up for Oscar to see.

"What are molars?" Oscar asked.

"Molars are the teeth at the back of your mouth, the ones that you chew your food with." Oscar's dad answered.

As he did, he gave the medicine to Minnie and then went away to clean up the cup.

Oscar's mom continued rocking Minnie back and forth and hugging her closely.

"I thought she had all of her teeth?" Oscar asked, remembering how Minnie had grown her front teeth a long time ago.

"Not yet." Oscar's mom answered.

"Will she be okay?" Oscar asked, worried about his little sister.

"She will be; she just has a fever and is in some pain because growing teeth hurt." Oscar's mom said.

"Maybe I can help?" Oscar said, climbing up into his mom's lap.

"You know what, I think that would be a great idea." Oscar's mom smiled.

Oscar cuddled his little sister Minnie in his mom's lap until Minnie stopped crying.

He helped her calm down by rubbing her cheeks gently, holding her hand, and singing quietly to her.

As he did, she started smiling up at him, and soon she started giggling.

"Hey, look, mom, I helped!" Oscar said, proud of himself.

"You did!" Oscar's mom smiled, squeezing her two children into a hug.

When she let go, Oscar hopped off of his mom's lap, and Minnie followed closely after him.

Not wanting her to feel alone, Oscar offered to come to play in Minnie's room to help her feel better.

Minnie giggled and ran into her bedroom, and Oscar followed behind her.

When they got to her bedroom, Minnie pulled out her tea party set and shoved it into Oscar's hands.

"Tea?" she grinned.

"Okay, Minnie, let's play tea party!"

Oscar collected all of Minnie's tea party toys and set them up on her small table.

He placed the teapot in the middle, then put the cups next to it.

He put the small milk jug next to the teapot and added some little plates with some pretend food.

Then, Oscar went into Minnie's toy box and pulled out a princess costume complete with a tiara for Minnie to wear.

He helped her put the dress on and put her tiara on, and then Minnie sat at the table.

"Tea?" she asked, grabbing the cup and pretending to pour tea into her cup.

"Tea." Oscar grinned, holding his cup out.

Minnie pretended to pour tea into Oscar's cup, too, and then they both pretended to drink their tea.

When they were done, they pretended to eat their snacks, and then they talked about all sorts of things that teething toddlers like to talk about.

After their tea party was done, Oscar's mom and dad came into the room to see how they were doing.

They checked on Minnie's temperature to make sure she was doing okay and that her fever was getting better, and then they checked her mouth to see how she was doing.

When they were done, they said it was time for a bath, and then time for bed.

As they were all leaving the room, Oscar's dad asked to talk to him.

"Oscar, can you come here please?" his dad said, walking away from the bathroom.

"Okay, dad," Oscar said, following his dad.

His dad crouched down to Oscar, the way he did when he wanted to have a serious conversation, and leaned forward, wrapping his arm around Oscar.

"That was a really nice thing you did for your little sister Minnie today." Oscar's dad said.

"Thank you, dad," Oscar said.

"Sometimes, your little sister is going to need your help in life. I'm happy to know she has such a wonderful big brother to help her when she needs you, you are a great big brother." his dad smiled, hugging him.

Oscar hugged back and thought about how lucky he was to have such a nice little sister and how proud he was of being able to be such a good big brother to his little sister. When they were done hugging, Oscar went to the bathroom to bring Minnie her favorite toy and her towel.

Then, he went back to his room to play with his toys by himself.

While there, he thought about how happy he was to have such a wonderful family, and how happy it made him be able to help his family out so much.

Oscar felt really lucky to have such a great family and hoped his little sister would feel better soon.

The Long Neck who Told Tall Tales

When it gets dark outside, dinosaurs tell many tales. Just like us, the inhabitants of Dino Land like to dream and talk about the things of legend. Dino's have their own idea of what is mystical and mysterious. To them, the stars in the night sky are like spirits that talk to them. They say sweet things to make them go to sleep. Bedtime is a time for sleeping and for saying goodbye to the day. One's eyes get droopy and their breathing slows down. With a big stretch and a loooong yawn, they are almost ready for sleep. Everybody thinks about different things before they close their eyes. They think about all of the good things that happened to them that day, and of all the things that will happen to them tomorrow. A good dinosaur thinks about what they will eat when they wake up. They think about growing big and strong like their mama and papa. They want to grow big, so big that maybe one day the can reach the stars above them. But it all starts with a breath. A simple breath that tells you that everything is just alright. A deep inhale, and a deep exhale. See? It's easy! All you have to do is take a big breath and then you hold it, hold it, hold it, and then you let it go, and as you let it go, you think about how wonderful this world is, and all the things that live in it. Every creature and thing is beautiful in their own way. From every tree to every little tiny rock, and from the smallest of critters like the ants on the sidewalk to the eagles that soar high in the sky. They are all connected. Now that the day has come to a close, it is time to say goodbye to everything that happened today. If it was bad or good, it doesn't matter. Because tomorrow you will say hello to a new day, and you will have a chance to experience life and all its beauty.

But before you go off to sleep and have adventures of your own in your dreams, you can listen to a tale about a little dyno and his friends. As you listen to the story try to picture what is being said in your head. Just like you are having a dream. But one that you are listening to. You will be glad that you did, I promise. By the time it is over, all you will want to do is go to sleep, and have sweet dreams of your own. Just relax, and allow your body to do whatever it wants to do. Breathe slowly, and get yourself into a comfortable position. Fluff some pillows, and throw on a warm blanket.

In Dino Land everybody knows that the stars are watching over the dinosaurs. They protect them from whatever danger there might be, and they show the dinosaurs the way home when they are lost. The stars are also a friend. If a dyno ever feels alone, all they have to do is look up and there will be hundreds of stars looking back at them. And when sleepy dynos go to sleep, they go to sleep underneath the stars. On most nights, the sky is clear and they can see the galaxies far away. The night sky is so pretty, don't you think. There is so much to see out there in outer space. Distant worlds that we haven't visited. Places that are so far away that we only seem them as little tiny stars when the sun goes down. Maybe one day we will reach them. In our dreams we can see what is there. All we have to do is imagine.

Stars are so important to dynos that they might become superstitious. They say that the stars can talk to you if you listen closely. Any dinosaur that can do that is said to have special powers. These are usually the old and wise dinosaurs that lead the entire pack. They know where to go to find all the best places to graze, and they know where to find water holes when it is needed. Those dinosaurs are said to listen to the world. They are very respected in Dino Land. They always seem to have all the answers. Whether it will rain tomorrow, if there will be a good harvest, or when it is time to migrate. Our story begins with a young long neck dinosaur, not much older than a baby. This dyno goes by the name of Sam. Sam is a sauropod, which in scientific lingo means "lizard footed". Long necks have four legs, long tails, and as you probably guessed, really long necks.

Dinosaurs like Sam eat the leaves high up on trees. Their long necks let them reach the leaves all the way on the top. They are also the biggest dinosaurs that walk around. The ground shakes everywhere they go, and nobody wants to mess with them because nobody wants to get squished by them. But Sam is a tiny sauropod. He hasn't grown as fast as his friends, and sometimes needs help to reach the good leaves that are higher up. Many of his friends think that Sam is weak. They say he is too small for a sauropod, and that he will never grow up to be big. They say he is always needing help from the rest of the herd, and that he will never be able to do things on his own.

Every morning, Sam goes to the water hole to get a drink. And every morning, the other sauropods are there flexing their long necks and telling jokes to each other. Sam wants to be just like them, but his neck isn't that long yet. Just wait a little bit Sam, and make sure you always eat enough food. You will have a long neck in no time. The water hole is really just a big lake. The sauropods aren't the only dinosaurs here either. Everybody needs to get a drink. And everybody gets along. Along the lake you see duckbills chattering about. Not too far there are triceratops feeding on the short grass. But not all dinosaurs are big and scary. Along the tall grass you can see movement, not too far away. There is something hiding behind the grass bushes there. One of the smallest dynos jumps out from behind, hungry for bugs. This is our friend Compsognathus, or just Compie for short. Compies travel in packs, and they are quite a sight to behold. No bigger than a chicken, compies need to stick together for protection. By themselves they aren't very scary. But in a group, they can be quite frightening. We shouldn't mess with the compies. Just like the compies, Sam is also small. At least for the type of dinosaur he is. For whatever reason, Sam hasn't grown as fast as he should. He is what you call the runt of the litter. A little smaller, and a little behind everyone else.

But if you were to ask Sam, he would say that he is strong and smarter than everyone else. According to him, he once fended off a group of velociraptors by making scary noises at them. Sam was known to tell tall tales. He also said that he once has flown on the back of a flying dinosaur and hitched a ride to an active volcano. Do you know what a tall tale is? They are stories or retellings of stories where the storyteller makes things up, or exaggerates the truth. Tall tales are fun to think about, but are almost never true. Maybe you have heard someone saying these types of stories to you. Did someone every say did they did something fantastic or that they something really cool? And did you believe them? When somebody tells a tall story, you want to believe it, because it is funny, or strange or just really interesting. But at the same time, you know that the story sounds a little made up. People like to make up stories. It's what we do. Even I am making up a story as I tell you it. And dinosaurs are no different. For a dinosaur like Sam, telling tall tales was the only way that he could get the other sauropods to like him. Ah, but it looks like Sam has just woken up. There he is, just on time arriving with the other Sauropods. He goes straight to where the long necks are hanging out. Everyone in dyno land has their own place to go to. Just like in school, when it is time to eat lunch we all have our little spots in the cafeteria room. And the sauropods are the big guys in the cafeteria. They can eat entire forests if they are hungry enough. They tower over all the other dinosaurs. Imagine being a compie, no bigger than a chicken and you see a sauropod that is three stories tall.

"Hi Fellas!" Said Sam to the other long necks.

"Hi Sam." they said back in their usual bored tone.

Sam had a reputation for being annoying. But it never stopped him from trying to fit in. Sam just liked to have a good time.

"Guess what guys?" Said Sam excitedly. "Guess what I saw last night!"

"What?" Asked Logan, a sauropod that was bigger than him, but not much older.

"You have to guess first!" Said Sam.

"Did you see your own reflection?" Said an even bigger sauropod named Bentley.

The others burst out laughing, which annoyed Sam.

"No!" He said. "I saw a star leaf tree and then some duckbills ran me off. But not before I got a taste of the star leaf tree!"

The other sauropods quieted down Sam said what he had to say. A Star leaf tree was one of the rarest types of trees around. A single star leaf tree could feed an entire herd. Each leaf was big, juicy and full of nutrients. Finding such a tree was like finding a treasure.

"Sam?" said Bentley the larger sauropod. "Where did you find that tree? Sam?" "I'm not sure," said Sam. "It was dark and I had wandered off because I get hungry at night. I think I found it somewhere in the forest. But then five really big duckbills showed up and scared me off!" Bentley didn't know whether to believe him or not. A star leaf tree is like a gift from the stars themselves. It had been a long time since the last star leaf tree was seen in Dino Land. And here was Sam, saying that he'd found one.

"Well what did it taste like?" Asked Logan.

"It was really crunchy," said Sam. "And at the same time, it was full of water. It was like eating a dead leaf sort of crunchy, but with all the nutrients of a healthy leaf. And it smelled really nice too. Something like flowers" Bentley nodded his head.

"That is exactly what a star tree leaf is supposed to taste like. They hold in water much better than other leafs. And the crunch is from being in the sun a lot. My mouth is watering just thinking about it."

"So, you are telling the truth, Sam?" asked Logan.

"Of course, I'm telling the truth!" Said Sam. "And those duckbills ran me off. I bet they know where the tree is and they are hiding the real location.

"I was thinking the same thing," said Bentley. "We have to tell this to the others, before the duckbills hog the entire tree. We should get everyone to search for it too. Thanks for telling us, Sam"

Logan, the other dinosaur wasn't sure if he believed Sam. But since Bentley was larger and smarter, Logan trusted him. And if Bentley said that Sam was telling the truth, then Logan would also believe it. The two sauropods disappeared into the forest, and left Sam alone on the lake. The truth was that Sam went into the forest last night and heard a scary sound. He was alone, and since he is small he ran off. But he didn't want to tell that to his friends. He made the entire story up. There was no star leaf tree, and there he didn't see any duckbills that night. But the others didn't need to know that. Sam finished up getting his drink of water and went to look for some nice trees to eat from. He didn't know that all around him the other sauropods were busy looking for that very tree. Everywhere he went Sam was hearing the rumors about the star tree leaf. The news spread fast through the sauropod herd. Everyone was talking about it. The little runt found a star tree leaf, they said. The duckbills are trying to take our territory, others said. Sam was really brave to take on five duckbills at once, said another. And everywhere he went, they asked Sam the same thing. "Where did you see the tree?" and "What did the star leaf taste like?" Sam knew what they tasted like because his mom told him a long time ago. He never actually ate one. You would be surprised how fast rumors spread. Even in dyno land, where they don't have computers or phones, important information can move really fast. When the stars went up that day, all of the sauropods where exhausted from looking for the tree. Nobody had seen it, and they looked everywhere. Up and down the forest. They looked around the lake, and in places beyond it. But there was no star tree leaf to be seen.

Did the duckbills pluck the tree dry? Maybe the flying dinosaurs came down from the mountains and snagged it. Nobody knew for sure, but the more that they thought about it, it seemed like Sam had told a lie. That night Sam slept alone, because he was tired of getting asked so many questions.

But just before he fell asleep, Sam saw something strange in the night sky. It was a bright light that flew across the stars. It left behind a big orange tail. Whatever it was, the light scared Sam. He thought that the stars were falling. When he woke up, Sam remembered everything that he saw. He ran to the lake, and started yelling that the sky was falling. But nobody paid him any attention. Not Bentley, not Logan or any of the others. They weren't interested in his story about the bright lights.

"You know Sam," said Bentley, "I talked to some of the duckbills yesterday. They said they didn't see a star leaf tree. The herd wasn't even in the forest that day"

"We spent all day trying to find it," added Logan. "Are you sure that you saw a star leaf tree?"

"But it's true!" Said Sam. "Those duckbills, maybe the ones I saw where different. I had never seen them before"

"Whatever you say Sam," said Bentley. Him and Logan walked off and left Sam all alone at the lake for the second time. Now they really didn't believe him. But what he said about the light in the sky was the truth. He didn't make it up, nor did he imagine it. And the others still wouldn't listen to him. Instead Sam decided to go talk to someone who would believe him. Somebody he knew he could trust. Sam went to see the Star Talker. One of the oldest, and wisest sauropods in their herd. The Star Talker lived deep in the forest. She was three stories tall, but the trees there were even bigger. The Star Talker liked to stay hidden in the forest, where nobody could see her. She spent her time looking for medicinal herbs to help heal the herd whenever somebody got hurt.

"She will know what to do," thought Sam. But finding her was going to be harder than he thought. When Sam entered the forest, all he saw was a wall of trees. Sam wasn't tall enough to see over them. And he didn't know where to look. Soon it was going to get dark again. Sam knew he had to warn the herd of the bright light he saw. But nobody wanted to believe him. Something bad was going to happen, he just knew it. And now it was up to him to tell the truth.

"Oh, Star Talker, where could you be?" Said Sam as he made his way deeper into the forest. Sam was completely lost in that forest, and the night time was getting closer. He didn't know how to get out, or where to go. The sounds of the forest frightened him very much. There was a sound like a loud screeching coming somewhere. And sometimes he felt like he could hear a dinosaur walking behind him, watching his every move.

"Oh, please help me, stars. Show me where I have to go" Said Sam.

He could see the night sky in between the leaves of the trees. And the stars all looked back at him.

"Show me the way"

The Great Guiding Star was shining bright that night. It was the biggest and brightest star that there was. Sam followed it, believing that it would show him the way to the Star Talker. But it was getting late, and it was possible that she was already sleeping. There was no time. Sam had a very important message for her. And even though the Star Talker was four times his size, he had to speak up to somebody. He only hoped that they would listen that what he had to say. Sam started to hear a loud humming sound coming from within the forest. It sounded like something of a song. Where the stars trying to talk to him? The humming got louder and louder, until it sounded like it was coming from the trees.

"What's that noise?" Wondered Sam.

But before he could look, Sam bumped straight into something big and hard. At the same time, the humming suddenly stopped.

"Oh, dear are you alright?"

It was the Star Talker! The forest was so dark that Sam never saw her there. The Star Talker was out looking for her herbs.

"They are best to find at night," she explained. "That's when the stars show me where to look"

Sam told her everything about what he saw the previous night. About the bright orange light and he thought something bad was going to happen.

"There is no need to be afraid little one," said Star Talker. "It is normal to see lights in the sky. After all, the stars are made out of it you know"

"But what if the sky falls and stars come down?" Asked Sam.

"Now now," said the Star Talker. "Let's not talk about the sky falling down. None of us know what the stars do and want. Not even I, who talks to the stars every night"

"You do? What do they tell you?" "They tell me that a certain little dinosaur has been saying made up things and spreading rumors"

"But I saw it!" Said Sam. "I saw the bright light in the sky with my two eyes! Why won't anyone believe me"

"Well I believe you," said the Star Talker.

"You do?" asked Sam, a little surprised.

"Of course, I believe you sweety. I know just what you are talking about. I see those lights in the sky all the time. The stars tell me that those lights are just other stars traveling through the sky. You don't have to be afraid of them"

"But they can fall on top of us and then what?" Said Sam. "What if the traveling stars fall down to earth?"

"Don't worry about that happening," said the Star Talker. "The stars tell me when they fall. And when they do, I will be sure to tell you and the rest of the herd"

"Now be a dear and help me collect these herbs"

Sam did as she asked, and helped the older dinosaur. Sometimes we have to help our elders do things that are easy for us. Since Sam was so small, he could help pick up the herbs from the ground with ease. The Star Talker was larger, and had to bend her long neck all the way down.

"You are very good at this," said the Star Talker. "Would you like to become my assistant? I could use a handsome young dyno like you"

Sam couldn't believe his ears. It was a great honor to become the Star Talker's assistant. He said yes immediately, and without question. That night Sam learned all about the duties of the Star Talker, and he did a good job being her assistant. When it was time to go to bed, the Star Walker told him the way out of the forest so he could make it home safe. Sam fell asleep quickly because he was so tired. But then in the middle of the night, something woke him up. He didn't know what, but one moment he was dreaming and then he was wide awake. He looked up to the night sky, and he saw a bright orange light. This time the light flew overhead and made a loud booming noise that woke up some birds in a nearby tree. And as hard as Sam tried to go back to sleep, he simply couldn't. At last when the sun started to rise Sam jumped out of his bed. Nothing seemed different. The mountains where still blue, the trees were still green and tall, and Sam was still small and short. Had anyone else heard the same boom that he did? Surely at least one other dyno must have heard the noise. Or seen the bright light that he saw. But none of the other dynos seemed worried. They were slowly waking up to start the new day, and none of them looked as scared as he did. One by one the herd of sauropods woke up from their nests. The massive creatures stretched their necks and backs, yawning just like we do.

The beginning of the day is always beautiful no matter where you live. Here just outside the forest the dinosaurs awoke to the pleasant sounds of birds chirping in the trees and of small little critters singing in the bushes. The sky turned from black to blue and then the sun rose in the east. And Sam couldn't wait to meet Logan and Bentley on the lake to tell them what he witnessed.

"Guys! Guys! You have to listen to me," he said panting after reaching him.

"Let me guess," said Logan. "You found another star leaf tree?"

"Did you get in a fight with a stegosaurus?" Said Bentley.

"No guys. None of those things. I saw the orange light again! And then there was a big boom!"

"A big boom?" said Logan. "I didn't hear anything. Did you hear anything?"

"Not a sound" said Bentley. "Maybe you heard it in your dreams Sam?"

But Sam swore he wasn't dreaming. He was wide awake the entire time. How could nobody else have heard the noise. It must have sounded from miles away. Bentley and Logan began eating their breakfast as usual on the trees next to the lake.

"You know Sam," said Bentley. "I heard that the Star Talker took you on as an assistant. Maybe next time you think the sky is falling you should talk to her first.

"It's true," said Logan. "The Star Talker knows everything about the stars. If there was something to worry about she would know"

"Aren't you guys scared?" Asked Sam impatiently. "How can you guys just sit around eating trees all day when the sky is falling on top of us!"

"The sky is falling?" Said Logan. "Sure, and my uncle is a Tyrannosaurus Rex"

Bentley started laughing so hard that he spat out his food. "Ooh that's a good one! I'm going to use that one next time!"

"The sky isn't falling Sam. I think you need to stop spreading rumors like that or you will scare the whole colony"

"I saw it okay! Said Sam "And I heard a big boom! Some other dinosaur must have heard it too. You'll see"

He went around the lake talking to the other dynos, but the results were the same. Everyone thought he was crazy. One duckbill even threatened to headbutt him if he didn't leave him alone. Something fishy was happening and he was going to get to the bottom of it. If the sky really was falling, more dinosaurs would be worried. The herd leader would call a meeting, and all the sauropods would have to think about a solution. Maybe they should all move to higher ground. Maybe they should make a shelter in the forest. Or go far away where the lights in the sky didn't happen. That night Sam went straight to the forest to meet up with the Star Talker again. The guys at the lake where right. The Star Talker sees everything. And he was certain that she also saw the light. Or maybe even heard the big bang.

Sam walked deep into the forest until he heard the familiar noise of the Star Talker humming into the night. It was such a sweet and soothing noise that Sam stood there a little bit just to listen. But the Star Talker sensed he was there, and told him to help.

"Well don't just stand there sweetie," she said. "Come here and help me pick up these herbs. These are the last of the season, and I really want to get all of them.

"Er, Star Talker?" Said Sam.

"Yes?"

"Yesterday—I mean last night did you hear something strange over the forest?"

"Strange? Why I hear strange things all the time. Even when the stars talk to me, I hear very strange things indeed. Why do you ask?"

Sam let out a big sigh.

"Because last night I saw another strange light in the sky. And then I heard a big scary sound, like a boom. I think the sky is falling and that we are all in danger"

But the Star Talker continued to do her work. She acted like nothing had happened.

"I didn't see any lights last night, Sam. And I also didn't hear any loud booming sound"

Sam felt like somebody hit him across the face with a frying pan. What did she mean she didn't see anything? She's the Star Talker! She sees everything!

"You don't believe me?"

"Of course, I believe you, sweetie," Said the Star Talker. "It's just that I didn't see or hear any of those things. It could be that I'm just a really deep sleeper that's all"

"But the others! Why doesn't anybody else believe me?" asked Sam.

"Well I don't need to remind you," the Star Talker said "That there was a certain little dinosaur going around spreading rumors about a star leaf tree"

"And that the same dinosaur said that he once scared off a group of velociraptors, or that the very same dinosaur also said he hitched a ride on a flying dinosaur and went to go see an active volcano"

"But this time it's different," said Sam. "I really saw the bright light in the sky. I really, really did. I'm not making this up. And the loud boom that I heard really scared me!"

"Now, now" said the Star Talker. "I don't think that the sky is falling. And just because you saw something bright in the sky doesn't mean that something bad is going to happen"

"It doesn't?" Sam said.

"Of course not. You are not the first, nor will you be the last dyno who sees the same type of bright light in the sky. So, trust me when I say that the sky is not falling down"

"But how come you are the only one who believes me?"

"Because I am the Star Talker. And I know lots of things. And I also know when somebody is telling the truth and when they are telling a lie"

Sam could see the moon rising through the trees in the forest. It was a full moon, and the moonlight helped him see inside the dark forest.

"Do you see that moon?" Asked the Star Talker.

"Yes, I see it"

"That moon will never tell a lie. Every night that the sun goes down the moon will always be there. Some nights you can see it, and other nights you can't. But every night you can be sure that the moon is out there, somewhere, looking down on us"

"What's so special about that?" Said Sam.

"It means that the moon is reliable, Sam. Every night the sun will go down and the moon will go up. No matter where you live, this will be true. No matter where you are, if you ask the stars if the moon is there, they will always tell you the truth. Even if you can't see the moon, the stars will tell you, yes, the moon is there. The moon cannot tell a lie"

Sam wasn't sure he understood, but the Star Talker was the wisest dinosaur he knew. So, he listened with all his heart.

"In other words, Sam, those who never tell a lie are reliable. Dinosaurs will listen to them, just like they listen to the stars and to the moon, because they know that the person is reliable. Do you get it now?"

"A little bit," Sam lied.

"Now let me tell you about the velociraptor," said the Star Talker. "A velociraptor is a trickster at heart. They will do anything they can do get what they need. This includes telling lies"

Sam began to understand a little bit better.

"We long necks say, never trust a velociraptor. They always lie and they are up to no good. My advice to you Sam, is to be like the moon and the stars. Don't be like the velociraptor that nobody trusts"

"But I'm so small!" Said Sam. "Nobody takes me seriously. All the other long necks think I'm a runt and that I always need help"

"So?" Asked The Star Talker. "We all need a little help from time to time. Just how as my assistant you help me collect my herbs. You see? There is nothing wrong with needing a little bit of help"

Sam didn't know what to say. He knew that the other dinosaurs wouldn't pay attention to him because of all the lies and tall tales that he said before.

"Look here Sam," said the Star Talker. "It's a good thing that you are smaller than all the other long necks. You can easily reach for the herbs that I need. And as long as you are my assistant, there will be a place for you right here" The rest of the night Sam helped the Star Talker collect her herbs, and she told him stories about what the stars are, and all the things they whisper to her. Sam learned a lot about himself that night. And he learned a lot about the stars too. Sam tried using the Star Talkers advice in the coming days. He wanted to be like the moon and like the stars, and he didn't want to be like the velociraptor anymore. "No more tall tales," he said to himself. "For now on, I will always be honest" Sam no longer talked about the sky falling. According to the Star Talker, the sky wouldn't fall just because he saw a few bright lights in the night. And even if the sky was falling, it wasn't nice to go around scaring people or trying to sound important. One day when he was having a drink of water at the lake Bentley and Logan approached him. And Sam didn't know it at the time, but the dynos wanted to make fun of him.

"What's the matter Sam, haven't seen any more of those star leaf trees?" Asked Logan.

"We may be thought the sky was falling again so we came to check on you" Added Bentley

Sam remembered what the Star Talker told him, about always being honest. But this was different. They were making fun of him for things he said in the past, not for things he would say now. How was Sam supposed to be honest when he already lied about seeing a star leaf tree?

"Oh, hey guys" said Sam pretending not to be bothered by them. "The Star Talker told me that the sky isn't falling after all. Those lights that I saw where just traveling stars. That's all"

The two dynos looked at each other and then looked back at Sam. They looked confused that Sam wasn't going off about something again. They were expecting another tall tale, but Sam wasn't going to tell stories like that. For now on, he was just going to be an honest dyno.

"Well what about the star leaf tree?" Asked Logan. "That was definitely a lie wasn't it?"

Sam didn't like admitting it to them. He really, really didn't want to admit it to them. If he did, then it meant that he was a no good liar just like a velociraptor. But if he was going to start being honest, he had to tell the truth about the past as well.

"That was just a dumb story I made up," he said. "I thought if I had a cool story to tell then dynos would like me more"

It hurt Sam to say those words, but he did so anyways. Because the Star Talker believed in him and because he believed in himself. He couldn't let Logan and Bentley get the better of him. They were just rubbing his past mistakes in his face. They were no better than bullies.

"So, you admit it was all just a big lie then?" Asked Logan. "And you also lied about the velociraptors and you lied about riding on the back of a flying dinosaur to a volcano?"

Sam looked at Logan with a look that said, "What do you want me to say?" Of course they were all lies. Sam thought that would be obvious by now. But they wanted him to admit it. They wanted to hear it come from his mouth.

"All made up" said Sam. "I have to go help the Star Talker now. Today we are planting new trees" And with that, Sam left Logan and Bentley with their mouths open. They couldn't believe that a runt dinosaur like Sam could be the Star Talkers assistant. Once Same started being honest everyone treated him differently. When he spoke, dinosaurs listened. Not only because he was the Star

Talker's assistant, but because he was one of the most honest and trustful long necks around. And just like the Star Talker said, the sky didn't fall down. And this is where our story ends my friend. I thank you for sticking around until the end, and for joining me and my journey to Dino Land. I hope you had a good time, and that you enjoyed it as much as I did. Always, always remember to be honest. Even when it hurts to be honest, we become better people by telling the truth. Be like the moon and the stars, not the velociraptor. Be more like Sam.

Now I must say goodnight and goodbye, until we meet again.

Baggi's Unwanted Slide

Baggi loves to dig big holes. For that Baggi is still such a small excavator, he is already really fast. Once he grows up, he wants to be as big and strong a digger as his dad. The dredge huge pile of soil and debris in no time from one end of the construction site to another. The construction workers needed it for days. A strong excavator, like Baggis Papa, can do it in a few hours. Baggi likes helping his dad with digging and so he has been to construction sites often. So often that he knows the environment like his own shovel. But that does not mean that things do not go wrong again and again. Today, a house is to be built. For that the construction workers need a big hole in the earth. Said and done. Baggi gets going. Although he can dig really fast, he has to work hard to keep up with his daddy. Shovel by shovel, the hole grows larger quickly. Shovel after shovel but it is also fast deep. Baggi is so energetic and anxious to show his father what he is capable of, that he becomes overzealous. He rolls faster and faster between the dug earth and the hole. It starts to drizzle. Baggis dad calls for a bad-weather break immediately - because safety first! But Baggi is at it right now and does not dream of stopping now. But the wetter the earth gets, the slipperier it will be. Suddenly Baggi starts to skid. With momentum he rushes towards the hole. Even frightened by the unwanted slide and full of effort the little Baggi tries to slow down. But once you're in the slip, even the best brake will not help. Baggi has an idea. He pushes his little shovel with all his strength into the ground. Now he is pulling a deep furrow and an ever-increasing pile of mud behind him. So the little Baggi tries to brake. And his plan seems to work out too, because he is getting bit by bit slower. But unfortunately, he came too late to this brilliant idea, because on the edge of the hole he is now on the loose and desperately trying to shift his weight forward so as not to slip into the huge hole. Baggis slide was so fast that Baggis dad had not heard the fast-paced drama. Seeing Baggi on the tip, he rushes to his son's aid immediately. The wet ground does not make it easy for him. And so, he comes to a tire length too late. Directly in front of him the small excavator slides straight into the hole. Behind him slips the wet earth, which he had accumulated during the slide. Smudged and smudged with mud and earth, the little excavator now squats in the huge hole. As much as he tries to come out again, he finds no support. The wheels spin in the wet soil and he digs deeper into the earth. Even his strong dad cannot reach him now. "Just stay calm my boy. We'll get you out of there! "Shouts Baggis dad. Then he looks up and sees the construction workers standing on the other side of the hole. They are sprinkled with mud from top to bottom. Baggi had been so eager to get out of the hole that the mud had flown in a high arc to the construction workers. These now stand like drowned poodles on the edge and wipe the muddy ground from the face. But on the job site, fortunately, one is a big family and not at all resentful. Because especially during construction can go something wrong. The important thing is that you help each other then. The foreman taps the dirt from the radio. Then he immediately informs the crane driver: "Excavator in need!". The crane operator sees what is going on and swings the crane over the hole to free Baggi from his predicament. Happy to have solid ground under the wheels, Baggi is relieved. But he is also embarrassed. For one thing, he should have listened to the security regulations and thus his dad. And on the other hand, everyone will surely make fun of him and tell funny stories about him. But to Baggis astonishment no one makes fun of him. But on the contrary. Everyone is really worried about the little excavator and asks him if everything is alright and how it happened? Baggi tells the story from the beginning. After a while, he realizes that he is telling a funny story about himself. And that is really funny! The construction workers have a lot of fun listening to Baggis story. And since it is raining right now, no more work is done today anyway. But still laughed a lot and Baggi laughs heartily with! One bed free and one for three? Today I tell you a story about a little girl named Lydia. Lydia is 4 years old and always nice and good. Mom and Dad are very proud that they have such a sweet child. Mum often even says "My Angel" to Lydia, because she is as good as an angel. But there is one thing that mom and dad do not find so divine. Lydia sleeps in her parents' bed every night. How come? Surely you are asking yourself now. Does not she have her own bed? But she has. And even a very cuddly. With many stuffed animals and a lot of space for such a little girl as Lydia. But Lydia just does not want to sleep in her own bed. She finds it much more comfortable with mom and dad. At the same time, Lydia does not know what it's like to sleep in her own bed. That was so long ago that she forgot.

Mom and dad love Lydia very much. But as big as mom and daddy's bed is, it's a little tight for three. Especially since Lydia gets bigger and bigger. When the dad turns around at night, he nudges Lydia. Then Lydia awakens briefly and turns around too. She bumps into her mom and the mom is awake and turns around. And when dad turns around again, the game starts again.

Sometimes Lydia twitches in her sleep. She then dreams something and begins to fidget with her arms and legs. Lydia herself does not notice. But depending on how she's lying, either mom or dad is lucky enough to get hit. Of course, one wakes up on it. And if you do not sleep enough, you are not well rested in the morning. If Lydia wants to play during the day, mom and dad are way too broken. You did not sleep much. And it was exhausting enough to do the work and the household. Lydia thinks that's stupid. The solution would be so simple. She would only have to sleep in her own bed. Then mom and dad would have slept well and cheerful enough to play with

Lydia. Lydia used to sleep in her own bed when she was younger. There she liked to cuddle with her teddy. But Lydia does not remember that. At some point she got a new bed - because she got bigger. And she did not sleep once in the new bed. If Mama Lydia had asked her if she would like to sleep in her own bed, then Lydia said, "No." Lydia said more. But today Mama said something for the first time that made Lydia think. "Your teddy is certainly very sad and misses you very doll." Lydia did not even think that when she sleeps with Mom and Dad, her stuffed animals are all alone. And indeed, her stuffed animals were already very sad. The little brown teddy, her doll, the white rabbit Mr. Schlappohr and her little pink unicorn were all alone. Of course, that had to be changed immediately. As Mama was packing laundry in the bedroom, Lydia scurried past her. The stuffed animals in her arms. Lydia placed the cuddly toys on Mom's and Dad's bed and said, "Problem solved." Then she rubbed her hands like daddy when he finished something. Mama did not have that in mind when she told Lydia about the sad stuffed animals. She knelt down in front of Lydia and said, "My angel. That's not OK. So, we do not have enough space in the bed. We can hardly sleep that way." Lydia thought for a moment. That's right, there was another problem. Mom and Dad were always too tired. Should she try to sleep in her own bed? Discouraged, she breathed out, "Phew. You and Dad are so far away. "She said. Mom looked at Lydia, "You mean when you sleep in your bed?" "Yes!" Lydia answered. Now Mom thought, "Hm." Then she said, "What do you think if we leave your door a bit open. And we also leave ours a bit open. Then we'll hear you immediately, if anything should be. " Lydia looked incredulous. But mom had an idea. "We'll try that out right away. That will be fun. What do you say? "Lydia nodded and ran to her room," Hello Mom! "She exclaimed. And mom answered, "Hello Lydia, my angel!" It actually worked. Lydia could hear Mama without Mom having to scream. So, the two spent a while and made all sorts of funny sounds that the other had to guess. When Dad came home, he went with him immediately. Now Mama called from the bedroom, Lydia from the nursery and dad from the room. That was funny. But dad had also brought two surprises.

Once a totally cuddly blanket and a great nightlight. The blanket was pink. Because Lydia loves pink. There were also little flowers on it, which almost looked like starlets. Asterisks would have preferred Lydia, but the flowers glowed in the dark and that was great. The nightlight actually made little stars. If you turned it on, there were little glowing stars all over the nursery. When Dad said that the night light is extra for the night and allowed to stay all night, Mama immediately said, "Well, you see. Not only can you hear us, you can see everything in your room at night." Now Lydia liked her room a lot better. And mom also had some news. Because if Lydia slept in her own bed now, then she was already big and brave. That's why Lydia was allowed to stay awake 15 minutes longer every evening. Lydia was happy and she felt really grown up. After supper Lydia got ready for bed. From the bathroom she marched straight into Mom's and Dad's bedroom. What was going on now? Lydia wanted to sleep in her own bed today. Oh well, the stuffed animals were still there. Well, they had to be fetched, of course. Then Lydia cuddled up with the new blanket in her cot. Teddy, Mr. Schlappohr, her doll and her unicorn around. The great nightlight sparkled and Mama read her another story. This Lydia could fall asleep really nice. She was sound asleep. And she even dreamed something nice.

The Night I Met a Ghost

Sam and his big brother Adam had gotten dressed up in their Halloween costumes and were all ready for trick-or-treating! Sam's favorite night of the year, when Dad would take Sam and Adam from house to house for loads upon loads of free candy. Sam sat at the kitchen table with his candy bucket, dressed as a vampire, waiting for his dad to come get him. Sam's mom walked into the kitchen and complimented Sam on his vampire costume and Adam on his mummy costume. The boys stood in front of her, smiling so she could take their picture, just like she did every single year. Just then, Sam's dad walked into the room with no costume.

"Are you going trick-or-treating without a costume this year, Dad?" Sam was confused.

"Actually, buddy, I'm not going to be taking you trick-or-treating this year. Your brother is getting older now and I think it's time that he took you out. It would be a good exercise in responsibility for him, and it would do the two of you some good to spend some quality time together." Sam could have pitched a fit. Adam and his friends were always picking on Sam when no one was there to say anything about it.

"Aw, Dad! I don't want to watch the twerp tonight! Toddy and I were going to meet up with Kyle and Skylar after trick-or-treating and I don't want them to see me with him."

"You're taking your brother and you will watch after him while he trick-or-treats. You can bring him home when you're done and then go back out with your friends.

In a huff, Adam took Sam outside and they went to their first house. Mrs. Biederman put two caramels in each of their buckets and wished them well. Sam went to walk toward the second house when Adam stopped him.

"Come on, we're going home. It's time for me to go meet up with my friends."

"What! We only went to one house. We can't be done yet!" Adam huffed at him loudly.

"Fine! I'm going to meet up with my friends. What you do on your own is your business." Adam stalked off into the night to look for Toddy.

Sam, not knowing if he should just go home, stood in the middle of the sidewalk. All around him, children bustled and rushed from house to house to get their candy. As he stood there, he saw a kid walking toward him in a ghost costume. He turned to say hello, but the ghost passed right through him! He turned around to look at the ghost, who floated next to him, watching Sam with worry in his eyes. Sam looked the ghost up and down, noticing that it was definitely floating above the ground. He reached out a hand, and the ghost did the same. The two hands touched and the cold, ghostly vapor of the second hand passed right through Sam's hand. Sam stood, staring at the hand in the middle of his own for a moment before looking back up to the ghostly eyes that were fixed on him.

"Before you start screaming, please let me explain." Sam bit his lower lip, focusing hard on not screaming in the middle of the street. "I am a ghost, but I promise not to hurt you. I just wanted to come out tonight to make some friends. Everyone runs away if I come out when it's not Halloween, and I thought this would be my chance!" Sam released the breath he had been holding.

"You promise you're not going to hurt me or do anything to scare me?"

"I promise! Cross my heart and hope to— Well... Maybe something else." The ghost and the boy laughed.

"What's your name? I'm Sam."

"Nice to meet you, Sam." The ghost put his hand on his chest and bowed deeply. "I am Francis." When Francis stood up and looked back at him, he looked around for a moment. "I don't usually see children walking around on Halloween without any friends to share it with. Where are your friends?"

"My friends live one street over. My brother was supposed to be watching me and taking me trick-or-treating, but he ditched me to go find his friends. My dad told me that I shouldn't be out at night by myself, so I was just about to go home."

"Go home! It's so early in the evening, and you only have... TWO CANDIES! Sam, my new friend, we can do so much better! And besides, you're not alone anymore. You have me!" Sam smiled, and he and Francis made their way to Mrs. Conklin's house next.

"Trick-or-treat!"

"Ooh! Happy Halloween, Samuel! And who is this with you? Is that Taylor?"

"No ma'am, this is my cousin Francis from upstate. We're trick-or-treating together!"

"Oh, how nice! Well, where's your candy bucket, Francis?"

"I, uh... It broke! Sam and I will be sharing a bucket this year!"

"Oh, how lovely. Well, here's some candy for Francis, then!" Mrs. Conklin dropped two more candies into Sam's bucket, and they went on their way.

Twelve houses later, Sam and Francis were face to face with Sam's friends! They had met in the middle, and now it was time to venture into the next neighborhood where houses had all the really good candy!

That night, Sam, Francis, Taylor, Bradley, Marcus, and Timothy all had a wonderful Halloween full of candy, laughing, stories, and memories. Francis promised Sam that he would meet him outside his house for trick-or-treating the next year and the year after that!

Rexy and Friends

When things get tough, a dinosaur can only look to their friends for help. When things get tough for us, we need to ask for help. And there is nothing wrong with leaning on a friend from time to time. Other times, we aren't so  lucky. But if you do have friends, and if they help you through tough times, then you are truly blessed.

We don't always appreciate what he has until it's gone. This is why having friends seems normal to us. When they are there, we like to laugh and play. But when they aren't there, we feel a little sad. And that's okay too. Do you have friends? How many? Do you prefer to have many friends, or do you like to have only a few really good friends? Take some time to think about who your friends are. How did you meet? What things do you like to do together? And have you been there for them during hard times? Have they been there for you? Friends are very special to us. A good friend is more important than having a million dollars. Good friends only come once in a life time. Friendship is truly a magical thing once you get to experience it. You will never want to go back to being alone. We have to take care of our friends and be good to them, because they are good to us in return. Sometimes a friend will need our help, and we have to give it to them. Sometimes a friend will need our support, and we have to give it to there. We have to be there for our friends. It is such a beautiful thing to have friends don't you think? Even big and strong dinosaurs need friends every once in a while. In Dino Land little dynos go to school just like you. They learn all their dyno facts and how to live out in the big wilderness.

But some dynos are all alone. They have a hard time making friends because they are different. Or because they look funny to the other dinosaurs. These dynos have to fit in with the crowd. Somehow, but who knows. I want you to imagine a wide open space, out in the wilderness. Not the jungle, with many trees and not the desert with only sand. Think of a space somewhere in between. A place where dynos of different types can gather and meet.

Dino school is very different from regular school. Dino's don't use pencils or chairs. They are too big for those things. Instead dynos sit and listen to what their teacher has to say. They don't have paper either. Everything that they learn has to go straight to their head. And you may not believe this, but dinosaurs have very good memory. Now take a few breaths to help relax your body. It is almost time for bed. I want you to fill up your mind with good, happy thoughts about you and the friends you have made at school, at home, and everywhere in between.

It's okay if you have only a few friends. Or if you haven't made any friends yet. I promise you that friends will come in time. Even if we don't have friends, we can still imagine what a good friend may be like. Chances are, a good friend will be just like you. Or maybe they will be very different. It doesn't matter. Anyone can be your friend.

Sometimes, your mom is the only friend that you need. Your mama will always be there for you no matter what. And everywhere you look, there are people that love and care for you. It could be your dad, your brother or your sister, your cousin or your teacher. Someone somewhere out there cares about you. And most importantly, you care about yourself. You love and care about who you are. You want only the best for you and your family That's why it is important to always believe in yourself. It is important to learn to accept who you are. And who are you? Well it all depends on how you look at it. Some people are short. Some are tall. Others are big, some are small. Some are strong, and others are skinny. People come in many shapes and sizes. And you know what? All of them are important. It doesn't matter what you look like. And it doesn't matter if you like reading books or if you like to play sports. Everyone is important in this world. But that is something that our friend Rexy the Tyrannosaurus Rex had to figure out on his own. This is the story about Rexy and his friends. And it is a story of how one baby Tyrannosaurs learned to accept himself for who he was. Even the mighty T-Rex has problems with the way that they look. In Dino Land they are the king, the most fearsome dinosaur to have ever walked the earth. But deep inside, a T-Rex is just like you and me. They all have their worries, their problems and so on. And just like you and me, they care about how they look.

Now I want you to imagine the first day of school. The first day is always the scariest day. You have to say goodbye to your parents for the entire day. For many of us, it is the first time we have to be away from them. And away from our house and our room and our toys. School can be very hard for some of us. Well in Dino Land it is no different, and early one morning Rexy the T-rex woke up to the sounds of his parents yelling at him.

"The sun is up the birds are out, and it's your first day of school!" Said his dad.

"Wake up sweetie," said his mom. "Today is a big day for you"

But Rexy didn't want to go to school. He wanted to stay in his comfortable bed. Why did he have to go to school when he could stay home and chase butterflies all day? School was boring and a lot of work. He tried his best to stay in bed, but his mama flipped him over and made him stand up.

"You better wash and get ready," said his dad. "You don't want to be late on your first day of school, now do we?"

"No father," said Rexy.

Rexy washed himself in the nearby creek. Rexy figured that he didn't have a choice, and that he would have to go to school. He didn't mind the idea of school so much as he did getting up in the morning. Why did school have to be so early in the morning? If school started just a few hours later in the day, like after lunchtime, Rexy would go running to school everyday. He would have the biggest smile on his face. But no, instead he had to wake up at dawn and get ready in the cold. And washing wasn't the easiest thing to do when you are a tyrannosaurus Rex. With that big head of his and tiny arms it was a miracle that Rexy could wash himself at all. But he knew a little trick. All he had to do was to dive into the water and scrape off the dirt using the nearby rocks. It was a hassle, but for Rexy the system worked out well. When he was all washed and ready, Rexy followed his mama and papa to the school grounds. Rexy was looking forward to making many friends in school. He couldn't wait to see the new faces that would be there. School is a time for learning, but it is also a time for having fun. At school you are away from home. Your parents won't be there to watch over you. So you must learn how to get along with others there.

School also teaches you how to make friends. It is truly an awesome place once you think about it. There's nap time, free time, and Rexy's favorite, snack time. So if you can get over waking up early in the morning like Rexy did, school is just another adventure waiting for you.

"How do we know when we get there?" asked Rexy. "He was still very small compared to his parents, so he couldn't see very far. But his mommy and daddy where big, and they were tall. They could see for miles and miles. And they had big holes in the front of their heads for better smelling. If a T Rex couldn't see you, they could probably smell you. Especially if you smelled tasty.

"Not too far now, Rexy" said his mommy. "We are just about there. I can already see the fence. Rexy walked with his parents and almost fell over with every step. A grown up T Rex makes the ground shake wherever they go. And here Rexy was in the middle of two of them.

Rexy could smell the other dinosaurs before he could see them. There were lots of smells that he didn't recognize. As they got closer, he could also hear the voices of all the baby dynos there waiting their first day of classes. Rexy and his parents went up a small hill, and below that hill they could finally see the other dinosaurs waiting behind the fenced area.

"You see those dynos down there?" Asked his mom. "Those dynos are your new class mates. So, make sure to say hello to all of them"

"And remember son," said his dad. "In school we cannot eat other dinosaurs. Am I absolutely clear? This is the best school on this side of Dino Land, and they only allow meat eaters under one condition. You cannot eat the other students".

Rexy said that he understood, and that his parents had nothing to worry about.

"Good," said his dad. "We can't get any closer than this, Rexy or the other parents will get scared. This is where we say goodbye"

"Wait. You guys are leaving?" said Rexy a little scared.

"Rexy, we talked about this," said his mamma. "We can't follow you into school. They don't allow meat eater grown-ups like us"

"But mamma--"

"Go on now, Rexy." said his dad. "At the end of the day we will show up on this hill to pick you up. Do you understand? We will be here once classes are over"

Rexy's parents left him all alone on the hill. At first, he was scared, and he even started to cry to a little bit. But that all changed when two Triceratops started to walk towards him. They were small—just like him. Where those his classmates?

"Hi!" said the green triceratops. "My name is Sarah. And this is Billy my brother. You must be Rexy!"

"Yep! I'm Rexy", he said.

"Then you can be our friend!" said Billy the brown Triceratops. "Come on, the others are waiting. Teacher said that school is going to start soon!"

Rexy walked with Billy and Sarah and met up with the other dynos. Once they were all inside the fenced area the parents started leaving one by one. Rexy saw them hug his classmates as they went and he felt a little sad. He still missed his mommy and daddy.

There where so many different dynos there that Rexy didn't know what to call who. He knew the two triceratops Billy and Sarah that said hi to him earlier. Apart from them, there where another three triceratops.

He also counted two duckbills, three flying dinosaurs, and one long neck. There was another dinosaur with spikes all around its back, but Rexy didn't know what kind of dinosaur he was. There were other dinosaurs too, but

Rexy was too nervous to try to name them. As far as he could tell, he was the only meat eater there. It made him feel a little bit alone. All the other plant eaters seemed to have at least one pair. The long neck was the only other dinosaur that was alone like him. But even a baby long neck is already a very big dinosaur. And this one could squash rexy like a bug. Their teacher was an old looking triceratops named Mr Dandelion. He got that name because his favorite food was the dandelion, and that's what everyone called him. When Mr Dandelion cleared his throat, all the other dinosaurs stopped talking and listened.

"Hello all," said Mr Dandelion. "Today I see some old faces and some new faces as well. Whoever you are, welcome to another school year here in Dino Academy. Today I would like all of us to get to know each other first."

One by one each dyno had to walk up to the front of the class, say their name, what type of dinosaur they were and finally say what their favorite food was. One by one the plant eaters went up and said their names. Rexy was so nervous he thought that the world was going to end. His heart went ba-dump, ba-dump ba-dump.

"My name is Sarah!" Said the green triceratops from before. "I am a type of triceratops. And my favorite food is cabbage!"

"Nice to meet you Sarah," said the rest of the class at once. Sarah smiled at everyone and then sat down in her spot.

"Okay let's see here," said Mr Dandelion. "Ah. The next student is a new face here at Dino Academy. Can Rexy please come up to the front and tell us a little about themselves?"

Rexy heard a bunch of whispering behind his back as soon as his name was called. His claws where so sweaty that he didn't know what to do with them. He felt like the entire class was looking at him.

"Uh hello," he said to the class. "My name is Rexy and uh"

From the corner of his eye Rexy saw that Sarah and Billy where giving him a thumbs up a big smile. That helped him a lot.

"My favorite food is seafood!"

"Nice to meet you Rexy!" Said the rest of the class.

When Rexy went to sit down his new friends Sarah and Billy where still giving him a big thumbs up. After introducing himself, Rexy didn't feel so scared anymore. Maybe school could actually be fun like his parents said. After the introductions, Mr Dandelion introduced them to the first school subject called memory skills. It taught dinosaurs how to remember things. Dinos don't have paper, so they have to remember everything. Mr Dandelion told the class that it took him only five minutes to memorize the entire class, their faces and their favorite food. Rexy was amazed that his teacher remembered everything, and he wanted to be just like him. After memorization skills the dynos were introduced to counting, and Rexy was very good at it. Rexy had grown up counting things all on his own. He counted how many hairs his dad had on his forehead and the number of dinosaurs at the lake. One time Rexy even tried counting the number of scales on his body, but he couldn't do it without losing track of which scales he already counted. Rexy was surprised to find out that he was one of the best students in his class. He never raised his hand, but he almost always knew the answer. Even when nobody else would know it, Rexy wouldn't say anything. I wonder why that was? Rexy was a T-Rex and T-Rex dinosaurs are not afraid of anything. Usually it's the other dinosaurs who are afraid of the T-Rex. But there was something else that was bothering Rexy. Something that he heard the other dynos talking about. Sure, Rexy was different from them. But Rexy was also strange looking. And the other dinosaurs didn't like it. One of the things that Rexy overhead them say was that he had little arms. Ever since they said that, Rexy didn't want to raise his hand anymore. Even if he knew the answer, because he knew that the other dynos would laugh at him. When Mr. Dandelion dismissed the class, all of the dynos walked to their friends. Rexy didn't know who to sit with, so he just stood there listening to the others talk.

"Did you see those arms?" Said the dinosaur with spikes on his back. "They look like twigs!"

"Tyrannosaurus Rex?" said a duckbill, "more like small-armasaurus"

The other dinosaurs that gathered around them started to howl with laughter.

"Don't listen to them," said Sarah the triceratops. "They are just bullies, that's all"

"You can sit with us Rexy," said her brother Billy.

But before Rexy could say anything he saw his dad standing on the hill from before.

"Thanks guys, but I have to go"

Rexy walked by the group of dinosaurs making fun of him and he heard their laughter explode as he passed. Rexy felt like he was going to cry. But since his dad was there he didn't want to look like a weakling"

"There's my boy!" Said his massive dad. "How was your first day at school?"

"It was okay" Said Rexy.

He didn't talk much on the way home, and his father knew that something was wrong. It wasn't like Rexy to keep quiet.

"Son, did something happen at school?"

"It's nothing dad, really"

But his father wasn't having any of it. Rexy saw his dad flare his nostrils in anger.

"You tell me what's wrong right now, or I will go back to your school and have a word with your teacher"

Rexy gulped. He knew if his father went over there and argued with poor old Mr Dandelion something bad would happen. Knowing how his dad got when angry, Rexy thought he might even eat Mr Dandelion. And Rexy didn't want that, because he really liked Mr Dandelion. And so, Rexy told his dad everything about what happened at school that day. About the name calling, the laughing, and being embarrassed about raising his hand in class.

"Well this won't do," said his father, "This won't do at all Rexy. Your education comes first. Who cares what those plant eaters say to you. You can't let them bother you"

"But they do bother me, dad," sad Rexy looking down at his tiny arms. "Why do I even bother having arms if I can barely use them?"

"Son you are a T Rex!" Said his dad snapping his mouth and showing his teeth. "We have small arms. But we also have powerful jaws. And we have strong legs. We can out run almost any plant eater out there, and you want to be sad about little arms?"

"What should I do"? Asked Rexy. "If I go back to school tomorrow they will just laugh at me again"

"Well you are still going to school mister!" said his dad. "I got an idea"

His dad put his enormous head next to Rexy's and whispered something in his ear.

That night Rexy went to sleep feeling a little bit better. And after hearing his dad's plan, Rexy was ready to confront his bullies. A T Rex never runs away. And a T Rex never lets somebody make fun of their little arms. When Rexy showed up to school he was full of confidence. His dad told him a trick, and that trick was simple. The only way to deal with bullies is to bully them back. Rexy's dad said that he used the same trick when he was small to get others to respect him. Well, when Rexy tried it the plan didn't go so well. During recess all the dinosaurs were having fun and playing, but Rexy was waiting for the perfect time to strike. He found his target, and he lined up for an attack.

"Hey you with the spikes!" Said Rexy to the Stegosaurus who was making fun of him yesterday. "What does it feel like to be a peanut brain!"

Everyone gasped. The stegosaurus looked at Rexy then back at his friends and then at Rexy again. And then they all burst out laughing.

"Peanut brain!"

"Did you hear what he said"

"He said peanut brain!"

As the dinosaurs howled with laughter Rexy saw that they weren't laughing at his jokes. They were laughing at him.

"You plant eaters are all the same!" Said Rexy. "All roar and no bite!"

But the other dinosaurs kept laughing at Rexy. His dad's plan didn't seem to work and now he didn't know what to do.

"Why I ought to..." Said Rexy, but he was stopped by a loud cough from behind him.

"Mr Rexy," said his teacher, "Can I have a word with you in my office?

Uh oh. Was Rexy going to be in trouble?

Mr Dandelion didn't really have an office. He just pulled Rexy aside so that the other dinosaurs couldn't hear what they were saying.

"Rexy," he said. "Our school is very strict about name calling and bullying. I don't want to hear you saying bad things to the plant eaters again"

"But--" said Rexy.

"I want to remind you," his teacher interrupted. "That you are a minority here. The parents of the plant eaters were very nervous when I told them that a T Rex would be studying here. Because of this, you have to be on extra good behavior. You have to set the example. Do you understand?"

"Yes Mr Dandelion," said Rexy.

It just wasn't fair, thought Rexy. Why did he have to get in trouble when it was the plant eaters who had started everything. They were the ones that were bullying him.

"Don't worry about them," said his friend Sarah the triceratops. "If Mr Dandelion sees them bullying you he will have a talk with them too"

"My sister is right!" Said Billy. "You have to focus on your school work and not let the others distract you"

But Rexy wasn't so sure. Every time he raised his little arm somebody always started laughing at him. How was he supposed to ignore them and focus on his school work then? He wanted to show Mr Dandelion that he was a good student who paid attention in class. But the others kept distracting him.

"Hey Rexy, do you want to play tag with us?" Asked Sarah when the school day was over.

"Okay!" Said Rexy. It was the first time he was invited to play since starting school. And he really liked to play tag. A T Rex is quick on their feet and one of their favorite activities is chasing things.

"Tag you're it!"

Rexy started chasing after his new triceratops friends and he was having a blast. They were pretty fast for plant eaters. But they weren't fast enough!

"You are it!" Said Rexy

It wasn't long before the other dinosaurs got interested in their game of tag. First a duckbill asked to play, and then another triceratops. Soon half the entire class was playing with Rexy and his friends. Some of his bullies watched from afar.

"Look at the T Rex!" One of them said. "He can barely reach with his little arms!"

Rexy pretended not to hear them, but the others started laughing. And he was having so much fun too. Rexy was really glad when he saw his mom waiting for him on the hill. He said goodbye to all his friends and ran home.

"How was your day at school, honey" Asked his mom.

Rexy told her everything that had happened, and how using his dad's advice didn't work.

"Don't listen to your dad!" Said his mom. "It is never okay to bully others, even if they are being mean to you. You can't fight fire with more fire. It just doesn't work"

"Then what should I do?" Asked Rexy. "They won't stop making fun of me, even when I am having fun"

"I have an idea sweetie," said his mom. "But I can't promise it will work"

Rexy listened to her idea, and he thought it was genius. He couldn't do anything to make his little arms grow, so all he had to do was get bigger arms! His mom helped him look for a big stick, and helped him wrap it around his little arm with vines. Then she did the other arm as well. When she was all finished, Rexy's new arms were much bigger than his old ones. He could reach for things easily. Rexy absolutely loved them, and he couldn't wait to show them off at school the next day.

The pieces of wood made noise when he walked, but he didn't care. He was so happy to have new arms that he ran all the way to school, clopping all the way. He must have looked a little ridiculous, but Rexy only cared about having longer arms. Rexy showed up to his school with the new arms. At first nobody noticed them, but after a while dinosaurs where staring at him.

"What are those?" Asked Sarah.

"Oh, these are just extra arms my mom made me. They are so I can reach things!" Said Rexy.

"Aren't those uncomfortable?

"Not really!" Rexy said.

"I think they are cool!" Said Sarah's brother Billy.

Now when Rexy raised his hand he didn't feel bad about using his little arms. He could reach high up in the sky. But his new arms had lots of problems. It was hard for him to sit on the grass, and he kept bumping into other dinosaurs and poking them in their faces. By the end of the day everyone was laughing at him again. He looked even more ridiculous than before. And now that he was bumping into the other students, he was causing a big commotion.

"Ouch that hurt!" Said one poor duckbill that Rexy accidentally hit with his wooden arm.

"I'm going to tell my parents about this!"

Another dyno almost got his eye poked out by Rexy's arm when they were playing tag.

That's when Rexy heard the familiar cough behind him. Uh oh.

"Rexy." said Mr Dandelion. "Can I have a little talk with you?"

"You can't bring those arms to school anymore, Rexy. I'm sorry but they are just too much of a distraction for the other students. If I see them again tomorrow I will have to confiscate them"

Rexy was heartbroken. He was really starting to like his new arms too, and now the teacher said that he couldn't bring them to school. "Now what am I supposed to do" thought Rexy. His dad's idea didn't work. And now his mom's idea was also out of the question.

Rexy walked home with his dad that day feeling sad.

"I give up!" He said. "I'm going to quit school and join the circus!"

"You won't be doing that," said his dad. "I worked really hard to get you into this school. You will be staying"

"And the bullies?" asked Rexy.

"We will just have to deal with them son. There has to be another way"

"But we already tried everything!" Rexy said. "Nothing seems to work!"

"We will just have to think about something else. Don't give up Rexy"

Rexy spent the rest of the day trying to think of ways to deal with the bullies at school. But every time he thought of something, all he could think about was the other students laughing at him. Or Mr Dandelion telling him he couldn't do it. But then Rexy got an idea was truly amazing. His idea was so good that he couldn't wait to try it. His idea was simple. The other dinosaurs didn't like because he was so different. So all he had to do was be more like them. He had to be like a plant eater. If a plant eater liked to eat trees and grass, then so would he. If a plant eater liked to sit around all day, then so would he. And if a plant eater liked to make fun of meat eaters, then so would he. Rexy was very excited to go to school the next day and try out his new idea. The first thing he would do is eat grass with the plant eaters, and show them that he could be just like them. The only problem was that Rexy had never tasted grass before.

"Good morning Rexy," said Sarah.

"Morning Sarah, morning Billy" Said Rexy.

Then without warning, Rexy stuck his face in the grass and started eating it just like the triceratops did.

The grass tasted terrible, but Rexy was determined to be just like them.

"Rexy stop!" Said Sarah. "You can't eat grass like us. Mama said you will get sick" But Rexy said that he felt fine. He said that he liked grass, and that he was eating grass ever since he was born. "I'm just a little different, that's all" said Rexy. "I'm not like other T Rexes"

As the day went on Rexy continued to eat more grass. The other plant eaters looked at him curiously. What was he up to? It was the first time they ever saw a T Rex trying to eat like them.

"That meat eater is eating plants," they would say. Or, "That meat eater is crazy"

"He's not a real plant eater unless he eats dirt!" Said the stegosaurus.

And that is exactly what Rexy did. He walked over to the river where the dirt was very muddy and he shoved a mouthful of dirt into his face.

"Yummm," he said.

The other dinosaurs couldn't believe their eyes. They laughed so hard at Rexy for eating dirt that they almost started crying.

It looked like his plan had failed. The other dinosaurs were laughing at him harder than ever.

When it was time to go home Rexy had a terrible stomach ache.

"Well did you eat something funny," asked his dad.

Rexy explained everything that had happened at school that day, and told them about his idea to become a plant eater. "That's not possible, son" said his dad. "Once a meat eater always a meat eater"

"I just wanted to be more like them. So they wouldn't make fun of me anymore for being different"

"It's okay to be different, son. We can't all be the same, can we?"

"Rexy," said his mom. "Sometimes the key to bullying is to simply be yourself"

"What do you mean mama," Said Rexy. "What do you mean be myself?"

"What I mean Rexy, is to go to school and just be you. Who cares if you have little arms. Or if you eat meat. Having little arms doesn't mean you can't be smart"

His mama was right. Rexy knew he was one of the smartest in the class. He always knew the right answer, but he was too embarrassed to raise his hand.

"You are a T Rex," said his dad. "You should be proud of that"

"I am proud!" Said Rexy. "And I do like being a T Rex!"

"So, then you should be also proud of having small arms," said his dad. "Because that's how T Rexes are made"

His dad was right. T Rexes have small arms, but that doesn't stop them from being one of the coolest dinosaurs around.

"Okay," said Rexy. "For now on I will be myself at school. Thanks mom, thanks dad"

Unfortunately for Rexy, he would have to pay the price for trying to be a plant eater. He had a tummy ache for the entire day. Show and tell was coming up in school and Rexy wasn't sure what he would take. He couldn't take his wooden arms, because Mr Dandelion sad he couldn't bring them anymore. Instead Rexy decided to bring a shiny rock he found the other day by the river. The rock was his favorite color of blue just like the sky. The other students brought many different things. One duckbill brought in their pet giant cricket, and another came in with their favorite stick. The triceratops brother and sister brought in really big feather. The long neck dinosaur brought in a necklace made out of twigs. Each dinosaur took turns talking about their favorite thing. When it was Rexy's turn, even his bullies listened to him talk. Everyone really liked his shiny rock. And he let them take turns looking at it. Overall, it was a really good day. And all Rexy had to do was be himself. He didn't let anyone bother him. He raised his hand, even though it looked funny.

"Oh no!" Said the stegosaurus. "I can't find my great-great-great grandfathers spike!"

The stegosaurus had lost his show and tell item. The dinosaurs all helped look and look, until finally one of the duckbills spotted it.

"Is that it? There, in between those two boulders!"

"Yes that's it!" Said the stegosaurus. "That's my great-great-great grandfathers spike!"

The only problem was that no dinosaur could reach it. There wasn't enough room to reach a hand down there. Rexy was interested in what they were doing over by those two boulders. And even though the stegosaurus used to make fun of his arm, he still wanted to help.

"What's going on here?"

"Nobody can reach the spike," said the duckbill. "Our hands are too fat and stumpy!"

Ah, but not Rexy's. Rexy's arm was short and small. It fit perfectly in between the two boulders.

He pulled it out without any help from the others and they all watched in amazement

"Wow! You did it" said the Stegosaurus. "I guess T Rexes aren't so bad after all"

When Rexy's mom came to pick him up on the hill, he told her all about what happened. Nobody called Rexy names after that, and they never laughed at him for having small arms. "You were right mom. I just had to be myself and everything worked out!"

The next day Rexy woke up extra early to go to school. He couldn't wait to meet up with all his new friends. When he got there, they surprised Rexy with a gift.

"Here you go Rexy," said Sarah. "I know it's hard for you to raise your hand in class, so we got you this" They made Rexy his very own hand! Well, not really. It was just a big stick with a wooden hand attached to the end. Every time Rexy wanted to answer a question in class all he had to do was pick up the stick high up in the air After that, nobody made fun of him for having small arms again. In the end things turned out just fine for Rexy. And all he had to do was be himself. Everyone has their own unique way of doing things and everybody is different. You must learn to accept those differences because it is what makes you, you. A meat eater could never turn into a plant eater, and that is okay. Some people are born with big noses, others have curly hair and some are just a little different from everyone else. But just like Rexy learned, it is okay to be different. So don't be afraid to be yourself. Being yourself is all that you can be. And with that, my friend, I wish you a goodnight. I am so happy that you decided to stay with me through this adventure we had in Dino Land. And I'm so glad that you got to meet Rexy and all his friends. I hope you enjoyed it as much as I did.

Until next time.

Scott and Nancy Learn to Get Along

Nancy and Scott are twins. They had spent their entire lives together. They liked the same foods, the same games, the same colors, and the same friends. For their short six years, they  had gotten along amazingly, but one-day, things changed.

Ever since their sixth birthday, Nancy and Scott had started liking different things. At first, it was simple things. Nancy decided she didn't like peas anymore, and Scott decided he preferred the color green instead of the color blue. It wasn't a big deal. But then their differences became bigger. They got so big that Nancy and Scott didn't know what to do.

"No! She's my best friend," Nancy shouted at the top of her lungs.

"She gave ME the train for MY birthday!" Scott shouted back.

"It was MY birthday party, too, and she gave ME the remote-controlled car."

"Nuh, uh! That was ours. I was the only one that got something special."

"NO! YOU! WEREN'T!"

Nancy and Scott had screaming matches like this often now. What used to be a quiet household with twin siblings who could always find something to agree on was now a house of yells and screams. They couldn't find a middle ground anymore. One of them always had to be right, no matter what. These fights could go on for hours if their parents didn't step in.

Cara and Brian, their parents, couldn't figure out what to do. They had sat them down time and time again explaining how to find common ground, and that it was okay not to always agree. But none of those meetings had ever helped. The twins seemed to be getting angrier and angrier with each other. Their parents were afraid that they might end up having a physical fight if they didn't learn how to get along with the changes to their personalities. Unfortunately, this present fight wasn't at home. It was in the park, and there wasn't anybody that could step in and stop their yelling. The park was just down the street from their house, so they were allowed to go there by themselves as long as they let their parents know. They had left just after noon, seemingly in a good mood, and said they would be home by four.

It was well past four, and Cara was getting worried. She was sure they were okay, but with the way they had been behaving, she worried that they had gotten into a fight. She was just about to walk down to the park when the phone rang.

"Hello," Cara said.

"You need to do something about your kids," a shrill old voice stated on the other side of the line.

"Excuse me?"

Cara knew the voice. It was old lady Whittaker. She lived right next to the park, and she was always giving her "advice" about the twins. Ever since they had started arguing more, Mrs. Whittaker would call, and in her nicest way possible, would tell Cara or Brian to make their kids shut up. She wasn't the nicest person, but Cara had learned to deal with her.

"Your children are at the park making a big scene," Mrs. Whittaker sneered.

"I was just getting ready to go get them, but thanks for slowing me down."

"I just thought you would like to know that your children don't know how to behave in public."

"Thank you, Mrs. Whittaker. Goodbye."

Cara hung up the phone. She grabbed her pursed and raced out the door towards the park. This wasn't the first time she had to pick them up from the park because they got into an argument. In fact, it had happened nearly every time they had gone to the park together since their birthday. As she got closer to the gate, she could hear them screaming.

"I want to invite her over for a sleepover, and I don't want you at home," Nancy screamed.

"NO! I'm having a sleepover, and she's coming, and you're not going to be at home!"

Nancy was taking a deep breath to yell something back at her brother when Cara stepped in.

"Both of you home, now."

She motioned for Nancy to leave first and for Scott to follow her, keeping herself between them. They walked home in silence, but Nancy and Scott were still filled with anger. Once home, Cara sent them to their rooms to let them cool off. After a few minutes, she went to Nancy first.

"Why were you two making such a scene at the park?"

"Scott wants to invite Susan here for a sleepover, but she's my friend. I want her at my sleepover, and I don't want Scott here."

"When your father and I said that you two could have a sleepover, we meant together. Now, if you want to invite friends and he invites his, you and your friends can sleep in here and his in his room, but you won't be able to have a sleepover if you two can't learn to get along."

"But mom…"

Cara left Nancy's room and walked across the hall to Scott's.

"What were you and Nancy arguing about at the park?"

"She thinks Susan is her friend, but she is really mine. She gave me a special present for my birthday."

"You both got a present from her on your birthday."

"No, the train was mine, and the car was both of ours."

"Scott, the package with the car had Nancy's name on it. You two can share it like you have done with toys in the past, but just like the train was given to you, the car was given to Nancy."

"Susan likes me better!"

"I understand that you're upset, but I don't like it when you yell at me. Like I told your sister, you two will not be having a sleepover until you can show me and your father you can get along for more than a few minutes and can reach an agreement on the friends."

Cara left Nancy and Scott in their rooms. She felt angry herself, now, but she knew screaming at them wouldn't help. Instead, she went to her own room and took some deep breaths and calmed herself. After a moment, she called Brian and asked him to bring in supper. She had some thinking to do to help her kids, and she didn't have time to cook.

Nancy paced around her bedroom. She still felt so angry with her brother. Ever since their birthday party, almost every day, she felt angry with him. When he spoke to her, she could feel her face going red, and her palms would begin to sweat. She never knew what to do, so she always yelled. Yelling made her feel good for a moment. She'd eventually calm down, and there were even times where she and Scott would get along, but that didn't happen often.

Scott was pacing as well. As much as he and Nancy had changed, they still had a lot in common. They felt just as strongly about each other. They both loved yelling when they were angry because that was the only thing that made them feel better. But Scott had an urge that Nancy hadn't experienced. He really felt like he needed to hit something. He had never acted on it, mainly because it scared him.

When Brian got home, he set the table as his wife told him what had happened today. He shook his head. He missed the days when his kids got along, but they were two different people, so they had to learn how to accept each other. Cara called the kids in for dinner. Nancy and Scott ran into each other as they stepped out of the rooms.

"Watch where you're going!" Scott shouted.

"You ran into me!"

"No, I didn't. You had your door open first and waited for me to step out before you came out."

"Nuh, uh."

"Kids," Brian yelled, getting their attention, "That's enough. Get to the kitchen and sit down. I don't want to hear any more arguing."

Nancy and Scott walked to the table, hitting, and shoving each other with their elbows. Cara pointed to the two chairs across from each other. They sat down and frowned at one another. They knew what was going to happen. They were only sat across from each other if mom and dad were going to try to teach them a lesson. But Cara and Brian didn't say anything. They served up the food, and everybody ate quietly. The only sound that could be heard was the sound of forks on plates. Once everyone was finished, Nancy helped her mom clear the table. The kids started to leave the kitchen to go play, but their parents stopped them.

"Sit back down," Brian said sternly.

The kids did as they were told and sat back down. Cara had picked up a couple of large pads of paper and some markers and sat one down at each kid.

"We're going to do something and try to figure out why you two keep arguing, okay?" Cara said.

"Okay," the kids mumbled.

"Alright, I want you both to write down five things that the other does that upsets you."

The children quickly wrote down their five things and looked up to their mom for further instruction.

"What did you write?" Cara asked Nancy.

"He's tall, he likes the color green, he thinks everything is his, he doesn't like the pool, and he talks funny."

"Okay, Scott, what did you put?"

"She thinks Susan likes her, she hates peas, she likes dolls, she wants to take dance, and she likes to read."

"Now, write five things that you like about each other."

Nancy and Scott started writing things down, but it took them a little longer to get to five things. Their likes didn't come as quickly as their dislikes.

"What did you get, Nancy?"

"He eats the peas I don't like, he yells at the guys that won't let me play cars, he sings, he likes cats, and he's my brother."

"Scott?"

"She eats the carrots I don't like, she shares her toys, she doesn't let kids laugh when I won't get in the pool, she helps me read, and she's my sister."

"Why did you two end with she's my sister or brother?"

"I couldn't think of anything else," Nancy said.

"Me, too."

"But that means you two still like being siblings, so why do you always argue," Brian said.

"Because she likes stupid things," Scott said.

"So, do you," Nancy stated.

"We're not arguing right now. You two want to have a sleepover?"

"Yes," they said.

"Then we have to figure out how you two can get along without fighting."

"Your differences are what make you two angry with each other, right?" Cara asked.

"Yes."

"Well, everybody is different. You get along with your friends, and they don't like the exact same things that you like, do they?"

"No, Susan likes playing soccer, and we both hate soccer," Scott said.

"But you two are fighting about who gets her at your sleepover."

"I suppose, but we can't both have her. And he is always trying to make me share something that I don't want to," Nancy said.

"Okay, I think it's time I told you, kids, something. You know Mrs. Whittaker?"

"Yeah."

"I don't care for her. She is always calling over here telling me how to raise you two, and how I am too soft of a parent. I don't appreciate how she always dismisses my parenting."

"But I never hear you yell at her," Nancy said.

"I know, that's why I'm telling you this. I don't yell at her because it wouldn't do any good. Sure, yelling makes you feel good for a moment, and it can help when somebody isn't listening to you, but most of the time, yelling isn't worth it. People listen better if you just talk to them. There is something about humans where we shut off our ears when somebody yells. There are going to be different people around you your entire life, and you have to learn how to work with them so that you aren't constantly angry."

"Being angry will happen, but you don't want to be angry all the time. By the looks of it, you two have been angry almost all the time since your birthday. Anger can cause a lot of problems if you let it stay inside of you," Brian added.

"But how do we do that?" Scott asked.

"Well, you can always come to us, and we can help you talk it out, but we might not always be available to help. So, the first thing is, if you feel yourself getting really angry, you need to go to your room. Take at least ten minutes to calm down and once you don't feel as angry, come back, and talk to each other. Also, it helps if you label your emotions. Nancy, you said you don't like it when he acts like everything is his."

"Yeah."

"How does it make you feel when he says something is his?"

"Mad."

"Okay, when he does something like that, instead of yelling, say, 'Scott, it makes me mad when you say that something is yours.' This lets your brother know how you feel. You can also do that when he makes you happy or another positive emotion."

"I think I could do that," Nancy.

"Me too."

"Now, how are you two going to have a sleepover without fighting?"

"We could just have it together," Nancy said.

"Yeah, we could do like we always do, and our friends can choose who and what they want to play with."

"We could sleep in the living room."

"Yeah, and make forts with the furniture."

"Yeah, mama, daddy, could we do that?"

"If you go this whole next week without having a screaming match, yes, we can make forts in the living room," Brian said.

The kids jumped up and hugged their parents. They felt lighter than they had in a while, and neither one of them felt angry when they looked at the other. During the next week, there were moments when they wanted to yell and scream at each other, but they didn't. They talked things through in a regular voice. Sure, there were times when they got a little loud, but their parents would step in and have them take a deep breath.

By the end of the week, they were helping their parents set up forts in the living room before their friends arrived. Their entire sleepover was a success, and they never once yelled at each other in front of their friends.

Magic at the Magic Show

Have you ever been to a magic show? Better yet, have you ever been a part of a magic show? What if I told you that you could actually be a part of a magic show right this moment if you wanted to? You can! You really can- In your mind! Your mind is capable of doing many incredible things, including something called Visualization.

To begin your visualization practice, close your eyes. Really, close your eyes (unless you are the one reading this, of course!) To build a very strong visualization, it is usually helpful to first center yourself and be sure you are giving your brain the very best tools it needs to work with. In this case, that means oxygen, and oxygen means taking some good, deep breaths.

You are going to take some slow, deep breaths now, following along with my instruction: Breathe in very slowly, 1 – 2 – 3 – 4. Now breathe out, very slowly, 1 – 2 – 3 – 4. Excellent. Now again very slowly, 1 – 2 – 3 – 4 and breathe back out very slowly, 1 – 2 – 3 – 4 very nice. Once more, very slowly in 1 – 2 – 3 – 4 and back out very slowly, 1 – 2 – 3 – 4. Great!

Take a moment to review how you feel. Are you comfy and feeling good? Okay, great.

Imagine yourself, in your mind's eye, in an audience in a huge, dimly lit auditorium. Looking around you, you can see this place is packed! Up on stage, there is a spotlight and one person standing front and center with a small table in front of him and a single chair next to the table. Look closer, who is that person?

He is tall with dark hair, and he appears to have some sort of a cape and top hat on. He takes the top hat off and looks to be rummaging around within the hat... how deep is that thing anyway! It looks like his whole entire arm is in his hat! And what on earth is he pulling out of it now? Oh, my goodness, look! It's a fluffy white bunny rabbit!

You and the rest of the audience applaud this amazing trick. How cool! This person is a magician, and you are at a magic show. Wow! Take a moment and take a long, deep breath in. You can smell the old auditorium with its worn leather seats and its maple wood stage. Just then, you hear the magician asking the crowd for a volunteer to come up on stage.

You have never been on stage as a magician's volunteer before, and you have to think a moment; what do you think the magician will need the volunteer to do? Will you be nervous? You realize your arm is already going up as you are thinking through it all because your excitement wins out over your worry every time. Now the magician is looking directly at you and motioning for you to come up! Wow! This is incredible!

You get up and out of your seat and make y our way out of your row. The other audience members are congratulating you on being picked. Everyone is very excited to see what will happen next, including you! You can feel the excitement in the air as you make your way up the steps on to the stage.

The magician welcomes you up on the stage and asks you to sit on the chair beside the table. You take a seat, and he immediately hands you the fluffy white bunny that he had just pulled from his hat. He tells you his bunny's name is Fluffy and that it is your job to keep Fluffy comfortable during this next trick, so you will need to pet Fluffy and keep her calm.

The magician reaches back into his top hat and begins rummaging around again. Oh, my goodness, seriously. How deep is that thing? He pulls out a large blueish black velvet drape and brings it over to where you are sitting with Fluffy. You are petting Fluffy and smiling. Fluffy's fur is so soft, and the lights of the stage are so warm as you sit petting this fluffy white bunny rabbit.

The magician drapes the bluish-black velvet drape over you and Fluffy and reminds you that you must keep petting Fluffy and keep her comfortable during this next trick. You are feeling so excited now to see what this trick will be! The magician takes his wand and waves it around both you and Fluffy a few times and says some silly magic words and voila!

The magician pulls the drape off of you and Fluffy bunny in one swift motion, revealing that instead of Fluffy Bunny in your lap, you are now holding and petting a stuffed bunny rabbit toy! You and the audience gasp together.

Your mouth drops open in disbelief, how did this happen? What on earth is going on? Where is the little fluffy bunny rabbit you had been petting? The magician motions to your head, and you reach up to feel that you are now wearing the magician's tall top hat on your very own head. You pull the top hat off and guess what's underneath? Fluffy Bunny Rabbit!!!!

The audience erupts into applause as the magician scoops the fluffy bunny rabbit up off of your head and returns him to the table with the tall top hat. The magician motions for you to stand up and take a bow as he thanks you for your assistance. You are still in absolute disbelief on how on earth he did this trick when he tells you that you can keep stuffed bunny rabbit toy as a souvenir.

You make your way back off the stage and to your seat, with the other audience members clapping for you and the magician. Once you've sat back down on the cool leather seat, you realize you are grinning ear to ear. You are so happy to be a part of this magic show, and you know that it has been an experience that you will never forget. Plus, you have this soft fluffy bunny rabbit toy to always help you remember it by. You feel so thankful that you have had this incredibly cool magic show experience!

You do not have to leave this magic show just yet if you don't want to. You can stay here in the audience, watching these amazing magic tricks as long as you want, and you can come back here anytime you'd like.

You can create anything you want in your mind. Imagine where you want to go and build the picture in your mind. Be sure to imagine how you want it to smell, taste, hear, and feel. The more detailed you can make your mental picture, the more you will enjoy being there.

It is all up to you. Perhaps as you drift off to sleep, you may find yourself back here in the auditorium with the maple wood stage, waiting for the magician to ask for another volunteer from the audience.

Finishing the Witch's Brew

Agatha was a witch who lived in the enchanted woods. In the enchanted woods, there was a great, big community of witched and wizards. All the witches would get together and cast their magic together, and all the wizards would do the same. A group of witches that work together is called a "coven," and a group of wizards that work together is called a "kiln." Every year on Halloween, the All Hallows Eve celebration was held for all the residents of the woods to enjoy. Every year, the witches and the wizards would both bring a delicious brew to the All Hallows Eve celebration for everyone to drink. The Wizard King, who was in charge of the enchanted woods would taste some of both brews at the celebration. The group with the most delicious, most tingly, most magical, and most bubbly brew would be crowned the winners! The winning group would be sent on a tropical vacation for the winter! A little-known fact about witches and wizards is that spending time in the sun and playing at the beach is their favorite type of vacation! They love having fun in the sun, playing volleyball, sunbathing, swimming, and sitting by the pool! The group that lost would stay in the enchanted woods and look after things through the winter. This year, Agatha was in charge of bringing four of the most important ingredients for the witch's brew and she couldn't let her coven down! Just days before the celebration, she had gone into town and bought the bat, newt, spider, and sugar for the brew. Now, these ingredients might not sound like something you would want to drink, but with the right amount of magic and sugar, they are absolutely delicious!

"You're sure you can handle this, Aggie?" Hilda, Agatha's best friend, had come over to drop off the cauldron of brew. "I know that sometimes you can get a little... well, forgetful."

"Yes, I can do it! I already have everything I need in order to make this the most delicious brew this celebration has ever seen! The spider I bought has been steeped in sour apple cordial for 200 years and is ready to bring a flavor to this party that the Wizard King won't soon forget!" Hilda and Agatha squealed with excitement as Hilda made her way out the door to leave the brew with Agatha. Agatha dashed straight into the kitchen to add her ingredients to the brew. When she got into the kitchen, she found that there was a terrible problem. Her spider had gotten up and walked away! She was sure that it had been petrified and that it couldn't have gotten up and walked away like that. She looked at the clock and it was only twelve minutes until the shop closed. She grabbed her hat, broom, and cloak and dashed out the door to go buy another one. She threw her cloak around her shoulders, plopped her hat on her head and zoomed off to the shop on her broom. When she arrived at the shop, there was a sign hanging on the door that read, "On vacation for All Hallows Eve, see you there!" Agatha's smile fell off her face as she read the sign. She had tried so hard to get there before closing time, only to realize that the shop had been closed all day long! She panicked for a moment as she thought of places where she could get another spider at this late hour. She thought about it some more and realized that Hilda must have a spider she could use! She hopped back onto her broom and zoomed back across the woods. She arrived at Hilda's home and knocked on the door playfully. She waited for a long moment and knocked once more, a little less playfully this time. Still, there was no answer. She knocked one final time before giving up, getting back onto her broom, and flying back to her cottage.

How could this be? How could it be that there was nowhere to find the spider she needed to make the perfect witch's brew? She wondered for a moment if she could find a replacement ingredient that would taste just as delicious as the spider. As she thought, she remembered that there were rules to the competition for making the brew. She was only allowed to put the approved ingredients into the brew. She had told the council exactly what she would be putting into the brew, and they were all expecting it. There was no way, with the other ingredients that Agatha had at home, she would be able to make the brew as delicious as she had wanted to make it. She flew home, feeling sad and defeated. As she opened the door, she thought of the ways she might have to make it up to her coven if it was her fault their brew lost the contest. They would never forgive her if they missed out on a tropical vacation because she lost one lousy spider! She arrived home and opened the front door. She hung up her hat and cloak, set down her broom and went back into the kitchen to start putting the other ingredients into the brew. As she added each one, the brew sizzled, bubbled, and changed color. When she added the sugar, the brew turned bright pink! When she added the newt, it turned a lovely shade of blue. When she added the bat, the brew bubbled, thickened, and turned a sickening shade of brown. Nervously, Agatha pulled her spoon out of the brew and took a little taste. To her surprise, it tasted okay! She looked down and thought that the look of the brew and the thickness was enough to keep The Wizard King from ever touching it.

How can we win this if The Wizard King won't even sip my brew! Agatha looked around the kitchen sadly when she noticed something poking out from underneath her spice rack. She walked over to the counter and pulled it out. The newt! She had found the newt! Agatha thought she must have swept it under the spice rack by mistake when she was cleaning up the dishes after she made breakfast that morning. She ran back over to the cauldron and dropped the spider into it, stirring very carefully. As she stirred, the brew began to thin out and brighten up. She stirred a little more and, as she did, the color turned a beautiful, gleaming green color. She spooned a little bit of the brew into a cup and took a taste. As she did, her eyes shot open, she leaped into the air and her socks flew off, all the way across the room! The brew was so delicious, it knocked her socks off! This would surely be the most perfect brew any All Hallows Eve celebration had ever seen! Agatha ran to the head witch in her coven so she could taste it. Immediately, a meeting of the coven was called, and everyone was asked to taste the brew that Agatha had saved! Everyone cheered for Agatha and praised her for her amazing ideas about how to make the brew delicious.

At the All Hallows Eve celebration, The Wizard King said that there was no question: the witches had won the contest! All the witches would get their tropical vacation and fun in the sun!

Mouse of Doom

The animal keepers at The Funmazing Circus thought that they were so clever when they named the new baby elephant Eleanor. However, Eleanor the Elephant is a mouthful and they have regretted it evermore.

Eleanor (Ellen for short) was the most adorable baby animal that the performers had ever seen. She was the color of clouds before a storm and tripped over her own ears more than anyone has ever tripped over anything. She was a bubbly little creature and would never shy away from learning new tricks. Ellen wore a periwinkle bow around her neck because she had always loved the color. A few of the trainers lamented that she was the sassiest little elephant and deserved her own hour in the show to perform her tricks. Ellen loved her job in the circus and had a natural presence on the stage. She was also a huge draw for the crowds, and they used her image on all the printed advertisements. Ellen had learned a new trick where she would lay down behind a large board that served as a wall to block her body. One of the trainers would play snake-charming music, and she would allow her trunk to slowly dance up above the wooden wall. The audience would think that she was a snake. She and the trainer would keep this illusion going for quite a while before she would stand up and reveal herself to the audience. They would scream and applaud her so loudly. She would stumble off the main stage, accidentally stepping on her ears once or three times.

Ellen was a wonderful performer and loved her life with her circus family. One fateful day, the trainers told her that she needed to work on her grace and balance. She was understandably upset. Ellen was a star! The audience seemed to love her exactly as she was, so why were they asking her to do something that was in opposition to her nature? It wasn't like they were asking her to do a new trick, they were asking her to change her nature. This brought Ellen to the point of tears and she felt as though they were telling her that she wasn't good enough. She didn't take the revelation well and ran to her specialized enclosure to sulk. The peppy pink and purple colors that adorned her walls were not enough to lift her spirits at this moment, as they had been in the past. She buried her head in a pillow and enclosed her ears around her, in a further effort to drown out the world around her.

Ellen sobbed for a while, knowing that's important to allow oneself to express one's emotions. As she began to calm down, she noticed a rustling in the stillness of her room. A tiny noise penetrated the quiet and caused the small elephant to take pause. She slowly pulled her ears from over her eyes to find the culprit. The movement stopped and Ellen decided that it must have just been the wind playing tricks on her very sensitive hearing. All the tears had worn our young hero completely out, so she repositioned her ears and readied herself for a nap. No sooner than she had covered her eyes again, that darn noise came back. She was determined to find the source, so she moved slowly and methodically this time. Ellen allowed her ears to gently fall away from her face, as though she were asleep. The tiny disturbance paused for a moment and then continued, probably safe in the knowledge that the elephant was resting. That is when she saw the creature responsible for the ruckus and her heart sank. It is at this point in our story that we must take a moment to understand a crucial fact about elephants. They have a natural aversion to small animals. This is a widely accepted fact, but we must understand why. In the chaos of excitement, it would be very easy for a tiny creature to misplace its' sense of direction and run right up an elephant's trunk. It is speculated that elephants are born with this disdain for smallness, and object to a tiny thing in the same way that you or I might object to a snake or a spider.

A small brown mouse stood anxiously in the corner of the room, looking for leftover straw for her own house. This tiny mouse had a nerve of steel and was mostly unbothered by the elephant while trying to be very mindful of its' awareness. She was a scavenger of other's junk but was also very careful not to take anything of sentimental value to anyone else. The tiny mouse occasionally glanced up at Ellen, and finally realized that she was being watched. They both let out a terrible shriek and the mouse scurried away in a blind panic. Ellen was still frozen with fear and concerned that the mouse might return to finish what it started. She stayed glued to her pillow for some time before she gathered her courage and went to find her trainer. The trainers searched her room from top to bottom and found no evidence that a mouse was ever there. They assumed that the small elephant was still upset about their earlier request to learn balance and was allowing that to cloud her perception. They informed Ellen that everything was quite alright and then left her again, to her own devices. What a terrible day for our elephant. Later that night, there was a tiny knock at the bottom of the entrance to her room. Ellen told the knocker to come in, half out of habit. The tiny brown mouse stood to wait in the doorway.

"I am so sorry that I gave you such a fright earlier. It was wrong of me to be in your room without permission. I was looking for straw for my own house. I really did not mean to frighten you. My name is Ida." The mouse said.

"Take anything you want, except for my bow!" Ellen screamed back. She was visibly shaken by the mouse's presence, and willing to do anything to rid herself of this tiny monster.

"Tell me Elephant, why are you so terrified of me?" The mouse asked.

Ellen explained that she was compulsively worried that something as tiny as this crafty little mouse might run right up her trunk. This seemed to be a fear that all elephants possessed, and she was surely not alone in this belief. Ida shook her head in dismay, knowing that there is no way that this elephant has ever had an experience even remotely like the one that she has been envisioning. This sort of thinking led to a lot of negative mouse stereotypes. Even if Ida had a habit of breaking into rooms and stealing trash, she'd never even think of clogging up someone else's nose tube thing (mice aren't hyperaware of elephant body parts). She did her best to explain to the elephant that she was actually a huge fan of her performance and had often wondered what it would be like to be on stage herself. Ellen found herself feeling more and more comfortable with the mouse as their conversation went on. She even confided in Ida about the trainers and their request that she overcomes her natural clumsiness. Ellen then talked at length about how she knew that she could never be as graceful as some of the other animals. Ida had always been a good listener. She took the time to really understand Ellen's hesitation with the request, before finally offering her advice:

"Please don't think of it as the trainers asking you to change a part of your personality. They're asking you to evolve into a better performer. You aren't going to be a baby forever, and someday you will need to know how to get around without hurting yourself. Becoming better is never a bad thing and if you think that you can't do it... well, you are just wrong. You need to change your thought process around change; change is a wonderful thing. Change is how you become the person that you're meant to be. Instead of tearing yourself down, you should build yourself up. Practice your heart and know that you can overcome this obstacle just like every obstacle." The mouse said.

Ellen was quiet for a moment while she considered Ida's words. She hadn't even considered that they were preparing her for the future. She thought that the trainers wanted her to change as an attack on her talent as a performer. She agreed to try her best to become more graceful and she asked her new friend to help her train. The next day the two set out to teach Ellen balance and awareness of her surroundings. Ida sat atop her head and pointed out every unlevel piece of ground as they traversed a field behind the circus. Ellen was unsteady on the first day of practice and became more and more frustrated as the day went on. She stumbled over her ears swayed from one side to the other. Ellen sighed and sat on the edge of the field, upset with herself for failing. Ida, still clinging to the top of the small elephant's head, was having none of this. She explained that failure is a necessary step in the process of mastering a skill.

"My first house was a wreck, easily found and destroyed by larger animals. The next time I built a house, I did so in a more secluded environment. Every time I rebuild, my houses get better and better. This does not defeat; it's only your first step in the process." The mouse explained.

The next day, the pair returned to the field. They tied Ellen's ears back with her favorite bow and there was an instant change. The little elephant was able to see all around herself now and no longer had to worry about tripping over every rock they crossed. Ida realized that this whole time, her ears had been the issue. The two of them still practiced all day, but the difference in Ellen's stride was remarkable. From that week on, the two were inseparable. Ida rebuilt her house in Ellen's room and two stayed up laughing late into the night, every night. If Ellen had let her fear get the better of her, to this day she would be a clumsy elephant with no best friend.

Soon Ellen had convinced the trainers to let Ida try out for the circus too. She was such a talented little mouse, that the circus was eager to have her. Ida and Ellen became known worldwide as The Unlikely Duo, and eventually, they performed all of their acts together. Ellen insisted that Ida take one of her favorite pink bows to that they could match on stage. Ida was especially nimble and excellent at acrobatic tricks, though ensuring that the audience could see her was not always the simplest task. One of the more industrious trainers actually invented a huge magnifying glass that became a staple in their acts. The trainers would roll out the enormous contraption and the crowd would go wild. Watching in eager anticipation as the mouse flipped around Ellen, who was always very careful to gently catch Ida with her trunk.

Then Ellen would dance around the ring as though rhythm and grace were gifts, she was given at birth. She would sashay around throwing out one foot at a time. The audience loved her, and her best friend Ida and they continued to be a favorite attraction for many years to come. The most treasured of their shows involved Ida pretending to scare Ellen, who would then run through a very difficult obstacle course that consisted of many challenging jumps and twists. In a playful spirit, they named this act The Mouse of Doom.

Neck Made for Dance

In the Funmazing Circus, every animal had a role and they were all considered important by both the staff and the audience. The animals that performed in the ring were given attention in a different and exciting way, but in the petting zoo, you were valued just for your existence. This made for a very easy and relaxed life for the animals that were not part of the show. They were required to be social every day for a few hours, and they had the rest of the day to themselves. No learning complicated techniques or crazy training. Life was laidback, and most of the petting zoo appreciated this. That is, except for a young giraffe named Jeff.

Jeff was addicted to the idea of being a performer. He felt as though it was something that he was born to do. He had so far, been unable to convince the trainers that he should be allowed to come up with a routine. They brushed off his requests because he was such a beloved member of the petting zoo. Children loved the idea of taking pictures of and hanging out with a giraffe that didn't tower above them, as Jeff's mother did. She had her own special place in the petting zoo though and was thrilled to have such an easy and reliable job.

Jeff's mother had often tried to talk him out of taking on an act in the circus. She felt as though the performers had too much responsibility and did not like the fact that Jeff could end up performing dangerous stunts for the entertainment of others. So, Jeff watched day in and day out as the other animals got to show everyone how talented they were, while he was stuck posing for pictures. He wanted to hear the roar of the crowd as they announced his name, and he wanted to see that large spotlight shining down on him. Jeff loved the clapping and was saddened at the thought that no one would ever clap for him. Time continued and as Jeff got older, his mother came to understand how being cooped up was affecting him. He just was not himself lately, and he hadn't been for some time. He smiled for pictures and enjoyed his time with the public, but it always seemed as though his brain was elsewhere. One day she nudged Jeff to the side. She told him that she would condone him having his own act, as long as it didn't involve anything dangerous. She also asked that before he approaches the trainers about being included in the show, he would take the time to figure out what his act would consist of. Jeff was overcome with joy at the revelation that his mother supported his decision to figure out who he really was. He began a process of extensive research in an effort to determine what his talent would be. He asked every animal that crossed his path how they realized what they were born to do. Much to his dismay, they had all been trained from birth for their particular acts, in the same way, that he had always been in the petting zoo.

The young giraffe spent many a night thinking about his decisions and trying to decide if he was making the right choice. He knew that he would be at a disadvantage, but he also knew that he could not just give up on his goal to become part of the stage show. Jeff was at such a crossroads in his young mind. He was so torn that one night he ran crying to his mother. She always knew just how to ease his thoughts.

She told Jeff that whenever he felt like he was not in control of his emotions to slowly breathe in through his mouth and out from his nose. Take deep breaths and focus on steadying himself before he worried about any of that other stuff. Just sit and breathe deeply. Jeff found this technique to be extremely helpful when he began to worry about his future and what his prospects might be.

His mother also taught the young giraffe to plant himself on the ground and focus on those same deep breaths. She told him to allow his thoughts to pass through his head without pursuing any of them. Just breathe in and breathe out. By following this advice, he was often able to take a step back from the situation that was troubling him. It allowed him to approach his problems from an entirely new perspective. Jeff felt renewed and ready to tackle his search. His mother was always his biggest fan and she knew that he was capable of anything he set his mind to. Being a performer had been his aspiration from the time he was born he loved the attention of a captive audience. One day Jeff managed to get the attention of his favorite trainer Sarah. He told her again about his desire to join the rest of the team under the big top. He went on and on about all of the areas that he would like to learn mastery of.

Sarah loved Jeff; everyone loved Jeff. She just didn't see the value in taking him away from something that he was good at, to place him in a new area. It didn't make sense from a business perspective and all of the other animals had been trained from birth in their areas of expertise. Sarah could not break Jeff's heart with this sentiment though, so she told him that maybe they would use him around the grounds more. He could try out some new things and maybe one day in the future, they could see if he had a talent for performing.

Jeff knew that this was mostly a no but was thrilled to have the opportunity to change up his scenery and knew that he would find a way to prove to the trainers that he had what it took to perform. He was even prepared to find his skills on his own. In his downtime, Jeff began trying to figure out what his talents were. He tried running quickly and jumping over obstacles, but soon realized that his size (even being a young giraffe) was a hindrance. He tried walking upright and balancing on his hind legs, but he just wasn't able to balance his weight. Jeff tried bouncing large beach balls on top of his head, but his head was so narrow that they all fell off. It was beginning to look like the young giraffe might have to settle in regard to his ambitions, but that is when the knowing hand of fate stepped in on his behalf.

One day after his shift at the petting zoo, Sarah approached Jeff and ask if he would like to help with the carnival portion of the circus. The Funmazing Circus had a small area set up to allow the children to ride fair-like rides and try their hands at games of chance and skill. The carnival portion of the circus was the first thing that visitors saw upon entering the ground, so the staff wanted to make a wonderful impression. It just so happened that on this afternoon, one of the game operators had come down with a bad case of food poisoning and was forced to take the day off. Jeff was not interested in running any of the games but also didn't want to let Sarah down, so he agreed to take the job. He was assigned to watch over the ring toss, which he thought had a fun sound to the name anyway. The young giraffe would do anything that he could to stay in the good graces of the circus and this sounded like a perfect opportunity to earn points. When he arrived at his booth, there was already a long line of eager players. The children were so thrilled to see a small giraffe that they almost lost interest in the game. The goal of this game was to throw decent-sized rings at large pins that were set up in the middle of a small tent. One of the children missed one of these pins and his ring landed squarely on the nose of the giraffe. At first, Jeff was taken aback by the shock of having something thrown on his nose. He then decided that he would entertain the children and began swirling the object around and around his narrow face. They all erupted in laughter. He loved the attention that his trick had gotten him, and so he began challenging the participants to hand rings on his nose. Young giraffes do not yet have the towering height of their older counterparts and at seven feet, Jeff was the perfect size for this game. Everyone that visited the tent that day, was thrilled and raved about the giraffe and his stunts with the rings.

Jeff was on top of the world and as he returned home that night, he realized that this could potentially be the talent that he had been searching for. He asked Sarah to sneak him a ring to practice with, and she happily obliged. That night, he stayed awake late into the evening working on new tricks. He even learned to balance rings upright on his nose. Jeff was such a hit at the ring toss, that he was allowed to return the next day. He was greeted by adoring fans that lined up specifically to see him and once again, he had a very successful day. The children adored him, and he was quickly becoming the most visited attraction in the carnival area of the circus. Management even insisted that he have his own booth. The rings were upgraded to hula hoops, which allowed for a much larger range of tricks that he was able to pull off. Rumor had it, he received such glowing reviews that the staff began to seriously consider adding him to the lineup in the big-top. Jeff heard such rumors and realized that he was not prepared for his dream to be realized so quickly. He was so nervous that he might mess everything up and have to return to the petting zoo forever. Jeff was having so much fun running his own booth, where there was not so much pressure placed on him to perform. He knew that if the trainers ask him to join the show, he would have to put effort into learning totally new stunts. He didn't realize that getting what he wanted would be so stressful. One night, after another perfect day at the carnival, Jeff returned home with a worried look on his face. His mother noticed these sorts of things immediately and ask the young giraffe what was bothering him. He told her about his fear of failure and how he was so comfortable now. He just didn't know if it would be worth the risk.

I am sure you remember this, but his mother always knew exactly what to say to make things better. She told Jeff that he would be wonderful because he was already a showman. He was using his current comfort as an excuse to not try for his dreams. She didn't want any son of hers being afraid to pursue the things that he wanted. Jeff and his mother spent that night working on new tricks to perform with the hula hoops and almost by accident, they discovered that he was amazing at dancing with the rings around his neck. She would throw the hoops from some distance away and he was always able to catch them and then swirl them around his neck while grooving to some music. The young giraffe was added to the show, only a short time after he and his mother found his talent. The fans loved Jeff and he took the stage as a fish takes to water. He was a natural performer! His determination finally paid off and he was so glad that he didn't let his nerves stop him from chasing his dreams. Jeff became known far and wide for his ability to dance with hoops on his neck, and for his charming stage presence.

Grandpa Heinz and the mermaid

Tamara sits at the dining table with her grandparents - it's supper time. Grandpa Heinz once again tells the best stories. He used to be a sailor and  experienced a lot. Granny Helene tells him over and over again he should not forget the food. But Grandpa Heinz is so in motion that he does not come to dinner. He tells of sea monsters, mermaids and waves as tall as houses. "You're going to spin your sailor's yarn again!" Says Granny Helene. "This is not a sailor's yarn Leni!" Says Opa Heinz. "Listen to me for the first time." "Oh," grins Grandma Helene. "You only give the little boy a fuss." After dinner, Grandpa Heinz proposes a walk on the beach. "Oh Heinz," says Granny Helene. "It's raining." But Grandpa Heinz is not deterred. "It almost stopped already. Plus, there's the right clothing for every weather, "he says, holding out the rain jacket to Tamara. "We'll be back in half an hour. Will you make us some hot tea? "He asks before Tamara and he walk out the door. And Granny Helene shakes her head and says what she always says: "You stubborn goat. Of course, I'll make tea for you. You should not get any snuff. " It is an uncomfortable weather. The sea is rough. But the rain has almost stopped. The rough sea reminds Grandpa Heinz of a stormy seafaring and he starts to talk. That's the beginning of a story that leaves Tamara quiet.

"I remember a seafaring trip that would hardly have survived your grandfather. It was a long time ago. I was still a young lad myself and did not go to sea much before long. The sea was even rougher than today and it stormed out of all the heavenly gates. The waves hit the cutter and the whole ship rocked back and forth. Some of the mariners were already afraid that the cutter would be full of water. So high hit the waves.

It was already dark and the rain whipped us in the face. In the dark we had lost sight and feared to walk on a sandbar keel. The best Kieker did not help you in the storm, you know? "Tamara looks questioningly at Opa

Heinz:" Kieker? "" Yes, "says Opa Heinz. "This is a pair of binoculars. And before you ask, running a keel means the ship is stalling. "Tamara nods wide-eyed and with her mouth open. Then Opa Heinz continues: "Eventually I did not even believe that we would arrive home safely. We did not even know which direction we needed to go. The storm continued to grow and I no longer saw the hand in my eyes. Something suddenly shone in the water. At the light, I saw a little girl. Potz Blitz, I thought a stowaway had gone overboard and wanted to make my way to the bell. Then I saw the girl jump out of the water.

I could not believe my eyes. She jumped out of the water and into it again. Like a dolphin. But I tell you, that was not a dolphin. And it was not a little girl either. When I jumped out of the water, I recognized a huge fin. I'm sure that was actually a mermaid. Again and again she jumped in the air and turned, until I understood that we should follow her. She swam ahead and shone the safe way into the harbor. This little mermaid has saved our lives! But then I never saw her again. Grandma Helene never believed me that. But it is the truth." Tamara looks at Opa Heinz with an open mouth: "I believe you Grandpa. How did she look? "" Like a little girl. You could not see too much in the dark. I mean she had blond hair and a huge caudal fin. It was really fast - faster than any boat I knew by then. "

The rain has stopped and the sea has calmed down. A gentle breeze blows from the water and Tamara eagerly listens to every word that comes out of Grandpa Heinz's mouth.

What they do not know is that the little mermaid from Grandpa Heinz needs his help this time. And right now. Her name is Amelie. At that time, she told Grandpa Heinz the safe way to the harbor. Now she needs help herself. Only a few hours ago she had been playing with the fish at the bottom of the lake. Then the sea freshened up and Amelie realized that she had swum farther out than she wanted. For such a brave little mermaid that's not a problem you might think. But even for mermaids, the rough seas can be dangerous. Amelie swam toward the local cave vault, so she was not watching properly and a current seized her. She lost her footing and poked her head against a rock. Unconsciously, she was flushed to the beach and the tide set in. It is the same beach where Grandpa Heinz and Tamara go for a walk. But the two are still too far away to help Amelie. However, a mermaid on land will not last long. Amelie wakes up and realizes that she is ashore. The ebb has pushed the sea far back. She wriggles like a fish on the dry land, but she does not get on well. She could have done a short distance. But the sea is much too far away due to the ebb. Discouraged, she gives up and bursts into tears. "Why does this happen to me? I've never done any harm. "She cries. "Oh darling, that has nothing to do with it." A voice suddenly says. Amelie swallows and wipes away her tears. But she sees nothing. "I'm up here," says the voice. Now Amelie sees a little fairy with beautiful wings flapping over her. "What are you?" Asks Amelie. "Well, what does it look like? I am a fairy godmother. To be more specific - your fairy godmother. But you do not have much to do as a fairy of a mermaid, "she smiles.

"Fairies do not exist!" Says Amelie. "There are only in the fairy tale." The fairy looks confused Amelie: "Oh dear. And that comes just from a mermaid? You know that mermaids are as mythical as fairies? "

Amelie shakes her head: "No, there are many of us in the sea. We're not mythical creatures. "The fairy touches his head:" Oh honey, what are they teaching you down there? "Then she makes two fists and holds them against her hips:" No matter, important now is that we get you back into the water. And fast! "

"But how are you going to help me? You are far too small to take me back to the sea. "Amelie says disappointed and close to tears again. "Sweetheart," says the fairy. "That has nothing to do with the size. Even little ones can help! "

Then the fairy thinks: "Hm, how was the spell for a stranded mermaid? You have to apologize. I'm out of practice. Most of the time you're in the water and I'm ashore. How was that again? " Then she swings her wand and murmurs a few words. The next moment the ground begins to fill with water under Amelie. The water becomes more and more, until Amelie is completely covered by water. The only problem is that the water is only around Amelie. She is swimming like a soap bubble now. The fairy exhales sadly, "It was not that," she says. Then she raises an eyebrow and says, "But we have gained time. Technically speaking, once you are back in the water. "Amelie nods and is happy to feel water again.

But as much as the little fairy thinks, she does not come up with the spell. "It's getting pretty dark," she says. "I'll light up first." She waves her wand again and a small light floats next to her. "At least we can see something now." A few meters further down the beach, go to Grandpa Heinz and Tamara. When Tamara discovers the light, she excitedly points to the glowing something: "Da grandpa. The light you have been talking about. "Opa Heinz scratches his head:" No, that's just a lantern. There's still someone who can walk. "" But it does not move at all. "Tamara exclaims excitedly. She pulls Grandpa Heinz's hand. "Come on Grandpa. This is your mermaid! "

Grandpa Heinz wonders if Granny Helene was right after all. Maybe he should not have told the story. Maybe he just puts Tamara in the head with It?

Suddenly he sees his mermaid floating on a beach in a bubble of water. He stands stiff as a stick: "What, but what?" He says, staring at Amelie. Tamara is quite outraged: "Da grandpa, you see? I told you. Is that the mermaid who saved you? "And Amelie recognizes Grandpa Heinz again. "You've gotten older," she says.

"But I recognize you!" Before the fairy could hear that, she's already flapping on Grandpa Heinz and boxing him with her little arms against his nose: "Stop!" She exclaims. "You will not touch Amelie, otherwise you will get to do it with me!" Grandpa Heinz carefully reaches for the fairy: "It's all right. I will do nothing to her. We know each other. "The fairy looks surprised Amelie over:" Is that true? "Amelie nods.

Grandpa Heinz comes closer to Amelie: "So your name is Amelie?" He asks. Then he points to Tamara. "This is my granddaughter Tamara." Amelie greets Tamara, who has now stopped babbling and standing with her mouth open. "You are beautiful!" Says Tamara and Amelie thanks.

Grandpa Heinz extends his hand to the water and says: "I could never thank you. You have saved my life! "At that moment, the fairy hits him on the hand:" Stay away from my water. "Then she waves her forefinger:" Touching the figure with the paws is forbidden. And now you go. We have work to do! "

The fairy flutters to Amelie and tries hard to push the bubble of water. But she does not move. Amelie is too heavy. "I'll help you," says Opa Heinz and just wants to push with, as the fairy cries out: "NO! I said do not touch! "Grandpa Heinz stops jerking.

"If you touch the bubble of water, it will burst or worse!" The little fairy is just catching her breath as she sees little Tamara push the bubble of water out of the corner of her eye. "But how is that possible?" Asks the fairy. Amelie nods to the fairy, "It's alright. Tamara is my soulmate. As I had felt with Heinz at that time, I feel it now with her. And I will eventually feel it with their children. "And Tamara pushes the little mermaid all the way back into the sea. As Amelie is back in the sea, she jumps happily in the waves around. Then she shows up and waves to Tamara: "Thank you dear Tamara. We will definitely meet again! But now I have to go back, "she says, turning around and disappearing in the waves. When Tamara turns around, the fairy is gone as well. Grandpa Heinz stands further back on the beach and beckons Tamara to himself. "Come on, little one, we have to go back, too. Granny Helene is already waiting for us with the tea. " When they arrive at home Tamara tells how a waterfall. The story gushes out of her: "And then I pushed the mermaid back into the sea. She waved me once more and then disappeared. Even the fairy was gone then. "Granny Helene strokes her cheek:" Well, you have experienced a real adventure. But now the tea is drunk and then it goes into the trap. " After Grandma Helene Tamara has gone to bed, she looks at Grandpa Heinz and smiles: "What did you do with her? She talked all the time until she fell asleep. The sailor's yarn that she spins does not fit any more. "Grandpa Heinz only smiles back and nods:" There's so much out there. And stories want to be told. Let her dream! " Then grandma Helene and grandpa Heinz go to bed. And Grandpa Heinz is happy that he now has someone who believes in him and shares his stories with him. Even if it will remain a secret between the two. Tamara and he know there's a little mermaid out there called Amelie, who will always watch over them at sea.

Noah Rides an Airplane

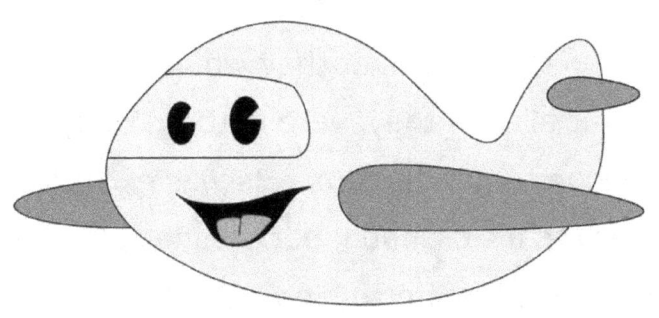

There are many ways to travel where you want to go. Trains, cars, trucks, buses, and boats are all great modes of transportation. Another great mode of transportation is airplanes. Airplanes fly high in the sky above everything, helping people get to their special destination with ease. For many people, airplanes are a mode of transportation that they use on a regular basis to help them get where they are going. For example, politicians and musicians use airplanes to get to important meetings or concerts that they are hosting all over the world! For Noah, airplanes were brand new. He had never been on an airplane before, and he had no idea what to expect. But, Noah's grandpa wanted to take him on a special trip to the other side of the country to visit a special museum, but he could only do that if they were going to fly. Trying to drive that far would take a very long time, and trains were more expensive to ride on and often took longer to get to their destinations. With an airplane, though, Noah and his grandpa would be across the country in just a couple of hours. Noah thought it was very cool that a plane could travel so fast, and that they would get there in almost no time at all. As they were getting ready for their trip, Noah began to get nervous. He was excited to ride in an airplane with his grandpa, but the idea of going somewhere new and then being so high scared Noah. He did not know what it would be like to go through the airport or to ride in an airplane. Noah worried that maybe he would get scared, or that he would feel uncomfortable while he and his grandpa rode the airplane.

While he packed his bags and got ready for his trip, Noah's dad tried to comfort him so that Noah would feel more comfortable with the trip he was going to take with his grandpa.

Noah's dad told Noah that taking the airplane would be easy. He told him that they would check in their luggage, and the airport attendees would make sure their luggage got on their airplane. Then, they would be checked through security to make sure they were not carrying anything that might be unsafe to carry on an airplane.

Next, they would wait in a big sitting area for their airplane to be called; then, they would get on the airplane. Once they were on, they would fasten their seatbelts and listen to the pilot tell them what to expect. Then, they could watch TV on the airplane while a flight attendant brought them snacks and drinks. Noah's dad told him that by the time they were done eating and drinking, the flight would almost be done, and they would get off. Then, they would get their luggage from the luggage trolley and make their way to their car so that they could go to the museum! Noah did not think that it sounded too hard to ride an airplane, but still, he was worried about all of these new experiences. That night, he had a difficult time sleeping as he wondered what it was going to be like and how he would do during his first time flying. Even though Noah was scared, he was still very excited to go on this special adventure with his grandpa.

The next morning, it was time for Noah's ride on an airplane. His grandpa came to his house and put his bags in the car while Noah said goodbye to his parents. By now, he was feeling both very scared and very excited about this special trip he was taking with his grandpa.

After he was done saying goodbye to his parents, Noah and his grandpa got in the car and headed toward the airport. Noah told his grandpa that he was scared and excited at the same time, and Noah's grandpa said he understood. Then, he told Noah the same things his dad had told him about what to expect and how easy it would be to take the flight. Noah started to feel more comfortable and tried to relax as they made their way to the airport.

When they got to the airport, Noah's grandpa parked their car in a special parking lot, and then they paid for a special ticket that let Noah's grandpa leave his car there until they got home. This way, they would have a car to drive home in when they got back from their trip! Once the fare was paid, they walked into the airport and started the process of getting ready to get on the plane. First, they went to the luggage area and gave their bags to the luggage attendants. As they did, the luggage attendants placed tags on their bags that let the airport know which flight those bags needed to be on. Then, they signed papers to confirm that their bags had been checked and kept a piece of paper for confirmation. Once they checked their bags in, they made their way to the security checkpoint. This part felt scary for Noah, as there were many sounds, machines, and people all over the place. Everyone had formed lines toward the checkpoint so that the security guards could make sure that everyone was safe and ready to travel.

This part took a while as it took time for each person to be checked in through the checkpoint in order for them to get to the waiting room. Noah watched as each person took off their jackets, shoes, and any jewelry that they might be wearing to put them in a bucket with their bags. The bucket would then go down a conveyer belt through a metal detector, and then the people would walk through a separate metal detector. On the other side, the security guard would make sure everything looked proper and safe, and then they would let the passenger through to the waiting area. Finally, It was Noah and his grandpa's turn to go through the security pass. Each of them took off their shoes and their jackets, and Noah's grandpa took off his wristwatch. Then, they put their carryon bags on the conveyer belt. One by one, they walked through the metal detector, and their bags went through the metal detector, too.

On the other side, the security guard checked to make sure that everything was okay, and then they were given their stuff back. They put their shoes and jackets back on, and Noah's grandpa put his wristwatch back on. Then, they grabbed their carryon bags and headed to the waiting area. The waiting area was just a big lounge filled with chairs and a few airport stores. One store was a convenience store with snacks and drinks, and the other was a book store. There was also a restaurant in case people wanted to eat before they took their flight to wherever they were going. Noah looked around at all of the people who were waiting, eating, and shopping for books. He was surprised by how many people were in the waiting area and wondered how many of them would be taking the flight with him and his grandpa. Noah and his grandpa found a seat and waited for the attendant to call their number so that they could board their airplane. When she did, they got up and went to the lineup, showed the attendant their boarding pass, and then started to board. Boarding the airplane was unusual: they walked down a long hallway and ended up on the plane at the end. Noah thought it was cool that they could attach this hallway to the airplane and that they could get on the airplane this way. Once they were on the airplane, Noah and his grandpa found their seats and sat down. It took a while for everyone to board the airplane.

Noah and his grandpa watched as families, men, women, and business folks all piled on. Each one found their seats, put their bags away, and then sat down and waited as the rest of the passengers boarded. Finally, after what seemed like forever, everyone was on board, and the airplane was ready to take off. They started takeoff with a message from the pilot.

The pilot talked to them about the flying conditions, and what to expect in terms of turbulence. Then, he talked to them about safety measures and what to do if there was a problem with the airplane.

This made Noah worry, but his grandpa assured him that everything would be fine. When the pilot was done talking, the big TV at the front of the plane turned on, and Noah was offered headphones from the flight attendant. He and his grandpa each accepted a pair and turned them on so that they could listen to the movie that was being played while they flew.

Then, they took off.

Take off was a cool experience for Noah. It started with them driving down the runway, but soon they were going so fast that the plane took off into the air. They took a sharp turn upward, and within moments they were flying through the clouds. Soon, they were above the clouds and flying straight to the other side of the country. Noah looked out the window to see the tops of the clouds and, when the clouds parted, the cities that fell below them. Most of the cities were too far away for Noah to see anything other than the texture of the ground, but he still thought it was very cool. While they flew, Noah looked out the window, watched the TV, and ate the snacks, and drank the drinks that the attendant gave him. Then, just like his dad said, by the time he was done, the plane was almost getting ready to land. As they got closer to their destination, the pilot came on the radio again and told all of the passengers about their landing. He let them know that it was time to put their seatbelts back on and that they would be landing very soon. He told them what time they would be landing at, what to expect, and what to do during the landing process. Soon after, they landed on the runway. It was a bit of a bumpy experience, but it was over quickly. Once they landed, Noah and his grandpa got off the airplane by going down a similar long hallway like the one they had when they boarded the airplane. Then, they went and collected their bags and went outside to catch the taxi to their hotel. The rest of the trip was very exciting for Noah. They stayed in a hotel, went to the museum, and enjoyed delicious dinners and breakfasts from the restaurants near the hotel. By the time their trip was done, Noah was sad to leave all of the fun behind but was excited for another ride on an airplane. Noah thought airplanes were so cool, and he could not wait to go on another trip on an airplane again really soon. He even asked his grandpa if they could go back to the museum again soon! Noah's grandpa just laughed and said sure.

The end!

Conclusion

These stories can and should be read over and over again and can become a healthy addition to any bedtime routine. The prompts are intended to give plenty of space for imagination, and hopefully, great dreams will follow.

It can be helpful to follow up with your children, either immediately after the story has been read or the following morning. This can be a nice moment of connection for parents and their children as they can then discuss together what their personal visualization was like. Asking questions that are both specific and open-ended like, "When you were on the hike in the woods, and you stumbled across the babbling brook, what did you think?" The idea is to ask the child about a specific part of the visualization but to leave the space for the child to fill in their own creative visualization details.

Meditation and visualization are powerful tools that can be employed by anyone of any age. Hopefully, the stories in this book have been useful.

Sometimes, in life, the best thing we can do is learn from others, and I hope that in reading this book, you have discovered many wonderful lessons from the little boys and girls who shared their stories with you here today. As you listen, be sure to keep your eyes closed so that you can fall asleep. After all, you cannot sleep if you have your eyes open! And you, my friend, need a great night's sleep so that you can wake up tomorrow and have enough energy to do everything that you need to do.

It is a widely used form of meditation and is suitable at any time of the day. In this approach, one is expected to focus on the experience and the environment. Even though mindfulness meditation may appear elementary it requires a commitment to pull it off. In, mindfulness approach, you should start by focusing on your breathing. Learn how to direct your attention to your breathing and allow distractions to emerge and fade off just like clouds in the sky. Picture the distractions as an approaching sheep that jumps over a gate.

Alternatively, you can also try to practice with other objects of meditation such as sensations. In other terms, allow your body to become aware of tensions and release the tensions. Through mindfulness meditation, an individual will become aware of what is happening within as well as become more adept at allowing distractions and frustrations to flow leaving the person more peacefully. Letting us know what you think helps other kids find this wonderful book, and helps me write more great stories just for kids like you!

Thank you, and sweet dreams.

Kids Sleep Meditation

A Complete Collection of Stories to Help Children Reduce Stress and Anxiety, Learn Mindfulness Meditation and Go to Sleep Feeling Calm, Happy and Confident

LILLY ANDERSEN

© **Copyright 2020 - All rights reserved.**

The content contained within this book may not be reproduced, duplicated or transmitted without direct written permission from the author or the publisher.

Under no circumstances will any blame or legal responsibility be held against the publisher, or author, for any damages, reparation, or monetary loss due to the information contained within this book. Either directly or indirectly.

Legal Notice:

This book is copyright protected. This book is only for personal use. You cannot amend, distribute, sell, use, quote or paraphrase any part, or the content within this book, without the consent of the author or publisher.

Disclaimer Notice:

Please note the information contained within this document is for educational and entertainment purposes only. All effort has been executed to present accurate, up to date, and reliable, complete information. No warranties of any kind are declared or implied. Readers acknowledge that the author is not engaging in the rendering of legal, financial, medical or professional advice. The content within this book has been derived from various sources. Please consult a licensed professional before attempting any techniques outlined in this book.

By reading this document, the reader agrees that under no circumstances is the author responsible for any losses, direct or indirect, which are incurred as a result of the use of information contained within this document, including, but not limited to, — errors, omissions, or inaccuracies.

Tables of Contents

Introduction 186

Chapter 1   The Chaos in Magic 189

Chapter 2   Mary and Miranda 210

Chapter 3   Herman Hermit Crab gets Crabby . 245

Chapter 4   Brother in Arms 252

Chapter 5   Chivalry Is Not Dead 265

Chapter 6   Garden Gnomes 280

Chapter 7   Topher's Ultimatum 286

Chapter 8   The Love in Fire 311

Chapter 9   Fighting Isn't Always the Answer . 323

Conclusion 353

Introduction

This book focuses on helping your children feel great about themselves, relax, and prepare for a good night's sleep. There are numerous tips in each meditation to help your children comfort themselves before starting to meditate and some tactics at the end of every script for them and you as their guardian. Most of the time, taking a few minutes at the end of meditation to speak about thoughts, emotions, or feelings that came up can be vital in helping your kids relax further before going to bed. Try to put aside at least five minutes after each meditation process to talk with your children about how they are feeling. You could ask them if anything came up that they want to tell you.

Children as young as three years have been known to benefit substantially from meditation sessions practiced regularly. Children who experience these meditation exercises plan tasks better and have a better memory. Moreover, they have the perfect ability to organize information as opposed to their peers. Additionally, meditation scripts have also been found to be vital in children dealing with fears they start to develop in their younger years. For instance, things like being afraid of monsters or darkness, or emotional worries, such as fear of not being perfect or fear of being left alone can all be dealt with by practicing meditation regularly.

To enjoy the most from this meditation exercise, advise your children to find a place in the house or wherever they are listening to these meditations where they can relax and settle down. It does not need to be the same place every time, but having a regular meditation routine helps their body start relaxing faster the more they repeat their meditation patterns. Tips on how to settle in before the meditation sessions are offered at the start of each chapter to help remind you and your child to start the relaxation process, but try to think of some now before you get started, so you feel prepared and ready for the first meditation.

A significant number of kids suffer from some form of sleep inadequacy. As earlier presented, depriving yourself of sleep will lead to poor concentration and irritability among others. The dangers of inadequate sleep can include depressed enjoyment of life and dangerous driving. Sleep insomnia occurs in two main forms which include one where you have difficulties falling asleep and where you have challenges resuming sleep after waking up. Fortunately, as seen hypnosis, guided imagery and guided meditation can help combat all forms of insomnia.

Remember that if you wake up in the night with thoughts going through your mind you are having a night of disrupted sleep. The mind is still active and cannot let the whole body rest when there is a pending business. Meditation is thus meant to help ease off these activities needs in your mind to help achieve threshold relaxation levels. One of the best approaches to trigger sleep meditation is to count the breaths you take. Begin the preparation to sleep meditation any scanning through your body and searching for areas of relaxation and tension. Now start counting breaths that are each inhalation and exhalation up to ten. The mind may wander but invite it back to the counting of breaths exercise. The goal is to shift away from the worrisome thinking and grant the mind a different object to focus on while the mind wanders off.

The Chaos in Magic

Hemlock always seemed to have the deck stacked in his favor. He was a handsome young wizard living in Spindle, one of the few mortal villages in Whimsy. Born to nobility, he was given an exceptional private education. His mother and father both had magical abilities, something that they'd passed down to their only son. Such powers were not the norm in his area.

The human villages were the most reminiscent of the Earth realm, during the era of the Victorian queen. The occupants knew of the mystical creatures beyond their borders, but as mostly defenseless humans, they did their best to segregate themselves from the rest of their world. For this reason, those with magic were fascinating to the population of Spindle. Those with gifts were given instant celebrity status.

Hemlock began receiving this extra attention from the moment he was born. His parents were both revered and famous. The birth of their son was anticipated by the villagers, well in advance. Parties were thrown for his arrival. There may have even been a parade right down the most central road of this community.

Hemlock's mother was the only one concerned with how this intense intrigue might affect her son. She was terrified of him becoming spoiled by the mass interest in him. She wanted her son to be virtuous and humble, and for the most part, he was. At first.

In the throes of his early childhood, he was kept oblivious to his own popularity. His mother homeschooled the young wizard, his public outings to nonexistent. She was so intent on keeping his head level, that she accidentally isolated her son. His mother also somewhat selfishly, wanted to keep her beautiful son beside her always. She wanted to shield him from the influences of fame. This was a completely unsustainable plan, but she treasured her child and would do anything to keep him safe.

Hemlock was a lonely boy, using his free time to further develop his magical abilities. His mother emphasized the necessity of keeping his identity secret. He longed for a friend, looking for someone else that could empathize with his plight.

Meanwhile, outside of the oppressive walls of his family's small mansion, the whole village was constantly lit up with rumors about the identity of the magical son. A mass curiosity that did not fade much with time.

Eventually, the need for companionship became so great that he began to sneak out of his gated family home when his parents were away. The village of Spindle knew of Hemlock's existence, but they had never seen his face. Being kept from the public eye allowed him to create a new persona for himself, to be used during these adventures. He called himself Herb and dressed as a member of the working class, as to not arouse suspicion.

He was jealous of the mortals and their sense of community. Every young villager roamed around with friends, something that Hemlock had never experienced. He watched from the shadows as they laughed and played among themselves. The envy gave way to a longing that created a deep ache within his soul. Their smiles were so free and natural.

It was during one of these outings that our hero was stumbled upon by a young lady from the village. She looked to be around the same age as Hemlock, which at the time was seventeen. By then, he had been wandering through public as Herb for years and years. He was well-practiced in avoiding attention by blending into the background of bustling mortal life. So, what could have changed about this day, you ask?

As Hemlock sat on a bench at the edge of a quiet garden park watching the people pass, he was spotted by a friendly dog that had only just slipped his owner. The canine approached the young wizard, looking for attention. His owner was close behind him, a mortal named Charlotte.

She ran as fast as she could in an effort to keep her dog off of the stranger, but alas, her pet was taken with the secret wizard and had jumped on his lap. Hemlock loved dogs and had always wanted a pet for himself, but his father had always fought him on such issues, being less allergic and more just not a fan of pet hair. The young wizard stroked the animal's head as it gazed at him in adoration.

Upon reaching the two of them, Charlotte immediately apologized and began to explain that her dog had a tendency to slip his leash and run. She stopped midsentence, though, as she was taken by the presence of the handsome young stranger. Hemlock was a tall young man, with a mess of brown curls atop his moon-shaped face. He had this look of innocence, courtesy of his round cheeks. He shared an icy pale eye color with his mother.

Charlotte introduced herself to Hemlock, who, of course, told her that his name was Herb. He could not help but feel very comfortable speaking to the young lady, as she had a very warm and inviting nature. He thought that she and her dog fit rather well together.

As the two sat together and talked, Hemlock did his best to keep the lying to a minimum. Anytime Charlotte would ask him questions about his past or family, and he would do his best to redirect the conversation. The pair bonded on that park bench for hours. He agreed to meet her there the next day so that they might further enjoy one another's company. Hemlock had never so candidly spoken to a stranger, and the whole experience left the wizard feeling lighter than air. In fact, he awoke from a dream that night to find himself floating above his bed. He only wished that he could be completely honest with her about his life.

Hemlock (or "Herb") continued to meet Charlotte in that park every opportunity that he got. Sometimes, he would even use his magic to shoot a suggestion to the young lady that she should really go and walk her dog. To spite Charlotte knowing about the wizard's true nature, the two became best friends. To Hemlock, she was his only and most important friend.

Charlotte was a short and spunky young woman with bright and lovely features. Long black hair fell around her slender face in waves. She had a nose that pointed up at the end, like what those in the Earth Realm might call a ski slope. Her large gray eyes had captivated Hemlock from the moment he made her acquaintance. He was hopelessly smitten with his first and only friend but knew that he would never ever risk their bond for romance. Hemlock had mostly resigned to never knowing a mutual love.

His favorite this about Charlotte was not her huge eyes or dainty and comical face, but the fact that she didn't hold back her feelings at all. Even when her opinions were in stark contrast to his own, she proudly spoke her piece. She was both calm and respectful. When the friends disagreed on a topic, neither would take the other's differing views personally. She was unlike anyone else in his life in that way. He had no idea yet, but he would come to value this even more in the coming months.

As time wore on, Charlotte introduced Hemlock to her family. He would often come and visit with them, sometimes even in her absence. Sneaking out of his own house was becoming more and more difficult, so he told his parents that he must commune with nature for hours every day, to keep his abilities sharp. In her family, he found an acceptance that he had never known anywhere else. He was loved and listened to and treated like any other relative. Their small brick house became his haven away from the expectations of his own family. His own parents loved him to death, too, but they were aloof and unaffectionate by nature. Charlotte's family was open and warm.

Hemlock had almost slipped up by using magic in front of Charlotte on several occasions, especially because the young lady was clumsy and accident-prone. He could not just watch her fall without intervening, thankfully Charlotte was very trusting and always found a way to explain any particular movement of objects or her own falling body, away. She slowly became very impressed by both her luck and the power of regular wind.

It is so easy to get carried away by your own desires. It is easy to become intoxicated by the universe, seemingly granting your most secret wishes. Hemlock being accepted by Charlotte's family, was a catalyst for him. He wanted them to know everything about him. He didn't want to hide his nature from her anymore either. He wanted the whole village to see him for the talented young wizard that he was. His magic was a large part of him, and he felt so much guilt from not being able to share it with the people that he had come to love. The longing to be honest with everyone was slowly eating away at his thoughts. He began formulating a plan.

On an unusually chilly August day, Hemlock transmitted a subconscious thought to Charlotte. She should go and walk her dog today after all this seemed to be the maiden breath of autumn (her favorite season). Hemlock's parents happened to be in town on this day, for what the village referred to as The Augustine Fair.

It was just one of many celebrations held in the large park at the center of the village; the same park where their son had first met his only friend. Hemlock picked this day for one important reason. It was the day of his birth, eighteen years ago. He was now an adult, and he would use this as a means by which to finally meet his peers. His mother would never have approved of his idea, but he refused to stay hidden forever. Hemlock could not be anonymous for the rest of his life, and he had no idea how much longer his parents would insist on keeping his face a secret from their community.

His parents both donated to and participated in the event. Proceeds were gifted to the less fortunate. It was a large festival with games, singing, talent acts, rides, and food. Hemlock's parents would perform feats of magic before their adoring fans, such as levitating audience members and performing acts of disappearance. The crowd favorite was a stunt that included his mother raising a perfect orb of fire above her head. Those who had watched their performance were always left speechless.

When Hemlock arrived at the large park, Charlotte was already there with her dog. He rushed to meet her, embracing her. This took her by surprise, as they had never hugged before. She blushed as the young wizard held her for a moment that passed too quickly. Hemlock pulled back and thanked her for meeting him here. She was understandably confused because the idea of walking her dog seemed to like her own. She was so pleased to see her closest friend, though, that she quickly brushed off the sentiment.

She was shocked by his dapper change in attire; he looked mysterious and otherworldly. He was wearing dark high collared shirt, vest, and jet-black trousers. His coat was also a crisp looking contrast to what he normally wore. His bowtie was the only pop of color within the outfit, and even that was a deep navy blue. He also wore a top hat, which lent even more to the sophistication in his appearance that day. These clothes seemed to compliment his personality much more than his usual loose brown vest and coat. He looked like an outwardly different person, but once Charlotte caught sight of his familiar facial expressions, she knew that he was still just regular Herb.

"I am so glad that you're here! I had completely forgotten that Augustine was today. We can walk around and make a real day of it. I just love the fair." Charlotte said.

"That sounds like the perfect birthday present! I have one thing that I must do first, though. I'd like you to promise me that you won't be furious at me for keeping a secret from you. It doesn't change anything; you know me more than anyone else. I was forced by circumstance to make a very difficult choice and today is the day that I rebel against all this unnecessary mystery. I know that your first instinct will be to hate me for misleading you. I just want you to understand that you and your family have made all the difference in my life. You are the reason I want to be honest." Hemlock said, his hands shaking from fear.

"It's your birthday!? Happy birthday, Herb! Is that your secret? Why didn't you tell anyone? I could never hate you." Charlotte said, confused but with a giant grin on her face.

"Well, it is my birthday, but I can only wish that were my secret. Today I am going to show you who I really am." A single tear ran down the young wizard's face as his chest rose and fell rapidly. This was going to be the scariest moment of his life so far. Seeing his distress, Charlotte threw her arms around him again and whispered to him that everything was going to be alright. She told him that no matter what happened, she would always be here when he needed her. This brought a measure of comfort to the terrified young man, and he did his best to slow his frantic breathing back down. Hemlock turned around just in time to see his parents walk out onto a large wooden stage that had been assembled for the event, in the center of the park.

"Aren't they amazing? What I wouldn't give to have magic. They are the most graceful looking couple that has ever existed. Did you know that they supposedly have a son our age? No one has ever seen him; some people don't even believe that he exists." Charlotte said while staring wide-eyed at his parents as they levitated an audience member. "They're so perfect that they don't even seem real. They're too beautiful. The magic, the wealth; they have everything. I bet they hate doing events like this with us regular folks." As Charlotte was saying these words, Hemlock felt his heart fall to his stomach once again. He could have thrown up.

"I...if you were to ask them, I bet they would tell you... this is probably the only fun engagement that they have this month." Hemlock said, choking on his words.

"Their idea of fun has to be much more sophisticated than ours!" Charlotte laughed.

"You would be surprised." Hemlock smiled weakly.

"What? How on Whimsy could you know?" Charlotte asked.

"Surprise!" Hemlock said with an unsteady voice as he turned and began marching toward the stage.

The first to see him was his mother. She accidentally released the mortal that she was levitating, and they fell two feet to the ground. Hemlock watched as his mother's eyes widened in shock and her mouth gaped open. He noticed that she had a look upon her face as though she were doing a very complex math equation in her head. Then, in an instant, her expression changed to one of resignation. A calm seemed to wash over her features, and she smiled at her son. His father made eye contact with his son, and it was the most unusual thing... a look of pride.

He had always secretly wanted to show off his son to the village but refrained out of respect for his wife. His father was beaming as his son made his way onto the small stage. The young man was so nervous that it felt as if his heart was trying to beat its way out of his chest.

"Attention, everyone! It is my sincerest pleasure to introduce to you, our son Hemlock." His father roared happily to the audience. He wrapped an arm around the young wizard, and a hush fell over the audience. Then thunderous applause.

The whole village had been waiting to meet Hemlock from the moment he was born. His mother wrapped her arm around him from his opposite side. "Would you like to see what he can do?" His father asked the crowd, and they responded enthusiastically. He then whispered to his son, making sure that he had prepared a stunt for his grand takeover of the stage.

Hemlock held his arms out in front of his body at a downward angle. As he rose them to be level with his shoulders, a ball of water began to form above his head. His mother took the hint and joined in his performance with her crowd favorite fireball. The two of them must have had the same idea because, in tandem, they began to move these orbs closer together. A loud and satisfying crackling occurred as the two forced joined and then disappeared into nothing. The hordes of onlookers went mad for this demonstration, clapping for the pair with an addictive intensity. The family then joined hands and bowed.

Hemlock had never experienced a feeling like this before. So many people cheered him on, and that sort of approval was something that never crossed his mind. His had been a life of blending into the background, until now. This new feeling lit a fire in his soul and spoke to a part of him that he didn't know existed.

Following the performance, the young wizard pushed through the jumble of fans in the park, looking for Charlotte. He found her right where he left her before the show. She looked positively shocked. So many emotions this young woman was trying to account for, all at once. She was furious that he had kept his identity a secret from her, but part of her understood that it wasn't a choice he wanted to make. Charlotte was also astounded by his magic and pretty sure that she was in love with him. She also felt a disconnect now, as though he and his family were miles above her. How could she even speak to him now? The thought of it made her knees feel weak. Hemlock? His name wasn't even really Herb! Goodness though, 'Hemlock' was a purely magical word.

She snapped out of her daze when the young wizard embraced her again. He was apologizing profusely and saying over and over again, that he was still the same man. His hug melted away all the angst that she had felt only a moment ago. It would take time, but Charlotte would forgive him. It helped that he explained the reason for his disguise was his own mother; he was trying to keep her from knowing about his sneaking out. Charlotte eventually came to sympathize with the story of his lonely childhood.

The pair slowly repaired their friendship, and he was finally able to be completely honest about her. The transmitting of subconscious thoughts was one of the few points of contention after a while. She eventually even gave in and forgave him for that too, because it happened to be extremely useful. Charlotte told him that he needed to make it known from now on when he sent her a thought. None of this is making her think things were her ideas when they were obviously not. She considered that to be an invasion of her privacy. Her family was also very forgiving of the young wizard, and eventually, he was able to bring his own parents to meet and visit with his second family.

The adoration from strangers in the village was a huge adjustment for Hemlock. They perused him, asking for magical favors or a demonstration of his power. He didn't mind any of this, because he was so grateful to finally be seen as himself and not Herb. He would not admit it to anyone, but he loved the attention. Hemlock had been ignored by the public for as long as he could remember, and now it was like he was a king or an Earth Realm Rockstar roaming among his fans. Slowly he began to crave their interest in him. Little by little his ego was growing.

Just as he was getting used to being loved for who he was, his magic began to go haywire. It was just little glitches at first, but of course, it got worse. Sometimes he would go to light a match with his mind, and he would incinerate an object near him instead. Hemlock was content to write it off as growing pains and ignore the issue until something happened that he could not ignore.

One afternoon while practicing, the young wizard accidentally set himself on fire. Luckily, he had already developed the water trick and was able to put it out immediately, even if he was soaked now. What if that had been someone else, though, what would he have done? His mind blinked back to Charlotte, what if he had hurt her. He would never forgive himself. Hemlock was pretty sure that he was in love with his best friend, which is a thought that he absolutely did not mean to transfer to her. His eyes widened, and he felt his heart fall into his stomach.

The fire had been nothing compared to accidentally bearing his soul to Charlotte. How would he ever face her now? The thought had sent, he felt it. He knew that it had to have gone to her. She had to know now. What if he just pretended that nothing happened? What if he ignored it?

He ran to his mother and begged to know why his powers were rebelling against him. She told him that he might be too wrapped up in the attention that he is receiving from is gifts. She mentioned that the universe always seems to know when you are misusing magic, and it has some pretty cruel ways to get back at you. He could feel himself blushing at her words. He asked his mother if there was any way that he could potentially rewind time?

"No, but you can meditate and find meaning in your magic again. That way, nothing else will happen. You need to be in this for the right reasons. If you can't handle the attention that being a wizard brings you, without your ego growing, then you need must step away from the public eye. Or learn to humble yourself. Do you want to talk about what happened with your magic?"

"No, I really don't. Thank you so much for the advice, though. I will find a way to fix my intentions." Hemlock said, nervously.

"Meditation and breath control always worked for me!" Said his mother.

Hemlock tried meditating later that day. He felt as though the magic glitching and ruining his life had humbled him enough, but he wanted to make absolutely sure that he was not going to be walking around, just broadcasting his innermost feelings to people. Hemlock felt amazing after quieting his racing mind. He concentrated on his breathing so that he could get into the right frame of mind, and everything else came naturally.

He decided that he would take a few days away from the public eye for more than one reason. The young wizard was content to hide in his parent's lavish house. He was too ashamed to go outside. That is when he heard a knock at the front door, he scrambled from his bed and cracked the door to his room so he could see what was going on. His mother had answered it.

"Hey, Charlotte, so nice to see you. I will go and get him!"

Mary and Miranda

Miranda turned six years old when her father got her a hamster for her birthday. He told her that he found the hamster on the street as if she were a stray cat. Miranda got many different presents that year, but this was her favorite one by far.

She wanted to spend all her time playing with this hamster she named Mary. They would run around together on the carpet, even though Miranda's father didn't like this at all. She still took Mary out of her cage and chased her around when he wasn't looking.

She tried to dress up Mary in her doll clothes, but the hamster didn't seem to like it. It didn't help that the clothes barely fit. Miranda's father came by a lot to check on them because he stopped trusting his daughter with her pet. He told her that hamsters are meant to stay in their cage, or else they might get sick.

But Miranda didn't see any fun at all in that. If Mary always stayed in the cage, she would only be able to pet her by sticking her hand inside. Plus, she figured it would get boring in there if she was never able to leave. Any time her father wasn't around, Miranda and Mary broke all of the rules, running around until they got tired. Miranda always got tired before the hamster did. Mary never seemed happy to go back in the cage, which Miranda understood. If she was in a cage herself, she would not be happy, either. This was why she tried to take her out as much as possible.

Even when her father was home, Miranda played with her pet. She would read stories to her, mostly rhymes that she found in the library. Even Miranda got bored when she was read to sometimes, so she was surprised that Mary seemed interested in all of the stories. She stood at the edge of the cage and listened intently. T the truth was, Miranda didn't even want to go to bed with Mary around. All of her other toys seemed boring now that she had Mary around. Her father made a big deal out of her birthday this year and got her all sorts of presents, but Mary was the only one that she cared about. She didn't even mind cleaning after her and feeding her, doing the things that her father said were teaching her responsibility. She would do anything for her pet.

Miranda had always said that she wanted a dog, but now she wouldn't want one, because she would be worried that it would hurt Mary. She even thought about Mary as she drifted off into sleep, thinking about all the fun things they would do together once she got up. Maybe tomorrow, they could play outside together. The possibilities were endless when the two of them spent time together because Miranda had a very good imagination.

Miranda had a lot of trouble falling asleep that night she got Mary, thinking about everything they would do the next day. She didn't even want to fall asleep. She wanted to get out of bed and think of the possibilities of what they could do, and then do them. Miranda was tossing and turning so much that she eventually got out of bed completely. She had to see what Mary was up to. Maybe she was having the same problem, and she couldn't get to bed either.

Miranda walked over to the cage and gasped. Mary, the hamster, was completely gone. She didn't hear her scamper away or make any noise at all, so she must have been so distracted by her thoughts that she wasn't able to hear her. Quietly, she flipped on the switch in her room so her father wouldn't hear. She looked around everything to find her: under her bed, in her closet, in her toy box. Mary was nowhere to be found. She was nervous about leaving her room and waking her father up, but she didn't want to lose her hamster forever. This was urgent: Miranda had to find her right this instant.

Next, she checked the bathroom. Mary wasn't in the sink, cabinet, or the shower. She was frustrated that she couldn't check in her father's room without waking him because Mary was probably small enough to squeeze under the door. But she couldn't check there, so she went into the living room. She looked inside the entertainment center, under the table, and behind the couch. Her hamster wasn't here either.

Then Miranda looked in the kitchen. She was starting to get nervous because there were only so many places that she could look. Even though she didn't know how she would get in there, she looked in the fridge last when she couldn't find Mary anywhere else. What if Mary went somewhere that she wouldn't even be able to reach? What if she went somewhere so dark and small that she would be impossible to find there? She tried to put these thoughts away. She checked under the dining room table. Nothing. Everywhere she checked, Miranda couldn't find her hamster.

Besides her father's room, there was only one more place where Mary could be: in the library. It was a small room in the back of the house with a few bookshelves. Her father was a big reader, so he liked to spend a lot of time in there. Sometimes he would even stay up late reading a book in there under a lamp, but thankfully that wasn't tonight, or Miranda would get caught being up late. To Miranda's surprise, there was a lamp on, but it wasn't her father who was in there. In fact, she didn't see anyone at all. And it wasn't like her father to leave lights on.

The lamp wasn't where her father normally placed it, either. It was where he picked it up from before he placed it on the end table next to his chair, but in this spot, it was on. Strangely, there was an open book placed next to it — and more strangely than that, she saw Mary on top of that book, looking down and staying still. Mary didn't even seem to notice that Miranda was there.

"Mary, what are you doing?" Miranda said. She could barely reach the shelf that Mary was on, but she looked up with her neck stretched far out to see her. "How did you get out of your cage without my help?"

Mary finally seemed to notice that her owner was there, as she stopped looking down at the page, and looked over to where Miranda was standing. Mary started to pace around on top of the book. She got a bookmark in her mouth and placed it on top of the page she was standing on.

"You're so funny, Mary. It looks like you're reading that book," she laughed. "I'm not a hamster, and even I can barely read right now. We are getting better at it in school, though. Oh, I wish I could take you to my school so we could spend all our time together! Then I wouldn't have to wait until I got home to play with you. Wouldn't that be fun?" Miranda asked.

Mary nuzzled her little hamster head to close the book she had been standing on top of. Miranda stretched up her hands as high as they could go so, she could grab the book Mary had appeared to be reading.

"Let's see what kinds of books you like," Miranda said, smiling. "*Storybook Classics*. I love this one! My daddy used to read it to me every night, but now he says I'm too old for it. He started reading me harder books that they give out in school, so I can read things a little harder than this one right now. Maybe one day, you'll be able to read chapter books too, Mary!"

Miranda put the storybook down on her father's end table, and she reached up again to take Mary into her hands.

"You really liked that last story I read you, didn't you?" Miranda said. "I'll be sure to read to you way more. When my daddy is around, we can't play outside your cage anyway, so that's a good time for me to read to you. Does that sound good to you?"

Miranda laughed again, knowing that her hamster wouldn't be able to say anything. But for the second time that night, Miranda gasped, because her hamster started speaking.

"I would love to read more stories with you, Miranda," Mary said.

Miranda nearly dropped her hamster in surprised, but thankfully she got her balance back and put her down on her father's chair.

Miranda was still extremely surprised, and while she was a chatty girl, she had no idea what to say to Mary. She was used to talking to her a lot, but when she started speaking to her, it was completely different. She never thought Mary would actually say anything back.

"It's like in the movies!" Miranda exclaimed. But she realized she might wake up her father, so she tried to quiet down. "I have many questions for you. Is it like in the movies where all animals can talk to each other, or can you only understand only hamsters? Do you speak in a different language with hamsters, or do you speak English too? Am I the only person who can understand you and other people just don't listen? Or do you just not usually talk around people."

"I'm glad to have a friend like you with so many questions," Mary said. "I can give you answers, too. Well, I don't know how to talk to any other animals, actually. Even other hamsters. Animals don't really have a language they can speak to each other in the way that humans do. That's what makes humans so special. In fact, I'm the only animal I know who can talk. I wasn't always this way; it was just the environment I was in that taught me how to do it. You might say that I got smart from reading books and listening to people. If you read and listen as much as I do, you'll get smart, too."

"Wow, you sound like an adult talking," Miranda said. She was trying to keep her voice down now. "If you're so smart, why are you reading a book that even a kid like me is too young for?"

"You don't have to be a kid to enjoy kid's stories," Mary said. "I love reading stories meant for children. I like adult's stories too, but sometimes they don't have the same sense of wonder that comes with childhood. You'll understand when you get older. You know, C.S. Lewis said that when he was a kid, he used to read kid's stories in secret, but as an adult, he read them in the open."

"I don't know who C.S. Lewis is, but it sounds like you've read a lot of books," Mary said. "So, it's okay with you if I read books that are below your reading level?"

Mary laughed. Miranda was surprised at how much it sounded like a human laugh. "Of course, you can. I just told you, I still like children's stories a lot. They're a great place to learn lessons, and even adults need to learn lessons. I like to think of children's stories as stories that everyone can enjoy, not just as for kids. Everyone can enjoy children's stories and bond over them and learn the lesson together."

"You're saying that I could be as smart as you if I read as much?" Miranda asked.

"I think you're very smart already, but anyone can get smarter if they read more," Mary said. "I can help you get better at reading if you want, but you can't tell your father about how I can talk. A lot of adults get scared of things like that."

"Really? But you're not scary," Miranda said.

"You're a child, so it's different for you. Your father might not even let me live here anymore," Mary said.

Mary started to look sad, and Miranda could even tell with her little hamster face. Mary crawled back up to the top of the bookshelf so she could talk to her properly.

"There's something I want to talk to you about, though, Miranda," Mary said.

"What is that? You sound like something is the matter. Don't hold your feelings in, tell me what you are feeling," Miranda replied.

"It's about living here with you. I really love playing with you at your house, but your dad actually found me when I got lost from my old home," Mary said. She nibbled on some food that she had found on the carpet.

"Where did your owner live before?" Miranda asked.

It was a long story, but Mary told it to her new owner.

Mary used to be a class pet for a class of second graders. The teacher's name was Ms. Webb, but she wasn't the only owner. Every student took turns being responsible for Mary. Almost all of them were very sweet children, but there was one little boy named Charlie. Charlie was where all the problems started.

It was Charlie's job to take care of her that week and feed her. But he didn't do what he was supposed to do; he didn't follow the rules whatsoever. In fact, he tortured her more than he took care of her. He would poke and prod at her, causing her a lot of pain. He even refused to feed her because he thought it was funny.

Mary didn't want to talk badly about any of the students, even Charlie. She thought maybe he had problems going on at home that would cause him to act this way. Miranda couldn't understand why a kid would be so cruel, but after all the reading Mary had done, she knew how awful people could be.

The last straw was when Charlie started to come to Mary with a sharpened pencil. Mary didn't feel safe in that classroom anymore. It made her very sad, but she had to leave for her own safety. That was when Mary learned how to escape her cage without anyone else's help.

When Charlie came at her with the fork, she rushed into the cage door and ran across the floor of the classroom. Charlie tried to chase her down, but he couldn't catch her in time. Mary ran through the hallway of the school, but she was so scared of the boy catching up with her that she just kept running.

Before she even knew it, Mary was outside in the playground. Kids were running across the field, and she was scared of getting stepped on, so she got out of there and went into the street.

Mary knew from books that roads were a dangerous place for a hamster, but it seemed like everywhere was dangerous for her. Miranda asked Mary what school she used to be in the classroom of, and Mary told her it was Ridgeland Park Elementary School.

"That's the elementary school I go to," Miranda said. "But I'm only in the first grade. I wish I could be in your class, but I'm too young. I'm really sorry about what happened with that mean little boy, Mary. I promise you most little boys aren't like that. I don't understand why he would be so mean to you."

"I know that most little boys are nice, Miranda. But I was so scared, and I didn't know what to do, so I just ran away. I'm afraid that even if I go back, he'll still get his turn to take care of me, and he'll do the same thing. And that's what I actually want to ask you about, Miranda," Mary said. She stopped nibbling on the crumb and looked at her new owner with hamster eyes. "I want to go back home, but I need you to tell Ms. Webb about what happened with Charlie; that way, he gets punished, and I know that I can go back safely."

Miranda almost started crying. She didn't want to lose her new friend, right after she had just gotten her. She was filled with emotions, because she didn't want to take Mary away from the people who loved her, either. The students in Ms. Webb's class must have really missed their hamster, Mary.

"I'm sorry, Mary, but I just can't do it!" Miranda cried. She couldn't control her volume at this point, and it was surprising that she didn't wake her dad up. "I know you like being in the class with all those kids where you got really smart, but I don't want to give you away when we just became friends! I'm not even in the second grade, so I would never be able to see you. Maybe sometimes, but we wouldn't get to spend a lot of time together like we do now."

"You could still see me, Miranda," Mary said. She had expected Miranda to react this way, but she was still disappointed. It was a lost opportunity: she shouldn't have even let Mary catch her reading in the first place or let her hear her talk, but she figured if she had, she might as well try to get Miranda to bring her back home. "I understand that you want us to stay as friends, though.

When I was a little hamster girl, I would have wanted the same thing. Don't worry about it. I can stay here with you, and you can be my new family, then. But for right now, you should probably go to bed. It's very late for a child your age."

Miranda was tearing up, but she was relieved when Mary said this. "Do you want to stay in here and read, or do you want me to take you back to your cage?"

Mary sighed sadly. "I'll go to bed. Don't worry about carrying me, though. I can get there by myself just like I got out. You definitely need to get to bed, though, Miranda. You have school in the morning, and it's nearly morning already."

Miranda did what she said and got under her covers. She has mixed feelings. She didn't want to lose her new friend already, but Mary seemed upset that she wouldn't go home. She didn't know what to do.

After that night, Mary didn't seem the same anymore. Miranda would take her out to play, but all she wanted to do was stay seated in the same spot and look down. She still talked to Miranda, but she didn't say much. Weeks went on like this, and Miranda felt like her friend wasn't the same as she was when she first got her as a pet.

She knew it was because she didn't take her to her old family, but the idea of losing Mary made her sad, too. It seemed like no matter what she did, either Mary would be upset, or she would be. Miranda wished there was a way she could make both of them happy without having to lose her.

But when the weather started to get warmer, Mary seemed to be in even worse shape than before. She barely ate any of the food she gave her, and she didn't talk to her as much as she used to. Miranda was at a loss. Did she have to let Mary go for her to be happy again?

She wasn't sure how she would help her, anyway. Her father didn't know that the hamster was originally someone else's, and she couldn't tell him that Mary could talk and that she told her about her last owner.

Miranda was lying in bed again, feeling really guilty about all of this. It was just like the first night after she got

Mary, but this time she was tossing and turning out of worry, not because she was excited for the next day. Once again, Miranda got out of bed when she couldn't get herself to sleep — and once again, she looked in Mary's cage, assuming she would be gone and out in the library reading.

But Mary wasn't. She wasn't asleep, either, but she was still in her cage, looking sad.

"Why didn't you go read like you always do?" Miranda asked, stretching her arms out as she got out of her bed.

"I haven't been doing that in a really long time. I'm just not in the mood for it anymore," Mary said. She looked down like she did when she was reading, but she just looked sad. "It does make me really happy to be your pet, Miranda. You're the nicest, brightest little girl I've ever met. But I can't help but be down about the class who used to take care of me. There were a lot of nice little girls and boys in that class, and I haven't seen them in months, now. But if you gave me back, you would barely see me anymore, either. And even the kids in that class will move on to the next grade, soon. So, don't worry about it, that's just how life works."

Miranda had figured this was what her change in mood had been about. "I'm sorry, Mary. The school year's almost over, too. Is that why you've been even sadder lately?"

"That's exactly why," Mary replied. "Even if I hadn't run away, most of those kids would never see me again after the school year was over, except for a few of them who would visit me. I've been a school pet for a long time now, and I know that's how it goes. It's just how it goes."

After hearing how Mary really felt about it, Miranda knew that she had to stop being greedy and help her friend. She didn't know how she would manage it under her father's supervision, but she had to bring Mary back to her family.

"I'll do it," Miranda determined. "I'm going to take you back to Ms. Webb's class. I shouldn't have kept you to myself for this long in the first place. I'm really sorry. I didn't want to share you, and it was selfish."

Mary suddenly perked up. Everything about her demeanor seemed to change. "You would really do that for me? I can't believe it — that's so kind of you!"

Miranda looked down like Mary just had. "It's not, really. I should have done this a long time ago, from the very beginning, when I found out who you belonged to. You haven't even been happy here, anyway. It's my fault you went through all that in the first place." Miranda almost started to cry, but Mary stopped her.

"Don't say that. You're a young girl who is still learning things about life. I shouldn't have expected you to give away your new pet so soon," Mary said.

Miranda took some very deep breaths to calm herself down. "I hope you're not mad at me... I'm just worried that things won't be the same if I give you back."

"They won't be, sweetheart. I wish I could tell you that they would, but in my years going through this, I know how things go. I'll stay in the classroom, and you'll go on with your life. Just like old students, you might see me sometimes, but not as much as I would want. You'll feel guilty, and I'll miss you most of the time. But then the moments that I do see you will be very special. They make everything worth it," Mary said.

Miranda didn't want to believe any of the things her hamster was saying, but she just tried not to think about it. She told herself that she would see Mary every day.

"I have to talk to my daddy in the morning and tell him who you belong to," Miranda said. "I know I can't tell him you talk, so what am I supposed to do?"

Mary thought about telling Miranda to simply say she ran away, but she didn't want her to think that lying was OK, either. At this thought, she realized she didn't know what the little girl should do. Anything that she did to bring her back to the school would need her to lie, and Miranda was an impressionable little girl.

Mary was impressed when she was the one to think of an idea that didn't involve dishonesty. Miranda said that she would bring a photo of her hamster to school, making sure that Ms. Webb's class saw it, too. Then at least one kid would recognize Mary and beg her to take their pet back. After that, Miranda would be able to say honestly that she found out the hamster was the classroom's, and ask her dad to bring her back.

"I have a question," Miranda said all of a sudden. "I named you Mary, but since I didn't have you first, that means they called you something else. Why didn't you tell me your real name? And what is it?"

"In class, they call me Rose," she said. "But it's just a name, so I didn't want you to think you did something wrong by calling me something else. I like the name, Mary, too. You can keep calling me that."

"I will," Miranda said, smiling for the first time in the whole exchange.

"Go to bed now, Miranda," her hamster said. "You have a lot to do tomorrow, and I don't want you to be tired for school, either."

"Good night, Mary."

The two of them went to bed. In the morning, when she went to school, Miranda did everything she was supposed to do, and there was one kid who said the photo was of his class's runaway hamster. She figured out it was Charlie, and remembered that she would have to tell on him when she took Mary back.

When she got home, Miranda was ready to do what she had been waiting to do all day. She dropped her backpack by the door and walked straight into her father's library. He was ready on his chair like he always did.

"Daddy," Miranda said. "I took a picture of Mary, and everyone at school was saying it was the class pet who ran away."

He slowly put down his book and took off his glasses. It seemed like he got very into the story he was reading and was taking a moment to reorient himself to what his daughter was saying.

"They really recognized their hamster? It sounds like they really liked her, then. But she did run away, Miranda," her father said. "I don't know that I want to trust kids to say when a hamster is theirs. Are you sure it was really their hamster?"

She wished that she could tell her father the truth about what Mary had told her, but she knew that Mary said that would frighten him, so she didn't.

"I am sure. They had a picture of her in that classroom, and she looks exactly the same as it. She has the same fur color, and she's the same size. Plus, everyone in that class swore to me that it was their old class pet," Miranda said.

"I'm sure they think it's their hamster, but that doesn't mean she is," her father said. "Either way, Mary is ours now, so don't let the other kids pressure you into taking her here."

Miranda went over to her room and told Mary what her dad said.

"I heard," Mary said. "It's okay. It sounds like there's nothing you can do about it, so just don't worry. I'll just be your pet. I'll feel better again, eventually."

Mary curled up into a ball and turned to the back corner of her cage. Miranda didn't think she looked like she felt better at all. But her dad said that she wasn't allowed to take the hamster back to her past owners. She was perplexed at what she should do.

She had an idea of what she should do, but she didn't want to sneak around her dad. Miranda knew that the school was opened early in the morning before she normally got there, and Ms. Webb was one of the teachers who was known to get there the earliest. If she got up early and took Mary with her, she could bring Mary back and tell the teacher what happened with Charlie.

When she thought about it, Miranda realized that there wasn't a way to do this while telling the complete truth. This was because even if she had her father's permission to return Mary, she wanted to tell the teacher about Charlie's treatment of the hamster as well. She knew for a fact that this had happened because of what Mary told her, but she couldn't just say that the hamster had told her what Charlie did herself. That meant she had to tell Ms. Webb that she had seen what happened when this was not actually the case.

What Miranda did was tell herself that maybe sometimes, it is OK to tell a little fib if it meant it would protect someone. She wanted to protect Mary from Charlie, and she wanted to bring her back home, too. In order to do those two things, her only option was to tell a few small fibs.

The following morning, Miranda scooped up Mary in her hand and put her in the back pocket of her bookbag. She hadn't told her about her plan the night before, because she knew that Mary wouldn't approve of her lying to her father. But as smart as Mary was, she wouldn't be able to get out of her book bag when she zipped it, and she knew she was doing what was best for her.

Mary had been sulking in her cage the entire time since she got home from school the day before and told her that she didn't have her father's permission. Miranda thought she was probably secretly happy about what Mary was doing. But she wasn't able to admit it to her.

It was so early in the morning that it was barely even light outside because the sun had just come up. Miranda took the long mile-long walk to bring her hamster to the school. The entire trip, Mary pesters her to walk back home at once.

"Your dad didn't tell you that this was acceptable," Mary kept saying. "I don't want you to get in trouble for this. Turn around this instant, Miranda. This isn't what you should be doing."

Miranda endured this for the whole long walk until she got to the school, and she needed help to figure out where the classroom was. Reluctantly, Mary told her which hallway it was in. It had been a long journey, but Mary was finally going back to her old owner. Ms. Webb was at her desk when Miranda entered.

Before speaking to the teacher, Miranda simply unzipped her backpack and took Mary out. She was extra careful with the hamster around Ms. Webb, much more careful than she had been when she was at home. She held her with both hands and slowly walked over to the cage that was still on the window, sill at the other side of the door.

"It's Rose!" Ms. Webb exclaimed. "I thought the children were out of their minds when they were saying Rose was still around. I assumed I would never see her ever again. Oh, my goodness! This is crazy!"

Miranda thought to herself that if she knew all the things she knew, it would be too crazy for her to handle. But she didn't tell her any of it, because of what Mary (now Rose) had told her: adults would be too scared to be able to handle knowing that an animal could talk.

She didn't say it directly, but Miranda did make some jokes about it for her former pet's sake.

"Rose is a very smart hamster, Ms. Webb," Miranda said. "One night, when I couldn't sleep, I walked out into my house's library, and Rose was reading a book under a lamplight."

Ms. Webb just laughed. "I'm sure that was a very strange thing to see."

"Then she told me that she learned how to read from your class," Miranda continued. She had realized that even though the hamster told her not to give away her secrets, it didn't really matter what she said to the adults, because they wouldn't think she was serious. Ms. Webb would simply laugh or smile at whatever claim Miranda made about her hamster.

But she didn't want to push things too far. She thought she owed the teacher a bit of an explanation. "I got her for my birthday. My daddy found her on the street and gave her to me as a present, but when I showed people pictures of her, they said it was Rose from this class. I called her Mary, but Rose is a very nice name, too," Miranda said. Before Ms. Webb could laugh again, Miranda took a deep breath and got ready to tell her little fib. "Oh, Ms. Webb, there's something very important I have to tell you. I didn't know it was the same hamster at the time, but before Rose ran away, I saw a student in your class treating her really meanly. He was poking at her with pencils."

"That must be why she ran away," Ms. Webb said seriously. "Thank you for telling me, Miranda. You're a very strong girl. You can be sure that she will be safe here from now on."

Mary walked about inside the cage. She didn't get settled right away, although Miranda could tell she was happy to be there. Mary faced Miranda, but saw that Ms. Webb was still there, so she didn't say anything.

"Ms. Webb, is it okay if I have a little time with Rose?" Miranda said. "I'm going to really miss her."

"Of course, you can! Let me go into the teacher's lounge and get some work done in there," the teacher said. She picked up some books and papers and headed out of the room. Mary was free to talk again.

"It's not too late, Miranda," she said. "Part of me doesn't feel right about not being your hamster anymore. And your dad is going to be upset that I'm not there. You can tell him that I ran away, but you've already lied for me, and you're too young to be doing things like this."

"I can't keep you away from your family," Miranda said simply. "But don't worry about it. Maybe you're right that we won't see each other very much anymore, but you were so sad without the kids from this class, and I couldn't let that go on. I got you something, too."

Miranda pulled out the storybook that she found Mary reading the first night that she discovered her hamster could talk. With some effort, she hauled the heavy book out of her bag and put it outside the cage where she could read it, leaving it on the page she was last on.

"This is where your bookmark was," Miranda said. "I don't know if this is exactly right, though."

"It's perfect. I hope you do see me again soon," Mary said sadly.

"Of course, I will. It won't even seem any different," Miranda promised. "I may not be in your class, but I'm going to see you all the time. I'll get you gifts, I'll read you stories, and when the teacher isn't looking, I'm going to take you out of the cage and we'll find new books for you in the school library."

"That sounds like a lot of fun," Mary said. "Thank you for being my owner, Miranda. I know that I wasn't that great to be around for the last couple of months, but you should know that I still loved having you around. It was just that I missed all those other kids too."

"I know that," Miranda said. She zipped up her bookbag. "Well, I have to run home now. If I don't hurry up, my daddy will notice that I'm not home. I don't want him to get worried."

"Yes, hurry home, Miranda," Mary said. "I'll see you soon."

Miranda ran home as fast as she could. Thankfully, he wasn't awake yet. She was really worried that he would wake up and notice that she wasn't home, but she knew that he was more of a night owl than an early bird, so she thought it was a reasonable risk to make. Next came the part of the plan that Mary had just told her she didn't approve of. But she didn't approve of being taken back home either, and this was the only way for Miranda to explain the hamster being gone without her father knowing that she had gone to school by herself.

"Daddy!" she shouted. "Where's Mary? Do you know where Mary is?"

She ran to her father's door with an urgency as if her hamster really had run away. She heard him start to get up, but he took a long time to answer her cries, so she ran into his room anyway. He was scratching his eyes like he didn't know what to say.

"She's not in her cage?" he finally said when she stood at his bed.

"No, and I can't find her anywhere," she said.

Eventually, he got out of bed and helped her look for the hamster, even though Miranda knew they wouldn't find her.

"It sounds like she's the kind of hamster that likes to run away," her father said. "I wonder how many owners she's had before us. Maybe she really was that class pet you were talking about…"

"Maybe she was," Miranda said, trying to sound innocent.

"I couldn't find her anywhere, and neither could you. There are only so many places to look in this small house, so we may be out of luck, kid," her father said. "I'm sorry.

You didn't even like any of your other birthday presents, did you?"

Miranda knew she had to seem upset, so she tried her best to act like it. "It's okay, daddy. Hamsters run away all the time. All the kids I know who had hamsters had them run away, too." The two of them spent some time that morning watching cartoons before Miranda had to go back to school. The whole time, she was thinking about all the things she and Mary could do after she was done with class. Maybe no one would notice that she was gone once school was out. After all, the kids in the class only took care of her during the day, so she thought they probably wouldn't even notice if she was gone for a little while.

"Daddy, I want to play with my friend Rose after school," Miranda said.

"Rose? I've never met this friend of yours, but as long as you just play in the neighborhood, it's OK with me," her father said.

Miranda nodded and smiled. It looked like things wouldn't be so different after all.

Herman Hermit Crab gets Crabby

He swings and hits the baseball and it goes soaring way to the outfield. Herman Hermit crab scurries down the base line-safe at first. He high fives the base coach and gets ready to watch and see if he can steal 2nd base. The next batter gets up and gets ready to hit the ball. Swish- STRIKE 1

"Come on buddy!" yelled Herman "you can do it- hit that ball."

The pitcher winds up and throws the ball. Herman starts to run and steal 2nd base. The batter swings again- SWISH-Strike 2. But Herman made it to 2nd base. He began clapping his claws and cheering on the batter again, "You can do it- Hit me home!" Herman yells from 2nd base.

Here comes the pitch and Herman starts to steal 3rd base…. "FOUL BALL." Shouts the referee of the home plate. Herman scowls and heads back to 2nd base.

Next 2 Pitches- "BALL" yells the umpire.

This is it Herman knew he could steal 3rd on this next pitch so he crouched down and got ready to bolt down the baseline. The Pitcher winds up and lets the ball roar across the plate and Herman takes off. The catcher throws the ball but Herman slides in and is safe.

"HaHa I knew it," Herman said proudly "I knew I'd make it," he tells the 3rd base coach.

The count is now 3 balls and 2 strikes; a full count. Herman watches the pitcher and looks at his coach for the sign to steal the base or wait. He gets the sign to wait. "Oh man, I could make it," Herman mumbles under his breath. He turns to his coach, "Let me steal home coach I can make it, I know I can."

"No wait here Herman, I think we can score if he hits the ball, if not we will wait for next batter." The coach encouraged Herman to wait. Herman made a grumpy face and stood on 3rd base kind of pouting. The batter swung and blooped it right down the third baseline. Herman wasn't paying attention, and he began to run. The 3rd base player picked up the ball tagged Herman and then threw it to first to get the batter out. A double play.

Herman stood there with a shocked look on his face. "Come on Herman lets go, we need to take the field," the coach said as he ran back to the dugout.

Herman walked back to the dugout very unhappy. He grabbed his mitt and headed out to the field. He walked out to center-field dragging his feet and taking his time.

"Batter up!" yelled the umpire. Herman was not even out to his position yet. He turned and scowled at the umpire as he made his way out to the outfield. Herman stood out there like he was waiting for a bus. He didn't move when a ball was hit and he didn't cheer on his team when they made a good play. Finally, they got 3 outs and Herman's team headed back in to bat.

"What's your problem, Herman?" Asked one of the players.

"Hello-I got out. Didn't you see that?" Herman snapped with a crabby voice.

"We all get out sometimes; it's not a big deal. If the coach sent you and you got out it's not your fault you were doing what you were told to do." Another player chimed in.

"Well he DIDN'T send me but I knew I could make it," Herman grumbled.

Herman team made it through the batting order and Herman was up to bat again. "Herman, you're up!" His coach called out. Herman grabbed his bat and slumped his way to the batter box. Herman stood there waiting for the perfect pitch. He just watched as the pitcher pitched 3 strikes in a row. Herman was out. He dropped his bat and grumbled all the way back to the bench.

"Hey, your crabby attitude is not helping the team." The next batter said as he walked toward the plate.

"Whatever!" Herman snapped.

The inning was over and Herman's team was taking the field.

"Herman, I'd like you to sit this inning out. We are a team and everyone needs to participate to do well." His coach said.

Herman flopped down on the bench and watched as his team fielded ball an made outs.

"Herman, you are a good player...but you could be great," His coach said as they sat watching the other players. "You need to be a leader even if things don't go as you hoped. Your attitude affects everyone. If you stay positive the team can be positive or at some point, they just won't want to play with you."

Herman sat, listened and thought about what the coach had said but he was still crabby about getting out. But what the coach had said seemed like a good point. Even if Herman got out if he could try to learn from the parts of the game, he didn't like he could learn to be a better player and maybe teach other players tricky tricks to play better.

"Can I please go back in coach?" Herman asked the next inning.

"I don't know Herman, how is your attitude?" Coach questioned.

"I am ready to do better. I understand that if I am crabby about what I did, it seems like I am crabby about what everyone does and I didn't mean for that to happen." Herman explained.

When the team took the field the next inning Herman ran out to his position and began being the team player, he knew he was. He was cheering on the team members who made plays and congratulated them when they made an out. Soon all the other players began to chime in on the team support. Herman stood in the outfield and felt proud that he was able to change his attitude and not be so crabby.

He realized that even when things don't go your way you can choose how to feel about it and choosing to look at the good things always makes you feel better.

Brother in Arms

Calvin and Alexander were brothers who grew up together in the same castle. As teenagers, they are both squires to brothers, learning how to be knights. Calvin is a year older than Alexander but Alex is a fast learner and is working hard to become a knight as quickly as possible. They were both working to prove they would be good knights. They commissioned their own weapons and armor, they just needed to spend some time learning to fight well.

Alexander is squire to Arthur. As a squire, Alexander is learning to battle on and off his horse. He practices daily and shows his allegiance to the King. Calvin is squire to Clifford. He is learning to fight and which horses are best in different situations. They are both learning the same thing, how to be a knight. They help their knights get ready for battle. They are each waiting for the time they will go with their knights into battle. For now, they practice. Calvin and Alexander have not yet had to fight each other, but they know they will eventually meet on the practice field. Alexander is rising through the ranks quickly so they will be matched against each other soon.

One day, Calvin was training with the other squires, practicing the hand to hand fighting by beating another squire in a cruel manner. Alexander happened to see the fight and stepped in to stop the unnecessary beating. Alexander did not know, at first, that it was his brother who was beating up the helpless squire. When he noticed who he was disarming, he was amazed.

"Brother? Why are you so cruel to this young man? You are far bigger and far stronger. We are practicing. Why would you want to lame this boy for the rest of his life?", asked Alexander.

His question was answered with a sneer from Calvin, "I am showing what I can do. That way, no one has to guess if I will fight well. They can see for themselves that I can fight. I show everyone each day that I intend to fight to the death for my King."

"Well, this will not happen if you kill the King's men each day. You should be helping the squires who are not as good as you. The purpose of the practice is not to hurt your fellow squires. It is to learn how to behave in battle. You should not be so brutal when it is not necessary," responded Alexander.

Alexander could see that Calvin did not enjoy being reprimanded. His eyes started to narrow and he looked like he was squinting. Alexander knows this is a sign of anger. He smiled to try to soften the words that he already said, and tried to think of a way to get Calvin to smile back.

"Calvin, remember when we were little boys and you saved that injured bird. You nursed it back to health and set it free. That bird stayed around you for many years after. He would fly away, but he always came back a few days later to check on you."

"Why are you bringing up all this stupid kid stuff," asked Calvin. "I was young back then. That was a long time ago. You know that we are nearly men and I am here to show everyone that I will be a great man and a great knight. If you are not here for the same, get out of my way or I will beat you down as well."

Alexander did not know why his brother had changed so much, but he did not want to fight with him. He turned around and walked away.

Alexander was taught early in his training to always face the battle in front of you. He was taking a chance by turning his back on Calvin, but he could not bear to see his older brother changed to such a hard man. Yes, he agrees with Calvin. They are nearly men. There is a difference between them now and they may never be able to be the carefree boys they were. It did not make Alexander happy to realize it.

Calvin and Alexander continued to train to become knights by acting as squires. They learned about weapons. Calvin learned, but he did not take the same care with his knight's weapons as did Alexander. Alexander understands that weapons are a means to an end. They must be cared for carefully to be sure the metal is strong to strike and protect the knight. Protecting the knight protects the King and the kingdom. Arthur taught all this to Alexander and they both believed in the rightness of this idea. Calvin was taught to inspect the weapons. If Clifford did not like the looks of a weapon or shield, he discarded it. He had a stockpile of weapons he took from knights beaten in battle. Calvin was responsible for making sure the weapons and armor were in good shape and at the ready. Clifford was a valiant knight and had many battle victories. He killed many men and took whatever he could use or sell from the battlefield. It made Clifford rich and he shared his bounty with the King. The King showed his appreciation by inviting him to the castle and Clifford was invited to all the best festivities as a guest of the King. Because of this,

Calvin learned that winning was the most important thing about being a knight. Clifford was very popular with the King and Calvin hoped to be as well.

To Arthur, a victory meant something different. Arthur had won many battles as well, but he did not like killing men and boys barely out of their youth. He did what was necessary took no pleasure in it. Alexander could see that each death took a toll on Arthur but that is how battles work. It is Arthur's life and is Alexander's life. Alexander and Calvin fought for the same King to protect the land and property of the King and their own family. Calvin loved the battles and the King's celebrations. Alexander loved the kingdom and the thought that his family and others would be safe for another time.

The King hosted tournaments for the knights to practice and prove themselves worthy of being part of his feudal forces. The knights used the tourneys and an opportunity to teach the squires in a military situation, but not a deadly one. The squires used all the skills they were learning during the tournaments. Many squires were noticed by the King for good and for bad. As it happened, the King liked the money he gained from the knights like Clifford. They couldn't use everything found on the battlefield and if Clifford was willing to share the spoils with him, the better for the King. Arthur had a pesky habit of letting the losing knights pledge their allegiance to him and the King. Having a larger army was nice, but money is better. Every knight added was gold he did not receive. He would never tell either of the knights his preference, but he really did prefer to fill his coffers. The tournaments were a way to see if any of the knights Arthur brought into his fold we're good at what they did. Many were and they seemed to like being part of Arthur's inner group. Clifford had people around him who liked to have a good time and they liked the adventure of battle. In the King's mind, there is room for both types of knights.

One tournament day, it seemed that the knights of both Calvin and Alexander were both signed up to participate. The tournament will be held at a vast estate of a nobleman not many hours ride from the castle. It seemed likely that their family would be there to see all the sights. Calvin sent word that the two would be part of the tournament and he wanted to humiliate his brother in front of Father and mother. It will be the best gift Calvin could give himself. A display of strength and intelligence in front of his family, Clifford and the King will do a lot for his goal of knighthood. Defeating his brother will do the opposite for Alexander.

Because Calvin was older, he had acquired more weapons and his armor was better fitted. Alexander was still growing and his armor would fit well one day and when he next went to put it on, it would be ill-fitting. But Alexander felt that Calvin was waiting for the opportunity to fight against his own little brother. Alexander had never been forgiven for breaking up the fight months earlier. Alexander was preparing for a long, exhausting tournament.

Calvin was very happy to have an opportunity to assist Clifford in his battle against the knights Arthur. Today would be the day that his brother would pay for daring to question the actions of his older brother. Calvin knows the noble art of knighthood and has been studying for longer. Calvin felt his brother was not only weak of body but weak of mind. He did not have what it takes to be a knight, from what Calvin could see. Calvin planned to conceal his attack during the melee. He felt sure he could take care of his brother and no one would be wiser. He was wearing the banner of his knight and saw that his brother was wearing the banner of his own liege. There will be lots of chaos as soon as the tourney starts and Calvin has plans to use the chaos to his advantage. He has a small knife he will use to cut the straps of Alexander's saddle. This will cause Alexander to fall off his horse in front of all the knights, the women, the noblemen, the peasants...everyone watching the tournament. His knight will probably dismiss Alexander as his squire. Calvin was happy. He wanted Alexander to be ruined.

Calvin saw a tunic with the coat-of-arms of Alexander's knight. He put it on over his own and made his way into the encampment of his enemy. Calvin had done this many times in times of battle so he moved easily among the knights and squires. Though Calvin did not notice, the camp noticed that the stranger moving in their midst. They were a close group and tended to know each other. A young squire was set to follow Calvin. He saw Calvin cutting the saddle straps on the horse normally used by Arthur's squire. He went back and reported what he saw to his knight. Arthur was informed and told Alexander to switch his saddle and get his own repaired. Alexander was angry that his brother tried to sabotage him in such an awful way. He was sure it was Calvin. He consulted with Arthur to see what he should do to end the feud with his brother. Alexander was not feuding, but Calvin was. Arthur suggested a long talk with Calvin to see if he is willing to stop the feud. Alexander set out to find his brother in the mob of people

When Alexander saw Calvin, he was with their family. They were all gathered together and looked happy to be together. Alex walked up and joined them all. They were happy that both their sons were safe.

Their mother walked to both of them and kissed the cheeks of each don. "Calvin, I'm so glad to let us know you would be near. We have missed you both so much." Calvin just smiled. As he hugged his mother, Calvin looked over his shoulder and gave Alexander a sneaky smile. Alexander knew then that the feud would always be there for Calvin. He did not care if their dear mother and sister saw Alexander trampled by horses or lamed in the tournament. So, Alexander bid goodbye to the group and set off to ride next to his knight

He checked and rechecked all of his equipment and all of his weapons

He did the same for his knight. And they set off for the melee. It happened that Clifford and Arthur were marched in the joust. As part of the tournament, the squires would do a joust first. Calvin was sure he would knock Alexander off his horse easily because Calvin was sure Alexander was weak and he was sure Alexander's saddle was weak.

Before the joust, the two brothers met in the center of the list (the path the horses run along the rail) and Alexander surprised Calvin with angry words.

"Brother. You have held a grudge for many months. I was trying to you from your own anger an inability to control yourself. Now, I see that we will never be true brothers again. Go in peace. I am at peace with how we will be forevermore."

Calvin was a little confused as to why his brother was speaking to him of peace. But he would not let him have the last word.

"Brother. It doesn't matter what you thought you were doing. Have your peace. I will have riches. Do you see my fine suit of armor? It is the armor of a true warrior. Go to your post and prepare to fall. The peasants are waiting to see you fail."

Alexander did not speak again he turned his horse and trotted away.

Calvin was sure of his victory over his brother. He had made it so things would go his way. He looked at his brother who was seated proudly on his stallion. Calvin turned his horse around and suddenly, his horse bolted. Because of the armor, Calvin was not able to move easily and soon he found himself leaning off the horse and tumbling to the ground. His horse left the arena and headed back to the stable. There was laughter. Everyone was laughing at him. He felt his face go red with the heat of embarrassment. Calvin's helmet became dented in the fall and was damaged so much that they had to call the blacksmith to remove it. All the while, people walked past him and laughed. Because Calvin was wearing Clifford's coat of arms, Clifford was not pleased. He can le by and tore the tunic off of Calvin and told him to report to the page section from now on.

Calvin was humiliated. For a minute, as he was falling, Calvin thought maybe God was getting back at him for trying to bully Alexander. But after it was all over, Calvin decided to find the horse and see if Alexander had caused the problem. Unfortunately, when the horse was found, what Calvin found was a bee sting. It wasn't even an act of sabotage. A bee stung his horse in the snout. The stinger was still in the nostril and the swelling was immense. An insect destroyed his life. He sold his weapons and armor by the end of the day and took his horse with the swollen face and returned home with his family. There is no way he could be a page. He might as well become a monk. Yes. He would get back at Alexander. He will join the church and crusade against the knights. If Calvin can't be a knight, he doesn't want Alexander to be one either.

Chivalry Is Not Dead

Alexander is a squire and has pledged his allegiance to the knight, Arthur. Alexander is working very hard to be dubbed a knight Arthur. He tries to be chivalrous at all times. He didn't realize how important the Code is, in life until recently. Alexander had a falling out with his brother. His brother was a squire for a knight who had a reputation for not exactly following the code of chivalry.

Alexander respects the code and wants to be sure when he is a knight, his fellow knights do the same. One day, when the band of knights was traveling across a pitted and scarred land they came across a village that seemed to be abandoned. One of the squires signaled that there was movement in the village. We were not sure if it was an animal or perhaps a squatter so some of the knights were sent to scout out the area. If nothing else, it would be a chance for the knights to rest. They had fought a long battle and were making their way back to their own lands. Their group was larger after the battle than before it. Though there were wounds that would need to heal, the loss of men was not as large as it could have been. Some of the defeated knights joined the ranks of Arthur's group. They pledged their loyalty to Arthur and his King. The scouts came back with the news that there are families living in the ruins of the village. This did not change our plans to stop and rest. We entered the village and called all to come forward and stop hiding.

"Come forward, people. We are not here to harm. We simply seek a place to rest our tired bodies and water our horses," announced the herald as we made our way down the main road.

People began to peek out from behind the corners of the buildings that were still standing. Arthur dismounted from his horse. Alexander did the same and gathered the reins of both horses. Arthur walked out ahead of the group. He was heading for the building where there was movement. Everyone seemed to be waiting to see what would happen. None of the knights and squires were expecting what happened next.

Suddenly, there were rocks being launched from above towards Alexander and the group of knights. The band of fighters was able to use their shields to protect themselves from the barrage of stones. Arthur kept going forward and soon Alexander was by his side.

Alexander left the horses under the protection of another knight and joined Arthur at a quick pace towards the building. Just as suddenly as the barrage started, it ended.

Arthur announced his good intentions, "I don't think you understood what my herald announced. We just want to take a rest. Why do you attack us so cruelly?"

A voice answered from an old man walking towards the group, "We are a peaceful group. We do not have men here to protect us. They didn't mean any harm to you with the stones. Water your horses and then, please, keep going. There is nothing here for you to take.

Whatever we had is already gone. Please, just leave us alone."

Arthur and Alexander had never heard such a defeated plea.

"What has happened here," asked Arthur? Why are you all hiding? You must have chores to complete and work to do. Why is everyone hidden away?"

The old man had reached us now. He did not have a look of fear in his eyes. He looked as though he would accept whatever happened to him. His shoulders were slumped in his ragged shirt. He was clean but frail. If this is a security force for the town there is something very wrong. He offered greetings to everyone, looking Arthur in the eye, finally.

Arthur did not back away from the meekness in front of him, "Don't make me repeat myself, old man. What is going on here?"

The old man seemed to be offended at being called an old man. Alexander wondered at the bold way this man presented himself in the rags and frailty of defeat. He answered Arthur in a clear and booming voice, "We have been ravaged by men calling themselves The Knights of Clifford. The men of fighting age were struck down, our food stolen and our women...it was just cruel and the knights acted without honor."

Alexander was appalled. This was not the way knights are to act. Because of the Code of Chivalry, Arthur did not curse the actions of the knights who were here before, but he did not defend them either. It was too much to think about for Alexander but Arthur was not taken aback at all.

"You have no reason to trust us, but we are not like the other knights. We just want to get something to drink. Take a rest If you have beds. We have a coin. It is not our way to take what we want and move on. We have honor that seems to be missing from some of our kind."

The old man looked wary but signaled to have water brought out for the men. A young boy brought out a bucket with fresh water. The knights did not move to approach the water. The old man looked confused.

"Here is the water. What are you waiting for?"

Arthur answered without pause, "We are waiting for everyone to come out from hiding. We have already been attacked once.

The old man seemed to understand and signaled that it was okay for his village to show itself.

There were people coming from behind every pile of rubble, every tree and every doorway. But it wasn't a typical village of people. They were the very oldest and the very youngest except for the women. There were women of all ages. Everyone looked very thin and old. Even the children looked old. As Alexander looked at the people coming into the open area, he could have wept. He did not know how men of honor, knights who should be the most honorable of men, how could they leave the villagers to die a slow and anguished death.

"Where are your men," Arthur nearly shouted.

"I told you, they were killed. It was that Clifford. And they took all of our weapons and tools. They killed the blacksmith. We have been able to hunt with traps and bows and arrows but we haven't made anything big enough and sharp enough to use on anything bigger than a rabbit. We have many days when we have only a few meager vegetables to share, answered the old man.

He spoke for everyone and we could see everyone nodding their heads in agreement.

The knights began to dismount after hearing the tale. Though everyone was tired and ready for a meal, it was apparent that there was no meal available. So, the knights began to unpack their travel provisions of dried meat, dried fruit, and hard bread. They made a pile between the villagers and the knights.

Arthur did not even have to turn around to know what his men were doing. He asked the villagers, "Who can turn this into the tastiest meal so that been may all eat a hot portion?" There was a rustling from the back of the group of villagers.

A girl no older than Alexander was pushed to the front and shyly spoke to Arthur, "I can cook. My family ran the inn. They are all dead except me. I know what to do."

"Good," answered Arthur. "Start on a meal."

A group of girls helped to gather everything in their aprons and they went to a building that had a sign hanging off its hinges that indicated it was, in fact, The Inn.

The knights passed around the water bucket and several boys brought more water. One of the older ladies showed the squires where they could take the horses for water and where they could munch on some grass and flowers.

The knights went along with the horses to try to wash away some of the dirt and sweat of the road and battle.

Arthur stopped to talk to a group of older men. Some had doubts about the integrity of the strangers. Others had hoped to be rescued. Alexander knew the knights would not leave without helping to put the town back together as well as they could and Arthur wanted to know what they needed most.

By the time it was worked out how the knights could help, the meal was ready and a plan was in Arthur's mind.

The village and the knights ate separately. The knights carried their meal to a field and ate noisily and happily. They had not had a hot meal in a few days and though it was not as hearty as they like, it tasted good.

The villagers gathered at the inn and ate well. They took small portions as they had grown used to eating very little. The taste, they were accustomed to. The portion of meat was not something they had eaten for months. They could feel the strength seeping back into their limbs by the time they finished.

As the villagers finished eating the knights were crowding the doorway. Alexander was elected to present the plans to the villagers. He started out shakily, his youth and inexperience showing in his red cheeks.

"Greetings villagers. Since we are here, we will help you with what you need to take care of yourselves."

As abruptly as Alexander started to talk, he finished and turned and left the building. The villagers thought him strange but began to clean up the tables in the inn. They needed to get back to the chores. They would have to try to check the traps and fetch more water. There were many things to do.

One of the knights set about the town looking for the smithy. He was used to caring for his shield and weapons and had some idea of how to make basic tools. He found the likely building, though the walls were no longer in existence. There was still a large hearth and workbench.

The knights had collected damaged and spare tools and implements from the other knights. He was trying to get a good fire going in the hearth when he felt eyes upon him. They belonged to a pair of young boys. Both of them were smooth-faced and scrawny. The older of the two, larger, anyway spoke, "Our family ran the smithy. Father was starting to teach us…." He broke off. He could not continue.

His brother moved towards the hearth and got to work getting the fire going. The brawny knight let him do it. As the boy made swift progress, the knight unloaded his pack of bits iron and leather. The boys watched and wondered, "Are you repairing your sword?"

"No. I'm going to make you a few tools so the fields can get planted and then harvested. I'm also thinking you need a good butcher knife and maybe a weapon. I think I can make something that's not too heavy so the ladies can handle them."

He was thinking the old men and boys could handle them too, but he didn't need to say it. Everyone still here feels something for not being able to stop the awful things that happened.

The knights spent more than a fortnight in the village. With knights there to protect them, they were able to get the word to other villages close by that they needed a few things. Their situation did not seem as dire and they felt okay to have people in the village. The women were able to make some of the wares they were used to selling to neighboring villages and the knights helped to hire men from other areas to rebuild the village. Things were not perfect, but they were a lot better.

During all of this rebuilding, Alexander and Arthur had disappeared. Though the knights thought it strange, they knew the pair we're good men and waited for their return.

When the returned, no one was more surprised than the villagers. The two knights brought with them a huge wild boar and men that looked bedraggled and dirty and familiar.

"We brought some things you have been missing," said Arthur as the entered the new and improved village common.

Women and children of the village dropped whatever they were doing and ran to the homely looking group. Some of their men had returned.

For some of the villagers, there was no happiness. They did not feel any worse than they felt that morning so no one was angry that only some of the men were able to return.

Arthur and Alexander tracked the band of knights who attacked the village. They were able to find them only a few days ride away. It seems the band would stop every few days and pillage a town. This made their progress slow. They would gather men along the way. The men could either pledge their allegiance to Clifford and his Lord, or they would be taken along and used to work for the band of knights. They were not fed well so there were often among the group of slave labor. It took some time for Arthur and Alexander to return because they wanted to be sure the other slaves were able to get back to their homes as well.

One of the men, a farmer whose wife could not stop hugging him, explained further.

"We were trying to figure out, us that was stolen, how to get away so we could return home. We got in the habit of taking whatever we could from them that calls themselves knights after the slept from drinking too much ale. We got some knives and such. We had figured out how to unbind ourselves and everyone was freed for a short time each day. We took turns. We were working together to get away, those of us who didn't join up with those evil men. Sorry love," he said while looking at an angry woman with 7 or 8 angry kids around her, clinging to her skirts and scratching in the dirt. "Anyway," he continued, "One night we started hearing some strange noises out in the trees one. With one or two of us always unchained, we could look for food and such. Those knights did not bother to wonder if we were hungry. The two who were unchained went to see what the noise was. It was Arthur and Alexander. They were looking for us and now, here we are."

The long speech from the farmer told enough of the story for all to know how the men ended up back in the village. Of course, it wasn't easy to get away, but they did not want to worry the families with what happened to them. The villagers were all happy and the knights felt they had stayed long enough. They were ready to fight a new battle and so started to gather their belongings so they could move on. The villagers had enough meat to last for months. There were tools and weapons. Most importantly, the villagers had a willingness to work together and help each other.

Arthur went around the village to settle the debts. The band of knights had been staying at the inn and the stables. They ate food the villagers had been saving and some they got from neighboring villages. Arthur felt the village would need coin in the coming seasons, but he knew the coin would not be accepted. He was right. No one would accept the coin.

The innkeepers' daughter said it best, "If it wasn't for you, we wouldn't even be here."

Arthur went to the church and left the money on the altar. He was sure the coin would be put to good use. He was a good man and a good knight.

Garden Gnomes

Do you know what garden gnomes are? They are the cute little statues that you see sometimes sitting outside on people's lawns and in their gardens.

Most garden gnomes have tall, pointy hats they wear and they are usually painted wearing brightly colored clothing that looks whimsical and fun. Have you ever wondered what it might be like to be able to paint your very own garden gnomes? What if I told you that you could paint your very own garden gnomes to put out in your garden right now, without having to move a single muscle? You really can- In your mind! Your mind is capable of doing many incredible things, including something called Visualization.

To begin your visualization practice, close your eyes. Really, close your eyes (unless you are the one reading this, of course!) To build a very strong visualization, it is usually helpful to first center yourself and be sure you are giving your brain the very best tools it needs to work with. In this case, that means oxygen, and oxygen means taking some good, deep breaths.

You are going to take some slow, deep breaths now, following along with my instruction: Breathe in very slowly, 1 – 2 – 3 – 4. Now breathe out, very slowly, 1 – 2 – 3 – 4. Excellent. Now again very slowly, 1 – 2 – 3 – 4 and breathe back out very slowly, 1 – 2 – 3 – 4 very nice. Once more very slowly in 1 – 2 – 3 – 4 and back out very slowly, 1 – 2 – 3 – 4. Great!

Take a moment to review how you feel. Are you comfy and feeling good? Okay, great.

Picture yourself, in your mind's eye, outside on a beautiful spring day. The sky is a pale blue above you and the sun is warming you where you sit. You have an artist's workspace set up with a wooden table that is about the same height as your waist, stocked with paints and paintbrushes of every color and every size. There are also several garden gnome statues beside the table, all the same light gray color of unpainted pottery.

You take a long, deep breath in and notice how fresh and clean the spring air is and you think to yourself that today is a spectacular day to be outside doing a lovely paint project. You look down and notice that you have on a long, black apron. Perfect! Now you won't have to worry about getting paint on your clothes.

You lean down to inspect the garden gnomes. Each one is unique and different. Some are smiling and others are making funny faces. Some are standing with their hands on their hips and some are crouched down petting a bunny rabbit or holding a little frog. There is even a garden gnome that is picking his nose!!! You laugh a little at this, gross!

That's when you see it: the perfect garden gnome for you! This garden gnome is wearing the typical pointy gnome hat but with a twist: it has a super-wide brim, like a sun hat and his hands are up in the air with his fingers outstretched like he is at a party or something! You know it will be so fun to paint and decorate this little guy. You lifted the fun party garden gnome up and set him on the table. You take a couple of steps back, wondering what color you should paint his hat. You pull a paint palette out and inspect the color options: there is a light aqua blue, tangerine orange, bright cherry red, pale buttercream yellow, and a sparkly midnight black color. So many awesome choices, but you think that this little gnome needs a fun party hat, so you decide to start with the bright cherry red!

You look at the many paintbrushes available and decide that the hat needs one that is a decent size, so you pick up a paintbrush that is about as wide as a quarter. You dip it into the cherry red, swirling the color on to the paintbrush. You begin to paint the awesome party hat and smile as you watch the vivid cherry red slowly cover the entire hat.

Now it's time to move on to the garden gnome's outfit. Hmm. You look at your palette and decide that sparkly midnight black color would be the perfect color for the shirt, so you choose another wide paintbrush and dip it into the midnight black color, loving how sparkly it is! You begin to paint the gnome's shirt, watching in awe as the sparkly midnight black seems to glitter more and more with every stroke of your paintbrush. You love it!

The next step is to paint the little shorts, and you think that the tangerine orange would be perfect, so you select another paintbrush and begin to paint the gnome's shorts a beautiful tangerine orange. You think that the tangerine orange is such an awesome color, you will keep the same paintbrush and just dip it right into the pale buttercream yellow to create a deep yellow-orange for the gnome's little shoes.

Now that you've painted your garden gnome's clothes, you step back from the table to look him over. His cherry-red hat, his sparkly midnight black shirt, tangerine orange shorts, and yellow-orange shoes are absolutely perfect! He is colorful and bright and looks like the perfect addition to your garden. You look over at all the other garden gnomes waiting to be painted and are very thankful that you get to paint all these cute garden gnomes. Next gnome is the one picking his nose!

You do not have to leave your garden gnomes just yet if you don't want to. You can spend as long as you want here and you can come back anytime you'd like.

You can create anything you want in your mind. Imagine where you want to go and build the picture in your mind. Be sure to imagine how you want it to smell, taste, hear and feel. The more detailed you can make your mental picture, the more you will enjoy being there.

It is all up to you. Perhaps as you drift off to sleep, you may find yourself back here with your paints and your garden gnomes, enjoying this beautiful spring day.

Topher's Ultimatum

Topher worked at an ordinary software company. When people asked what his job was, he  just told them debugging. If they were interested, he could tell them more about the intricacies of what he did, but no one ever was. Even he wasn't.

Not that he had many qualms with his life. He would often say that things being boring was a sign that he was lucky. It meant that he didn't spend his days fretting over big problems.

He spent his days dealing with very small first-world problems: the slightly more interesting to describe his job was to say that he fixed issues that people had with their cell phone software. He was one of the people who fixed the code behind what makes everyone's personal devices work.

Again, he had no complaints about the life he lives being mostly uneventful. Topher didn't mind it at all, but there was one thing that made it worse, and it had to do with his boss, Sam.

He knew it was common for a person to hate their boss, but when Topher talked about how much he hated Sam, he didn't think they understood the gravity of his hatred. The reason he hated him so much was that even though Sam didn't do a much different job, he was paid significantly more.

What was more, Sam always seemed to be flaunting the nice things he could afford with his salary. If Sam didn't have a family, it would be different, but he knew that he did, so watching Sam's Corvette rolling into the parking lot every morning nearly drove him mad.

Topher had a family too: a wife named Wendy and two boys. He was paid relatively well, all things considered. But after everything was paid for as far as bills, he always seemed to be broke. Retirement seemed like a joke at this point. If there was an unexpected medical expense coming in the future, he wasn't sure how he would cover it. He knew for a fact that the insurance that Sam had for his family was much better, because he accidentally stumbled upon these records when doing normal work one day.

The thought of that accident gave Topher an idea, though. It was possible that there was something unsavory in the more detailed financial reports deep in the records that no one read. It was a long shot, but perhaps if he took a look, there would be something that he could use against him.

Topher felt vindicated when he found what he was looking for. He didn't find it in the financial records for Sam, but for the company. When he added up all the accounts receivable and compared them with the accounts payable, there was a huge discrepancy. Why did the company systematically end up with tens of thousands of dollars every week on the whole? There had to be something here that no one else was paying attention to.

Since they worked for such a big, powerful company, he could see how something like this could go unnoticed.

But that didn't mean that corporate would be able to ignore it if it was brought to their attention.

Topher couldn't say for sure if Sam was the reason for the discrepancy, but no one else could control the money that went in and out more than he could. He didn't really have to prove that he did it in the papers as long as he was scared enough of the accusation. Sure, there would be some consequences if he was wrong, but Topher was a programmer. He could always work somewhere else.

And he didn't think he was wrong. It made everything made sense. Sam's salary was significantly higher than Topher's, but with him having the pay the same expenses for having a family as he did, it just didn't make sense for him to have so much more extra money all the time. The missing money from the company accounts would explain it completely.

Now, he didn't really want to just rat Sam out. He could get no benefit out of that. What he wanted was some power that he would be able to attain if his hunch was right, and his findings would put Sam in jeopardy. Topher didn't want to be the boss himself; he was fine with staying in the position he was now. But he thought if Sam knew that Topher knew what he was doing, there was a lot he would be able to get away with that he wouldn't otherwise.

His life had gotten stale, and this could lead to something new. And he hated his boss. He was killing two birds with one stone.

It wasn't that Topher wanted a promotion or a raise. It was that he was sick of being overlooked for these things. He told Sam as much when went to his office and made a deal with him.

Topher dressed noticeably differently that day. Even the men took a second look at him when he passed by. He was wearing a suit in place of his normal button-up and khakis. Only Sam, the boss, would ever wear a suit. But Topher was wearing a suit to send a message: a message that he would be the boss from now on. He didn't make a meeting with Sam beforehand. He planned to do this on a Monday morning, just after he arrived. Sam always arrived at the building around 6, while Topher always got there around 8. This meant Sam would feel like he was settling into his weekly routine when Topher would suddenly come into his office and slam the stack of accounting papers on his desk.

Sam didn't say anything at first. He seemed absolutely confused as to what this would be about. But seeing the look on his usually non-threatening employee's face let him in on what was happening.

Still, Sam flipped through the pages first. Topher didn't say anything, because he thought the documents should speak for themselves. He also thought that on the off chance he was wrong, he could say that he saw a clerical mistake in the funds. But he really didn't think that was what was going on here.

Just as Topher expected, Sam didn't deny it. He came out with it pretty quickly.

"So, you started to read about what we really do around here," he said. "Shut the door, please."

Topher did. The two of them sat on either end of Sam's desk, quiet for a long while. Topher knew what he wanted, but he thought it was smart to see if Sam would have anything else incriminating to say first. This might go even deeper than he originally assumed.

Sam didn't say anything else, though. Not wanting to lose his moment, Topher finally spoke up. "What 'we' do around here? Your name might not be on this directly, but your signature is all over the code. This wasn't written by anyone else. I don't think this has to do with anyone else besides yourself."

"I meant that I'm not the only one who's doing this, Topher," Sam said. "Look, I understand where you're coming from. I used to be a moral person like yourself. But when I talk to my boss — the one who really ones this place — I start to see things more clearly. No, you're not the one in control here. Do you think I am? I most certainly am not. The ones in control here are the ones who own the damn place. I don't own any significant portion of the company — just the small piece that legally has to own. That's it. I don't control any of this," Sam said. "And the money — do you think they're missing it? Of course, they aren't. What thousands are to them are what coins are to us. They don't even notice it leaving our accounts. It's hard to believe for people like you and me, but it's true."

"People like you and me," Topher scoffed. "I know how much you make. And now I know how much you really make."

"Trust me, pal. If you really knew how much a billion dollars was worth, you would understand that you and I are truly in the same class. To the guys at the top, we're insignificant. Nothing that we do really affects their bottom line. All we do is our small parts in making their machines operate. That's it."

Topher noticed that Sam was chewing gum, which made him mad. He was already dominating the conversation, even though he was the one who should be. Sitting in there with just him made him pretty nervous if he was being honest with himself. Come to think of it; he thought this had to be the first time they had a one-on-one conversation. Every other time they had talked, it was in the presence of many more ears. But with the door secured shut right now, there was no way anyone was hearing anything they were saying.

"You misunderstood me when you said I'm being a moralist," Topher said. "I'm smart enough to know I don't have anything to gain from turning this in. I wouldn't get money or a trophy. You would just get in legal trouble, and I would probably have to show up in court. I don't want that at all."

"Let me make a wild guess, then," Sam said, sounding bored. "You're threatening to show this to someone if I don't give you a cut."

"Exactly right," Topher said. He was perplexed. Somehow, everything seemed to be going the way it was supposed to and wrong at the same time. He thought he wished that Sam had acted surprised at his finding or something. Instead, it was almost like he had been waiting for this to happen all along.

"I don't mean to take away all the excitement, buddy, but as you saw in our papers, it is all right there," Sam said. "Anyone who bothered to read what the code actually said, rather than just performing the operations, would be able to see that I was stealing. To me, this is the perfect crime. Who gets hurt? Do you really call some billionaires getting thousands less of their shares injustice? And if and when someone did find out, as you did, what would happen? I figured they would just want a piece of it, which you did. As far as I'm concerned, there's no harm done here. Obviously, I would have liked it more if I kept all of the money, but I don't need every penny of it if I'm being truthful. It's much more than I can spend or plan with. The fact that there are people out there with more money than this is pretty insane if you ask me. What are they doing with it? Just holding it?"

"You're getting a little political, Sam," Topher said.

"Whatever you say," Sam said. "I thought we were just chatting. Well, I suppose that does it, then. I know your bank. I'll start wiring half of it to you as the price of your silence. Does that sound all right with you?"

"It does," Topher said. He had already given up on having a big moment. He had thought for a bit that this would be about more than the money, and it was disappointing to see that at the end of the day, this really was just about money — which made it all seem like a typical part of his typical life.

The other reason for revealing these papers to his boss was to make Sam uncomfortable since he had harbored this resentment against him for so long. But now that he knew he could have found out this secret a long time ago and gotten a cut, he didn't feel like he made Sam feel on edge at all. If anything, Sam just made him feel like an idiot.

Topher didn't know how to react to all this. Somehow, even with how his life would surely change from this new influx of funds, he felt like he didn't get what he wanted out of this ultimatum at all.

He went home and gave Wendy the reason he had rehearsed for why they were about to have much more money than they used to: he had gotten promoted to Project Manager at the company. Wendy had never shown any genuine interest in his job, so she simply pretended to be proud of his accomplishment, but in truth, Topher had never cared about being promoted, either.

He didn't want to have more responsibilities than he already had, and he didn't get a power rush out of leading people as some people did. He only told Wendy about the promotion because it felt good, and because he needed some sort of rationale for all the things, he was going to buy with all his new cash.

Topher knew Wendy would tell him he was going overboard with the raise, but that was part of the fun of it all. He didn't want to worry about money anymore now that he was getting more than he knew to do with. His idea of luxury was buying a new hybrid vehicle, the newest gadgets; he started investing in new products based on their promise rather than the market history.

He could tell his family was much happier with money, too. Everyone who said that money couldn't buy happiness must have just never had it, because although the happiness he earned from it was fleeting in a way that he could tell, it was very much real happiness. His sons got their own credit cards, because he thought, why not? Now, he could afford it.

Contrary to the homemaker stereotype, Wendy did not actually spend money much differently than she used to before his promotion. Instead, she complained to him about how he was teaching their children bad habits. She said it was almost better before, because at least then they had a limit they had to stay inside. When they didn't have these limits, they became something she didn't recognize.

To Topher's dismay, the second person to express such concerns was his boss. Just as Topher had come into Sam's office that Monday morning, Sam went into Topher's cubicle. But instead of slamming down a stack of papers on his desk, he just started talking.

"Are you out of your mind, Topher?" Sam said. He kept his voice slightly down, but everyone was gone at the moment to eat lunch, so no one could hear them. "You can't have a closed-door meeting with me one week and then drive to work in an electric car the next. It looks very suspicious. I thought you had to be smart in order to notice the discrepancy in the account papers. But instead, it seems like having just a little bit more money has completely gone to your head. Did you even find the discrepancy because you were reading it normally, or were you just trying to find something against me? Because I'm starting to think the latter."

"People don't know what investments I'm making. Maybe I took out a loan for the car," Topher suggested. He was indignant that his boss continued to act this way, dragging out the feeling of dissatisfaction he had had when he showed him the paper in the first place.

"No one takes out a loan out of the blue like that, and if you were making investments that good, you wouldn't be here," Sam said. Topher hated how he always acted like he knew everything. "And you know you have to have money in the first place to make investments that pay off that much. Just think a little bit, please. You really need to settle down with all the spending. People might start asking questions. Every employee's pay is public, so we can all see that I didn't give you a raise."

Topher desperately wanted to catch Sam off guard, just once. "I could let the truth out at any time. So, what if I'm implicated? I was pressured by you. You wouldn't let me tell the truth. You intimidated me. I didn't think I had another choice."

Sam looked at him, expressionless. "You really don't think. What kind of crap do you think people really believe? Not that, I'll tell you. You don't get to play the victim in this; it won't work out for you. Though I have to admit, you would make for quite a convincing one, with how dim-witted you've been acting. It's hard to believe you're the one who threatened me. On what grounds do you stand on now, anyway? You are just as complicit in this as I am. No one is going to believe that you were threatened into having more money than you had before. No one."

"What do you want from me? I'm the one who discovered your secret," Topher said. "I would play nicer with me if I were you."

Sam sighed. "Sure, I will, Topher. I am just trying to help us the best I can since both of our names are on this. There's no going back for either of us, so it's in our best interest to keep this as clean as possible."

Topher was tired of being treated like this. He was the one who could uncover Sam's secret any time he wanted, yet he treated being treated like some kind of idiot. "I have an addendum to add to our agreement, boss," Topher said. He grabbed his laptop case and started stuffing his things inside of it. "I don't want to come in here anymore. If you need me for someone, you can send me a call. Or an email. Better yet, don't try to reach me at all. I'm done coming into this place. With what I know, I don't have to anymore."

Sam didn't skip a beat. It infuriated Topher even further, but it didn't matter. He was already walking out of the building. "It's for the best, probably. The longer you stay here, the more questions people are going to ask. You won't even need a title here anymore. You'll have all the money you ever needed sent into your account."

"When you put it that way, this is the arrangement I should have asked for in the first place," Topher said. He went on his way home.

Topher's peace from quitting didn't last long. Even just hours after getting home, he started to get paranoid. He didn't answer calls or emails. He didn't know if his former boss had even tried to reach him, because if he did, Topher certainly hadn't answered them. The way he tried to keep his sanity was rocking back and forth, trying his very best not to check any of the ways he could be contacted.

He knew he should try to think about something else, but he became obsessed with it, and it didn't seem possible to do anything but stare at his blank computer screen without opening the email application.

The amounts he was receiving were astronomical right now, but he started to get worried about how things could change. Was it really as much as it seemed in the beginning? Would it cover his sons' college tuition now that he didn't earn a salary from his regular job any longer? Would he have to sell his electric car?

The thoughts didn't stop racing through his head, and he felt like this had to be the last straw. Without reading any messages or voicemails that may have already been sent to him, Topher sent Sam an email saying that he was cutting all ties with the company: he didn't want to be contacted by anyone from there ever again. All he wanted was what he already had set up. He didn't say what he meant directly since email was a traceable mode of communication, but he figured Sam knew what he was talking about.

In other words, he still expected his cut to come virtually into his account. He had things to pay for, and knowing how devious Sam could be, Topher had a bad feeling he wouldn't be able to work at any other tech company after this. Sam had probably put Topher on a blacklist that would prevent him from getting hired anywhere else. This was the end of the road for his real career. His only choice now was to leave.

He discussed it with his wife in a different way than he truly saw it, but they were moving out of the country. After thinking of all the different places, they could go, he eventually landed in Granada, Spain. He thought they would probably not be bothered there. After just a month of preparations, he, Wendy, and their two sons flew over to their new home in Spain.

Spain had never been at the top of his mind before, but he chose it now because he was not willing to go anywhere where he could understand the language around him. Not now, when his paranoid was getting so out of hand that a few simple words in the next room might drive him berserk. As long as the people around him were speaking in Spanish, he didn't worry about things like this.

Of all the places they looked at online, Granda seemed like the most beautiful. There were many areas they could visit as tourists, but it was also a friendly place for foreigners without too much English being spoken there. They could expect many people to be able to understand them so they could take care of their errands without any issues, but English was not so common as to trigger Topher's paranoia.

Of course, Wendy did not know about this problem at all. As far as she knew, he was continuing to work remotely. She had no idea all of their money was coming from the illegal deposits he was getting through Sam.

Things were looking up after the move, mostly because it greatly helped him not look at his modes of communication for a short while. But when he did, he noticed something very disturbing. When he checked his bank account, he had stopped receiving half of the cut from Sam. From what he saw, he was getting the full 50%. On the surface, this was a good thing, but he had a bad feeling about this. He knew that Sam had to be setting him up.

But Topher didn't know what he could do about it. Sam stopped answering all of his calls. He figured this had to be his fault because this is what Topher asked him to do. But now, he didn't even have a way to confirm what was going on.

Then a month passed, and his worst fear was realized. He did not get the deposit on the day he was supposed to. His paranoia went to extreme levels at this point. Then, a day passed, and another day. The most still didn't come.

Topher knew what he had to do. He had to make his withdrawals before his bank was totally frozen. He wasn't able to withdraw all of it at once, but he was pleased to find out he could get most of it in euros.

It seemed like Spain was a very cash-friendly place, so he hardly had any problems with this at all. It was not all of the money that he would need throughout his whole life, but it was more than enough for the next couple years while he figured out what he and his family should do next.

He didn't hear back from Sam for two years. When he did, it was nothing good. He and Sam had a short conversation about what happened and what Topher should do. Topher was right: knowing that him moving away suddenly seemed suspicious, Sam started sending all of the money to him, instead of just the 50 percent. Then Sam sent this information to the corporate office, who had no choice but to send it to the authorities, or else they could get into trouble themselves.

If Topher ever went back to America, he would be in deep trouble. He knew it; his paranoia had been affirmed to be unclouded judgment. Topher hadn't been crazy at all to think they had to leave. If he wasn't in Spain right now, he would probably be in jail. Now he, Wendy, and the kids had no choice but to find a new life here in Granada. He didn't know what came next for them, but he did know that it couldn't be in his home country.

Topher started working under the table for a bar, and even picked up some Spanish as he did it. The money wasn't nearly enough to pay for his sons' eventual college tuition or for his and his wife's retirement, but at least he felt like he was doing something about the problem.

He even started to sincerely enjoy the job. He had never worked with his hands before and made real, physical things. As a programmer and a software developer, he had only typed to create code that made pixels, which could technically be counted as physical things, but it was not at all the same.

Topher started to find a sort of happiness in doing this work. But things took a turn when Wendy came to the bar and saw him there. It looked like she had only gone in there for a drink — she did not expect to find her husband behind the counter at all. He hadn't expected to see her either, so he didn't know what to do or say when they saw each other. She demanded to know what was going on.

Topher told her the truth, knowing that by now, there was no coming back from it. He had lost the job a long time ago, and he had even lost the large illegal deposits that had been sustaining them thus far. They still had plenty of money for basics, but there was no money for the future.

He could tell that this wasn't the first bar Wendy had gone to that night. The way she reacted broke him, but it didn't surprise him, because he knew how many mistakes he had made. Wendy walked out on him on the spot.

Topher didn't know if his family would be home when he got back, but he had a bad feeling that they wouldn't be.

When he got off his shift, he came home, and indeed his family was no longer there. They left no note, and the only traces of them that were left were the Spanish learning books that none of them had ever really mastered.

He sat on his bed and thought about how things could have gone differently. All of the money that they got for a short while was not worth all of this. He had lost everything: the money, his wife, his kids. He could have kept doing his normal job; he could have left the financial records alone, and just minded his own business.

It wasn't right that Sam got away with all this. He had a glimpse of hope, thinking that he could prove what Sam did, too. Then he thought back to what Sam had said: no one would believe him. And he was right. It was apparent that Topher had done wrong. He had even moved out of the country.

Meanwhile, Sam was already richer than everyone else in the office before Topher made all these mistakes. It was far more suspicious for Topher to be doing the things he was doing compared to Sam. He should have known that he couldn't get away with the same things.

But it was too late. The realization struck him so hard that he didn't know how to react to it emotionally. He was simply despondent. But not completely.

He had become a bartender in Spain. He had participated in a fraud that made him very rich for a period of time. He may have never been able to push any of Sam's buttons, but at least his life had seen some excitement.

It wasn't much of a comfort, but when he looked back on it, he had taken these chances so that he could have stories to tell. And now he did.

The Love in Fire

There was once a young dragon named Romulus, who roamed Whimsy hundreds of years ago. His family and friends referred to him as Rom. His scales were the color of slate with sharp white teeth that could frighten even the most seasoned warrior. His eyes blazed brilliantly, the essence of lava. Rom had an enormous wingspan with sharp boney protrusions at the tip of each. His tale was exceptionally long at fifteen feet, and he could wrap it around his body. The horizontal plated scales on his chest shone golden in the light of day. Rom was a rather regal looking dragon, poised enough to look both elegant and terrifying. Strangers always noted his eerie beauty as his breastbone puffed out in front of him, like a lion's mane.

Should you ever met Rom, you might initially be scared out of your mind. Getting to know the young dragon is another beast altogether. He was not the most graceful creature to ever sail the skies of Whimsy, frequently becoming distracted and running into trees. He was lucky that dragons have such hard heads.

Rom was also not possessed of the same fierceness that was commonplace among his species. He loved getting to know other creatures and spent his days watching the various beings of Whimsy from above. He was a loving and curious dragon, with a taste for adventure. Any other dragon that he's ever met just loved to fight. They were a ruthless species that often found their use in being contracted by villages for protection from enemies that mortals would not be able to guard against.

Dragons were not cruel or uncaring; it was just in their nature to spar. They would never just terrorize others for sport, but should they be tasked with protecting a town...they would enjoy the battle. All except for Rom that is. He was hardly ever around to be involved in these great wars. He could be found in the forest, making friends with any creature that was not immediately terrified by the way that he looked.

The young dragon was especially fond of elves. He found them to be lovely and mysterious. The elven race in Whimsy was tall and pale, with their skin reflecting a pale blue. Hair like the night sky fell around them, usually to their waists. They were a wise species that also valued learned and knowledge above everything else, not dissimilar to Rom himself.

Rom's most favorite elf was also his best friend, whom he referred to as Blue. Elven words are some of the most difficult to pronounce, so they were often given nicknames by those they meet. The race has a distinctly different vocal cord arrangement, making their mother tongue very trying for strangers. Luckily, they were all educated and fluent in the various other languages of the realm.

Blue was one of the first creatures that Rom had ever met who did not immediately flee from the sight of the imposingly statured dragon. The two shared many of the same interests and loved going on adventures together. They crafted a very special saddle that allowed the young elf to safely ride atop of Rom as he flew to their next destination.

One cold and dreary day, the pair decided that they would venture out in search of a tropical environment. Both had heard tales of a beach with pristine white sand contrasting against the vivid azure of rolling ocean tides. This was a land far south, where it was rumored to be warm all year round. Exotic species supposedly peppered the land, which made both Rom and Blue very eager to set sail. They treasured the relationships they formed with new beings.

They had no concept of how important their adventures were for connecting the various creatures of Whimsy. Rom specifically had broken many harmful dragon stereotypes that others hold about the race until they met him. Blue served as the diplomat in their operation, and he was responsible for establishing the first contact. Elves were much more approachable, which allowed him a chance to explain the kind nature of his scary-looking best friend.

The pair bundled the young elf up because the frigid air would be almost unbearable for Blue as they cut through the cold rain at lightning-fast speeds. He would fashion a cocoon of sorts that they would stabilize around the saddle with ropes. They used thin pieces of wood to structure the mass. Large leaves would encompass the mass of fabric to repel the precipitation that they would encounter. A tube of steel would run from inside this cloth cave, to the outside air, so that Blue would not feel as though he was suffocating under the weight of his protection. The two were quite inventive about preparing for their travels and would do their best to anticipate obstacles ahead of time, mostly with the intent of keeping Blue safe. Dragons were fairly durable in comparison to elves.

Rom took to the sky with his passenger hunkered down and warmed on his back. The trip was made slightly more difficult with the added weight, but the young dragon was strong enough to keep flying. Hours passed, and it seemed to the pair like the coast might be a myth. They'd never been this far away from their stomping grounds before. As Rom passed a large canyon carved into the countryside, a man seated atop a cliff waved at him. He waved back before realizing that this man was far larger than a man should be. Rom felt his heartbeat sped up; he had just met his first giant! He could not wait to relay the experience to Blue!

Finally, night began to fall as Rom was beginning to lose some of his energy. He wished that he would have told his family where he was going; he just never dreamed that it would be so far away. The climate was getting warmer, but there was no ocean in sight. He hoped that his parents weren't too worried about him.

The pair stopped for the night, finding shelter in a forest. The trees were all very strange looking with rust-colored bark. They seemed to be spaced even distances away from one another, lending a very clean look to the woodland. They seemed to be swaying back and forth to a gentle wind. Blue swore that he heard the trees whispering to one another.

Rom and Blue had a serious talk about if they should continue onward or return home. They knew that eventually, their families would grow concerned about them, but they also didn't want to have wasted all the time and effort that their journey had taken thus far. They came to the conclusion that they would press on for now. They two set by a fire that Rom had created eating an elven herbal soup that Blue made from the plants around them and some dried meat that the two had packed for the journey. They laughed and told stories late into the night.

In the morning, Rom hunted down a cave where he would hide their cocoon contraption until they were on their way back. The climate was more like spring and less like the oppressive winter from back home. They set off once again to find their ocean, refusing to lose hope.

Again, the pair spent hours in the sky, watching the midday sun travel across the horizon and dip below. There was a stillness in the night air, as the two decided to continue their trip through the darkness. Rom was encouraged by a strange smell that hung thick around them. It was a saltiness that he had never experienced before. He harkened back to the rumors of the mysterious sea, as it was said to be filled with a briny water solution. The moon dusted a pale glow upon our flying heroes from her mysterious throne in the starry night sky.

Day broke in tandem with a miraculous visage. Crystalline waves rolled into one another and crashed against a creamy beach. Palm trees and flowers halted their approach toward the sea line when the soil turned to sand. From his position in the sky, Rom could see dolphins and mermaids playing in the water near the shore.

He was overcome with the majesty of such a vision. Blue was fast asleep atop the dragons back, doubled over his saddle. Rom dipped in the sky to wake the elf from his slumber. He knew that his plan had worked when he heard his friend gasp with delight at the sight in front of them.

Rom quickly landed right on the beach. A few of the mermaids covered their mouths in shock and darted underneath the water. He had forgotten for a moment that he was a dragon. He breathed deeply, taking in the smell and taste of the brackish air. Rom had always imagined the ocean would be beautiful, but in person, there was a profundity to the image.

Blue hopped off his friend's back and began looking around. He waved to a curious mermaid who smiled and returned the gesture. He approached the young mermaid and introduced himself and Rom. Her name was Cora, and she said that she had never met an elf or a dragon before. She was taken Rom and how majestic he looked standing in the sand before her beside his stately blue friend.

The three of them became deeply engaged in conversation, comparing, and contrasting their environments. Cora said that the sunsets on the beach were breathtaking, and they must stay to see one. The pair agreed and were not at all eager to make the journey back home. The young mermaid asked to see Rom breath fire. This was something that Rom had not mastered in the same way that his peers had, but he was willing to give it a try.

He turned toward the beach and tried to silence his thoughts. This was a technique that he had always used to maintain control over his emotions when he was anxious. He had discovered by accident one day that it also allowed him to focus his fire. Rom took a deep breath in through his nose and slowly let it out through his mouth. He found that if concentrated quite hard, something within his chest engaged with the breath, and it would turn into flames.

He was able to breathe out this fire toward the sand, and he watched as something miraculous happened. The areas where his breath had touched had turned clear and fluid. Rom had somehow fused the pieces of sand together under the heat of this exhalation. Cora and Blue were just as shocked as the young dragon was. He had created something that they had never seen in their realm before, glass. They watched as the clear liquid hardened in a puddle. The dragon picked up a piece of this hardened glass because his skin was highly temperature resistant. He turned it over in his claws, in awe of the beauty of his creation.

Blue and Rom sat down immediately to brainstorm ways to use this new material. You could build things out of it, but it also seemed to shatter very easily. It was a stunning substance and could be used in any manner of art. The two shared ideas for the longest time, trying to decide how to approach this new object and its' potential usefulness. It was Blue on the beach that night, who came up with the idea of windows. The transparency it allowed was its most functional aspect.

The pair stayed to watch a coastal sunset with Cora, soaking up the natural beauty of their new favorite place. They packed up a sample of sand to bring to their communities so that they might demonstrate the usefulness of their discovery. They were hailed as inventors upon their return. The dragons and elves combined forces to set up a glass making operation right on the edge of the beach. Rom and Blue offered to travel there and oversee the production of the new material, as windows became one of the most in-demand items in all of Whimsy.

All of this took place a long, long time ago, and the people of Whimsy have been enjoying the benefits of the pairs trip for hundreds of years. They laid down the foundation for all sorts of new art and functional bowls, lightbulbs, windows, and even eventually mirrors. Mirrors being very important to a magical land filled with beautiful creatures. Every student in Whimsy learns the legend of Romulus and Blue.

As for our heroes, they traveled back and forth to the coast for their invention. They lived happily alongside their mermaid friend and their families back home. They served as an example of the good that can come from getting to know creatures that differ from yourself. They believed strongly in a free exchange of ideas among cultures. For the two best friends, this was just one of many adventures that they were fated to experience together as they split their time between the land they called home and the majestic sea.

Fighting Isn't Always the Answer

Arthur was a knight. He had his own convoy, or army, of knights and overall, it was a good group of knights. He had a squire named Alexander. Alexander was ready to become a knight and Arthur was planning the dubbing ceremony for after the next battle.

The convoy of knights was traveling through the countryside searching for a rogue band of knights. Arthur considered them rogue. They did not follow the Code of Chivalry and they were consistently breaking all the rules of conduct. Even though they pledged allegiance to the same liege lord, Knight Clifford needed to be taught a lesson and his convoy needed to be broken up. Arthur was taking the matter into his own hands. It troubled him little that he was possibly breaking the knight's code of chivalry because he was not breaking his own personal code. He felt that the world would be better without this group of marauding knights.

Arthur sent Alexander ahead to see how he does at scouting out the enemy camp. Arthur has seen signs all day that Clifford is slightly ahead of them but they are moving quickly and carelessly. Alexander should be seeing the same signs. Arthur will see just what skill Alexander has in finding the enemy. And then he will see what kind of strategy Alexander comes up with to invade the camp and conquer Clifford and the other knights. Alexander's brother, Calvin, had been squire to Clifford for some time but Clifford released him from service. Actually, Calvin was thrown out of the convoy. Though there were many reasons why Calvin would not make a good knight, Calvin was actually a perfect fit for Clifford and his convoy of knights.

Alexander returned in the middle of the night with news of where Knight Clifford could be found. The large group was in a town nearby. They had basically invaded the town and were tormenting the residents by demanding food and drink.

"I can see the camp is spread out along a hillside," explained Alexander. "They have a good source of water, so they may be planning to stay for several days."

"Do you think we can battle them where they are right now?" asked Arthur.

"I think the hillside is would make it hard for a battle. Once the fighting starts, it will have to take place up the hill. The valley is narrow but it looks like the water is a little stream and would be easy to cross. It is lined with rocks, so it would be hard for horses to get across quickly."

Arthur asked about Clifford. "Where is Clifford? Does his squire seem to be organized and able? Alexander thought about it for longer than Arthur expected. He finally answered, "Ay, his squire seems comfortable. I was watching the movement of the squire amongst the men. I think it is my brother, Calvin."

Arthur was a little surprised at this, but no totally. Calvin was with Clifford for a longer time than Alexander has been with Arthur. It would be hard to train someone new. Calvin may have been humiliated, but he was probably able to work his way back into the good humor of Clifford. He would probably just paid Clifford extra coin to be able to get back to being his squire. And Clifford probably wanted him back. They made a team.

"We will assume it is Calvin. What do you suggest we do? How should we take over the convoy?" asked Arthur. He wanted to know if Alexander was able to strategize and he would see how he is able to execute the strategy.

Alexander had been thinking about how to start a battle that would be a win for Arthur. He was thinking about it for the whole trip back to camp.

"I will go to the camp tomorrow with a list of ways they have not lived up to the Code of Chivalry. I am sure they will laugh in my face. I will then tell them that if they are not going to change, which I'm sure they won't, we will battle on a field just north of their camp on the following day. I will tell them it will be a fight to the finish."

Arthur understands that it must be this way, but he wants to be sure Alexander, and all the men, know that Clifford and his knights are not chivalrous and will fight until death. Arthur also knows The King likes Clifford because he always adds much gold to the King's coffers. The King does not care about chivalry and neither does Clifford. His men don't seem to care if they are chivalrous or not.

"Alexander, are you prepared for battle?" asked Arthur. This was not a question about whether the weapons were ready and the shields strong. This was about whether Alexander is ready to fight his brother.

"Sir, I am ready to serve you, my Liege," was Alexander's easy reply.

Arthur set about planning the battle. He knew the number of knights should not present a problem for him. There were several men in the ranks of Clifford's army that did not have a true loyalty to him. Arthur knew this because he had freed several men and knew Clifford's army was full of men who like to cause mayhem. They like to rob and steal and were not keen to fight. Arthur expected about 10 percent of the men to run off as soon as the trouble starts.

The men who stay to fight vary in terms of their abilities. Arthur noticed at the last tournament that the knights in Clifford's army have grown lazy and sloppy. They obviously did not practice with swords and lance. They were also, a lot of them, fat. Some have horses that seemed to strain under the weight of their master. Arthur planned to weed out the least skilled and push them to the side where they would be kept at bay by a few of his own men who were older and not able to fight for long periods of time. Arthur looked over to Alexander. Alexander was inspecting all weapons and shields that he and Arthur owned. This included things that had not been used in several years. Alexander felt that it was a waste to carry a weapon that was not in useful condition. Arthur had to agree with him.

Arthur was surprised to find Alexander sleeping that night. It appears that he is not worried about his plan to upset his brother and his brother's world. It was surprising, but Arthur was pleased. He picked the right boy to be his personal squire. The boy was now a man. The next morning, Arthur had all the men gather around. Alexander was surprised when Arthur asked him to kneel and pledge his allegiance to the church and the king. Arthur then dubbed Alexander as a knight by touching his sword upon the shoulders of Alexander.

The men cheered and Alexander was pleased and surprised. He was expecting to be knighted after the battle. But there was work to be done and Alexander set out to do his part. He left to find Clifford and Calvin, knights of His Highness, the King. He entered the camp full of snorts and snores. Calvin was awake and checking his armor and looking for any issues with his chainmail. Alexander had done all of this as well, plus checking the armor and chainmail of Arthur. Alexander did not see Clifford, but he was here somewhere.

"Calvin. Where is your liege?" asked Alexander.

"Alex, I thought I felt you. It kept me up most of the night. Why are you here?"

"I am here to see your master. I have no quarrel with you. Not today, anyway."

"No quarrel with me? You are daft. I don't care if you have a quarrel with me. I have a quarrel with you. You left me humiliated on the field at the tourney. How could you do that to me, brother?"

"Oh, don't play the victim. You tried to cut my saddle so I would fall off my horse in the middle of the tournament. I have a true grievance. You fell off your horse by yourself. I was lucky to have found your sabotage before your games destroyed my life. Now, fetch me your liege," said Alexander in an angry voice Calvin had not heard before. His little brother was always showing a new side.

"Please, enough yelling!" yelled the liege, himself. I am trying to sleep here," came a drowsy voice from just behind Calvin.

"Sir Clifford, I bring a message from Sir Arthur."

"Because you have failed to uphold the Code of Chivalry and you do not live the life of a true knight, we challenge you to cease your nefarious behavior and uphold the values of which all knights are held to a high standard. Failure to do so will result in immediate physical removal of you and the knights of your allegiance. How say you, Sir?"

Clifford laughed. He laughed and laughed and laughed. He thought it was funny to have a boy tell him what to do and how to behave.

When Clifford was done laughing, he spat at Alexander. He missed his mark, but Alexander understood the sentiment.

"Tomorrow at sunrise, Sir. The battle shall begin tomorrow at sunrise."

Alexander rode back to his own camp. He took a direct route and did little to conceal his travel. He tried to make it seem that he did not know Calvin would follow him, but he knew he would. That is why he did not even bother to say where the battle would take place. He discussed it with Arthur before he left and Arthur agreed. Clifford and Calvin would not fight fairly. They would rather ambush the camp than follow code to fight fairly. This is precisely why they need to be stopped.

Arthur had been following out of sight to make a note of how many men were set to fight against him and his knights. So far, it was only Calvin. Calvin was moving stealthily. He did not want to be seen. When Calvin was close to Arthur's camp, he turned around and returned to Clifford. Arthur followed him to try to get an understanding of their plot.

"Calvin, how many men are there?" asked Clifford.

"I counted 20. It is a small group. It will not be a problem to overtake them if we go now before the rest of the knights come back from town."

Arthur listened to the two talking and was expecting them to put a little more thought into the plot against him. They were just going to wake up a few men and take them to fight a battle against the "unsuspecting" knights.

Arthur was sure there would be more to the plot and so he followed them as they rode with a total of twelve men in full armor on their warhorses. Alexander was in charge of getting the men ready at the camp. It was true that there were only a few men at the camp when Calvin saw them, but the others were simply lounging on the other side of the hill. They should all be ready for battle now, ready to disband the evil in the most permanent way.

Calvin and Clifford did not notice the quiet that was settling around them. The birds were not chirping because they flew away when the men settled in the branches of the trees. One by one, the men leaped out of the trees and landed on the backs of Clifford's men as they passed beneath. The men in the trees were not in armor. They were a lot more mobile than the men dressed for battle. The knights knocked the armored soldiers off their warhorses and someone on the ground knocked the man unconscious with a large mallet. Because they were in armor, Clifford and Calvin did not hear all of the commotion going on around them. They were riding fast and it was until they were the only two left they realized something was very wrong.

By this time, Arthur and Alexander were riding side by side toward Clifford and Calvin. I would be a duel between the four of them, knight against knight, brother against brother. Shields were lowered and lances were readied and they charge at each other. There were maces swinging and the lances were used to know the riders from astride the horses. The noise was deafening. Alexander knocked Calvin off balance with his lance then turned back and hit Calvin with the mace in his shoulder. Calvin tried to raise his shield but he was too late. He was heading to the ground.

Clifford was not having better luck. His mace had fallen to the ground after the lance brushed him with more force than he was prepared to take. Though he was still on his horse, he was shaken. It was not to be believed. He thought of all the tricks he has used in the past. He had many, but he needed Calvin next to him to pull them off. Calvin was not there. He is on the ground and he isn't moving. There isn't any blood, but the side of his helmet is bashed in quite badly. Tired of wasting time and not sure where his men were, Clifford decided to flee back to his camp.

Clifford's camp was not controlled by the knights of Arthur. They took over the camp. The rowdy knights were corralled into a quickly made cage. It was Alexander's idea on a previous campaign to have everything they need to set up a large cage for prisoners. It works very well and they had the laziest of the knights locked inside. Some of the knights fled. They were followed and they appear to have no intention of fighting. They are simply running away. Around the time the sun was setting, Clifford came racing back to the camp. He was surprised to see his knights caged like the animals at The Colosseum. "What a disappointment," he thought. "You can't count on anyone, not even yourself."

Calvin was still not awake. He was kicked in the head by his horse after he fell. Both Calvin and Clifford were stripped of their armor and weapons. Their clothes were inspected and their boots removed. There were many weapons hidden in their clothes and boots. They were truly ready to fight to the death. Instead of death, they were placed inside the cage with the other knights where they stayed until a tournament was organized and the men were paraded through the tournament grounds while a list of offenses against the Code of Chivalry was read. Many of the townspeople they had harmed were there to see their shame. They would never be accepted as knights again.

Alexander was a good and strong knight. He formed a convoy of young soldiers and they vowed to abide by the Code of Chivalry and to protect the Church and the King. They killed as few soldiers as possible, but they did as they must in the name of their liege lord. The problem they saw was that battles were won; the loser regrouped and came back to fight again. It was a cycle that just kept happening again and again. Alexander and his soldiers made sure to be alert and have weapons ready so they would always be ready for an attack. It was the choice they made, to love God and to fight. So that is what they did. They served their King well, always bringing coin from the sale of armor and weapons. They did what they could to destroy the weapons of the men defeated on the battlefield. They hoped it would deter the survivors from setting out to fight again. The usually found more money to buy more weapons and challenged the King's knights again. The circle of fighting battles is never-ending.

A Pyramid Discovery

A long time ago, there lived a king. His name was King Toba. King Toba was generally a good king. He reigned justly, and therefore it was hard for his people to be hard complaining. King Toba valued hard work and honesty, and he urged his people to adopt these virtues. Every morning during the peaceful time, he will lead his people in cultivating various cross for food. He firmly believed that his people would be vulnerable without food. So as a result, the food stores were always full of the trim with the grain. People were happy.

King Toba also had a beautiful daughter, princess Lia. The princess was so gorgeous that whenever she passed, the king's square everyman would stop to wonder at her exceptional beauty. She was also very respectful and friendly. However, the princess was the apple of her father's eyes and was therefore well guarded. No man was ever allowed anywhere near her without direct permission from the father.

So, it happened that the was one young man called Tibe. Tibe was the blacksmith. He was so skilled at his work that sometimes he would win the praise of the king. Tibe's interest, it would appear, was not only in working on sturdy iron. He was also interested in the princess. He was so much in love with her. He dreamt about her every day. And when he told his mother, the mother dismissed him

"mother, one day I will marry the princess, "he will begin. The mother will smile inwardly and then say, "my son, please don't aim at the sun when the gods intended you to reside on the moon. Look for a nice girl, your status, and marry her. The princess is not for you."

"But I love her so much mother, what shall I do?" Tibe would ask.

"There are other beautiful girls around who admire you Tibe. Look at Han's daughter, beautiful, hardworking, and respectful. And I know for a fact that the girl loves you. Look at the way she looks at you. Marry her and forget all about the princess."

Although he was popular with the girls, he couldn't find any girl who resembled his dream girl, the princes. He had to find a way. He had to. He then resumed his work, but his mind was racing with many thoughts. He was wondering how to attract the princess' attention. He decided the next time she passed through the square; he will present her with flowers. He might find a chance to talk to her. But he knew it would be difficult bearing in mind the mean guards who always accompanied her wherever they went.

He knew the princess would be touring the square on the following day. So, with his savings, he went to the flower shop at the corner. He wanted to buy the best flowers available.

"I need flowers, the best available. Flowers that can talk to a girl, "he asked the shop attendant.

"Any special occasion?"

"yes, there is this girl, whom I love greatly need to impress her tomorrow morning," he replied wryly.

"Well, there are flowers. Then there are special flowers. But since you are not using them today, why don't you come in the morning. Let me prepare the special ones for you."

Tibe then paid for the flowers. He will pick them the following day then wait for the princess to arrive. He was starting to feel confident. He hoped the girl would like him. He prayed.

The following morning, he woke up very early, and he was at the flower shop even before it opened. The shop attendant was surprised to find him standing there.

"morning prince charming, I can see you are already up," the attendant greeted him cheerfully.

"Yes, as you know, our forefathers warn us that man should wake up ahead of the sun. that is why I am here this early," Tibe replied.

"True, my friend. A man who loves sleep always invites Poverty through the windows. Anyway, your flowers are ready, let me show you," the attendant said.

Once inside, Tibe was presented with the most beautiful flowers his eyes had ever seen. Not that he was an expert in the knowledge of flowers, but he knew a lovely flower when he saw one.

"my friend. I had to get this beautiful flower for you after hearing about your mission later today. This flower carries luck. Go and present it to the girl of your dream. You wot come back disappointed, "the attendant explained

Tube thanked him profusely and headed out to the square, the flowers on his hand. He didn't know the time the princess will come. So, he sat down and waited. He waited and waited but still the princess as nowhere. He waited some more, but the princess didn't come out of the palace. He was about to give up when he glimpsed the familiar chariots of the palace's first family coming from a distance. He stood up and squinted his eyes towards it. He hoped it was the princess' chariot.

His heart started pounding hard as the chariot drew near and nearer. It was indeed the princess being driven around the kingdom. He recognized the princess's flag, which was always mounted on the leading chariot. There was a problem though. It was simply impossible to walk up to the princess without passing through the guards. He quickly thought up an idea, but none was forthcoming. So, he did the craziest thin no sane man would do.

He jumped in the middle of the way, blocking the chariots' way and shouted the princess' name

"princess Lia! "he shouted so loudly that everyone stopped doing what they were doing and turned to look at the Youngman in the middle of the road. His shout was also heard by the princess, who looked through the window only to find an energetic man with flowers on his hand. She didn't know what to make of it correctly. And his actions brought the wrath of the overzealous guards who descendent on him with fists and blows. But Tibe was so determined. He fought his way to the princess' carriage and threw the flowers to her. The flowers landed on her seat. She picked the flowers and smelled. It had a pleasant smell. She next stepped out and ordered the guards to leave Tibe alone.

"Am so sorry my princess to come to you this way," Tibe said

"What is your name?" asked the princess.

"I am Tibe. The blacksmith. Please accept my flowers."

"Thank you for the flowers. And for your troubles, I invite you to the princess' party next week at the king's palace. I will keep the flowers," the princess replied. And the chariot moved on.

Tibe was injured, but he seemed not to feel any pain. He was so happy with himself for accomplishing the mission. He was exalted at the invitation of the princess. He hoped she liked the flower. He walked very fast to his home. He had to let his skeptical mother know about the good news. He found his mother kneading bread. She immediately stood up in alarm.

"What happened to you, did you have an accident," she asked.

"no mother, there was no accident. I met the princess..." he started explaining, but his mother cut him off.

"I knew it. That princess will kill you," she said and then rushed inside to pick the healing oil which she administered gently on Tibe's wounds.

"mother, I met her today. She is adorable. And she invited me to her party," Tibe explained.

"She did what?' Her mother asked. She was surprised at the turn of events. But still, she didn't want Tibe associating with the mighty princess. She reasoned that such actions would only lead to her being hurt. But her son was getting obsessed with the princess with each passing day. She didn't know how best to stop him.

Meanwhile, in the palace, the princess placed the flowers on the table next to her dressing mirror. She just loved the smell of the flowers. It was so unique. She had never seen such adorable flowers, and she kept wondering where it came from. That night, when she slept, she dreamt the flowers had grown into a big umbrella, and she was flying around the kingdom while holding the knob. The experience was magical, and when she woke up from the dream, she walked to the dressing table and picked the flowers and smelt again. She then returned to bed, and soon she was deep asleep.

When she woke up the following morning, she was surprised to find the flowers fresh again as if it had just been picked straight from the field. Usually, her flowers would wilt within a day. But these flowers remained fresh for days, and so was its smell. Questions rang in her mind, but the only person who could answer was the man who presented her with the flowers. She told herself she would have to inquire more about the flower from the palace's servants.

She summoned some of the experienced servants to try and explain all they knew about the flower, which never wilted. But no one seems to know anything about that particular flower. No one had ever seen the flower before. She decided to wait for the princess party, which was due in a week. She hoped the young man who presented her with the flowers would turn up. From then on, the princess carried the flowers wherever she went. It was observed that she was getting obsessed with the flowers.

She ate better, laughed better, and was happier when she had the flowers on her hand.

Back to Tibe. The boy was simply over the moon. His mind was focused on meeting the princess again. He wondered what to wear to the party. He also wondered how he would best behave in the palace. He had heard that the king never condoned some behaviors from those around him. His mother, however, was concerned with the boy. He seemed to find interest in no one or anything else. He was not eating well anymore. He even failed to report at work once or twice that week. This was something that had never happened before.

Finally, the day of the party arrived. Tibe woke up very early. He took a long slow bath then dressed in the impeccable brand-new clothes he had bought a few days ago. The clothes had cost him an arm and a leg. He headed for the palace immediately after breakfast. On arriving at the gate, he was informed that the party was for that evening and he had come a little earlier. He was then told to wait outside until the event started. He sat outside the palace gates and waited for hours. And finally, his long wait bore fruits. The gates were opened at exactly four in the evening.

Tibe, with everyone else who had been invited, stepped into the palace in awe. The building was beautiful and clean. It was a vast place with countless servants who seemed to carry out their duties in a seamless pattern. They were directed to the ball area room, the location of the party. They were served with drinks and various food. They enjoyed some music pelted out by a live performance band. Food and beverages were in plenty.

As the party progressed, more and more guests arrived, including the prince of the neighborhood kingdom. Prince Charles was rumored to have an interest in the princess. The prince had proposed to the princess once or twice, but his offer was turned down. The princess needed time, but the prince was getting impatient. He intended to see the king's help to convince her daughter to marry him. Soon the first family's arrival was announced, and everybody offered their welcoming clap. Tibe, for the first time that day, saw the princess. She was so beautiful and adorable. The princess was wearing a beautiful white gown, and on her hand, to Tibe's delight, she was holding the unique flowers he had given her several days earlier. Tibe wondered how the princess had managed to keep the flowers fresh and beautiful for days.

The king then gave out his speech to the crowd. He welcomed them to his daughter's event and reminded everyone about the need to maintain peace and harmony in the kingdom. He repeated his clarion call of the need for hard work. After that, he welcomed everyone to the dance floor. This was the moment Tibe had been waiting for. Feeling confident, perhaps from the several glasses of wine he'd had droned, he told himself he must find a way to dance with the princess. He knew it was not easy, but there was always away.

The princess was also secretly scanning the cord for Tibe, the flower man, but she seems to be having trouble locating him. After several attempts, she finally discovered him. He was dancing awkwardly alone in the middle of the dance floor. She moved to where he was.

"Hello, care for a dance?" she asked, startling him.

"Princess, ooh sure," then they headed for the floor. As they were dancing, the princess asked him several questions, but of most interests to her was the flower. She wanted to know where Tibe had fetched it from.

"A friend gave me. It is a special flower," Tibe replied.

"Yes, I love it so much it is now my companion," replied the princess. Tibe was so pleased to hear the princess say that. They danced some more and soon the party was over. They had to part. That night, the princess couldn't trace her favorite flower. It had just disappeared mysteriously during the party. Someone must have kept it for her. The following morning, she summoned all her servants, but nobody seemed to have seen the flower. A frenzied search was carried out in all the chambers of the palace, but still, no flower was found. Several days of searching bore no fruit.

Then the princess became depressed over it. She wanted her flower. She refused to eat or talk to anyone. The king and the queen became concerned for their daughter. So, the king ordered an investigation to be done on the source of the flower. And soon, the flower was traced to Tibe, who was summoned to the king's palace. He, however, explained he bought the flower from the flower shop. The king ordered the attendant to be summoned, but when the guards reached the shop, it was closed, and there was no sign of the attendant. He, too, like the flower was missing.

Meanwhile, the princess's condition was getting worse by the day. After several days of not eating, she collapsed into a coma.

The king, in his desperation, made a declaration. Whoever will find the unique flower will marry her daughter. Tibe swore to use all his power to find the flower. He thought of the best way to locate it. And so, he spent several days thinking and searching for the flower with no success.

One day as he was buried in sleep, he had a strange dream. He dreamed he was inside the Pharaoh's pyramid situated several miles away. And while inside, he came across thousands of the unique flowers like the one he had presented the princess. The following morning, he woke up early and headed for the pyramid. After walking for hours, he finally arrived. He entered inside and started the search. After searching every room, he couldn't locate the flower. Tired, he decided to sit down and rest next to a big statue of a lion. He was dozing off when the statue started to talk to him,

"Tibe, I will help you find the flower if you help me," the lion statue said in a clear voice, startling Tibe. His first instinct was to flee, but he then thought of the princess and her suffering.

"How can I help you?" he finally gathered enough courage to ask.

"Simple, touch at my brow, and I will come back to life again. That is the only way I will defeat the spell," the statue said. It explained that a terrible witch had cast a spell on him and ever since it was turned into a statue.

The moment Tibe touched the brow of the lion, the statue changed first into a lion, then into a man. The man then led Tibe into a hidden room where several flowers like the one the princess was looking or were growing. He

Picked several of them, thanked the man, and quickly rushed to the palace.

The king received the flower cheerfully and took it to the princess' room. He ordered the flower to be given to the princess to smell. She regained her consciousness immediately; she sniffed the flower. She was starving, and after eating to her full, she asked for Tibe.

Several days later, the princess fully recovered, and soon the king allowed Tibe to marry her. They lived happily after that. And that is how Tibe discovered the flowers which never wilted inside the pyramid.

Conclusion

In summary, this book acknowledges that the reader is looking for a solution and is already disturbed by the difficulties of not getting sleep or not realizing quality sleep. The author makes an effort to present guidelines, proven guidelines, of how to attain guided meditation to overcome anxiety and insomnia that adversely affect the sleep patterns and the duration of sleep. The book systematically addresses guided meditation to induce children to sleep. The layout and the flow of the book are meant to allow the user to benefit from whichever chapter that the reader starts with. However, the author recommends the audience reading through from the first chapter to the last chapter.

Lack of sleep and lack of quality sleep affects the physical, physiological and mental health status of children. In this manner, lack of sleep and lack of quality sleep can lead to anger, irritability, and lack of concentration when executing routine duties which can be dangerous. The meditation scripts given in this book are itemized and simple enough to suit children engaging in guided hypnosis or guided meditation for the first time including seasoned kids with respect to meditation.

Meditation are excellent tools for helping your children feel more confident, creative, and relaxed. At its necessary foundation, just sitting still and quiet for a length of time is a powerful tool. This space that you create for them ignites their imagination and focus on just breathing. It also gives them a time and place to feel their emotions. It is also a message to them that feeling, expressing, and talking about their views is a good thing. Meditation also gives children the chance to be their true selves, even when all the other time in the day they may feel like they need to act or say or be a different way. In the space of meditation, your child can be whoever they are or want to be. That is a powerful moment to give!

The meditations you and your children are about to go through are a mixture of techniques to reach children in different ways. Focus on sounds, breathing, or a specific thought aids your children to start developing essential skills to help their coping and their focus skills as they continue growing. Besides, every meditation script presents a chance for your children to demonstrate their creativity through imaginations and visualizations. They provide compelling images to picture in their minds as the intended message and support sink deep in their brains.

Mindfulness Meditation for Kids

A Complete Guide for Kids, with Daily Exercises to Relieve Stress, Anxiety, Build Responsibility and Promote Peacefulness and Positive Thinking.

LILLY ANDERSEN

© **Copyright 2020 - All rights reserved.**

The content contained within this book may not be reproduced, duplicated or transmitted without direct written permission from the author or the publisher.
Under no circumstances will any blame or legal responsibility be held against the publisher, or author, for any damages, reparation, or monetary loss due to the information contained within this book. Either directly or indirectly.

Legal Notice:
This book is copyright protected. This book is only for personal use. You cannot amend, distribute, sell, use, quote or paraphrase any part, or the content within this book, without the consent of the author or publisher.

Disclaimer Notice:
Please note the information contained within this document is for educational and entertainment purposes only. All effort has been executed to present accurate, up to date, and reliable, complete information. No warranties of any kind are declared or implied. Readers acknowledge that the author is not engaging in the rendering of legal, financial, medical or professional advice. The content within this book has been derived from various sources. Please consult a licensed professional before attempting any techniques outlined in this book.

By reading this document, the reader agrees that under no circumstances is the author responsible for any losses, direct or indirect, which are incurred as a result of the use of information contained within this document, including, but not limited to, — errors, omissions, or inaccuracies.

Tables of Contents

Introduction 360

Chapter 1. An Introduction To Mindfulness 364

Chapter 2. How To Teach Mindfulness Meditation To Children 385

Chapter 3. Techniques And Trips To Relieve Stress And Promote Peacefulness 399

Chapter 4. Daily Exercises 407

Chapter 5. Tips and Tricks to Improve the Effectiveness of Meditation 429

Chapter 6. Guided Mindfulness Meditations for Deep Sleep 442

Guide Meditation to Improve Insomnia 442

Guide Meditation for Depression, Anxiety Relief 446

Relaxation Scripts 456

Sleep Scripts 468

Chapter 7. Bedtime Meditations For Kids 476

Chapter 8. Traits You Will Pick Up from Practicing Mindfulness Meditation 499

Chapter 9. How to Increase Focus with Mindfulness Meditation 512

Chapter 10. Meditations for Everyday Life 520

Conclusion 535

Introduction

Meditation is not only about sitting in silent concentration, although it is central to the practice. It's also about a series of active techniques that enhance the mind-control ability that is used not only during this sitting, but also in the rest of the awake (and perhaps even the dreaming) life. Meditation thus touches on most aspects of human experience, making them potentially richer, deeper, and productive.

In one form or the other, meditation has been practiced by all the great spiritual traditions, and their origins are lost in the fog of time.

Some of the early teachings on the basic technique of meditation (breathing observation) were made by the Buddha around 500 BC. Patanjali, the semi-legendary founder of Yoga philosophy, offers even more details about the Yoga Sutras, which date back to the second century BC. The unbroken tradition of meditation goes from Patanjali to the present day, where more people than ever have meditated.

Meditation is essentially a state of balanced, high-leveled concentration that is not focused on a thought or idea train, but on a single, well-defined stimulus. Meditation is the opposite of wandering thoughts or even of a directed train of thought. Buddhaghosa, a fifth-century Buddhist monk, spoke of meditation as a training of attention. Other early authors have more generally referred to it as training the mind or as a way to dig and analyse what is going on in the mind. Over the years, other authors have defined meditation in various ways, as a standstill of the mind, a concentration of mental energy, a discovery of the true self, attainment of inner peace, harmonization of body and mind, or simply sitting still and doing nothing. But it is a very special way to sit still and do nothing in which the mind is kept clear and still, alert and watchful and free from losing oneself in thought.

Phrases like training the mind are a surprise to many Westerners. Isn't our formal education system in schools and universities meant for training of the mind? Isn't' the mind being trained by learning the facts, figures, and techniques of the various academic subjects being taught by our teachers and faculty?, Why should we have to deal with something as seemingly esoteric and time-wasting as meditation?.

Unfortunately, the mind is not quite categorically trained by the facts and figures and techniques taught in our school and universities. The knowledge we acquire over these years is of tremendous value to us and in many cases, to our fellow human beings, but it is not spiritual training.

Anyone who is still in doubt can go ahead and do a simple test. Close your eyes and stop thinking......

How did you progress? Very few people can handle a seemingly simple task for half a minute. So, who is responsible for your mind? One thing is for sure, if you cannot stop thinking for 30 seconds, you certainly are not thinking.

We tend to think that "thinking" is a good thing, provided we have some control over the manner in which ideas are created and the direction to which they are going.

Chapter 1. An Introduction To Mindfulness

Many people are guilty of doing things quickly, without thought. When you are not focused on the things you are supposed to or whatever is stressing you out, you experience life more fully. Mindfulness is about not worrying about the past or future but being aware of the moment. By living in this way, you can invite calm and rational thought into your life. You learn critical skills that can benefit you through life, and so will your child. Here are some of the benefits.

General Benefits of Mindfulness

#1: Better Decision Making

Mindfulness helps with identifying emotions that might hinder the decision-making process. Have you ever been tired or stressed and made a poor decision? For example, your spouse may have done something to upset you. Instead of confronting them, you make assumptions and lash out. You decide to be passive aggressive, 'forgetting' to pack them lunch or giving them short, snappy answers when they ask you how your day went.

Instead, you could decide to confront them. Tell them what you know and ask them what they have to say about the situation. Think about it critically and decide if they are telling the truth. Then, take deep breaths and decide how to respond. Yelling does not solve anything—you must decide if you are going to forgive them and move forward or respond in another way. For example, if they cheated, you might decide to end the relationship.

#2: Improved Social Interactions

Both children and adults can benefit from improving their social interactions. Mindfulness teaches a deeper connection to emotions. It helps teach empathy. This empathy helps us understand ourselves and not be so critical, but it also helps us understand others. This deeper understanding can give us an idea of why people may react the way they do in certain situations. It teaches us to be kind to the mother with screaming children in the store or the homeless people on the street because we have no idea what life has handed them.

#3: Ability to Deal with Stress

Life rarely goes the way that we intend it to. It is normal for people to experience problems like job loss, the death of a loved one, sickness, break-ups, and other unpleasant situations in their lifetime. However, the people that succeed in life are those that learn to overcome the stressful situations.

For example, imagine that you lost your job. There is the option that some people turn to—drinking away their worries or finding some way to numb what they are feeling. However, this numbness will not help them find a new job. It is an unhealthy reaction to stress. Instead, the energy spent drinking or numbing the stress can be used constructively to create a resume or fill out job applications.

Mindfulness Benefits for Children

In addition to the general benefits of mindfulness, there are specific advantages of teaching your child mindfulness.

#1: Their Minds Are Less Busy

Have you ever reflected on your childhood, wishing you could go back to a time when everything was simpler? As you age, responsibilities grow and there is increased pressure from the world to keep busy. Even high school students have more responsibility than younger children, having to juggle extra-curricular activities, homework, and a social life. Once children grow into adults, their minds become busy places where you cannot enjoy what you are doing sometimes because you are worried about the future.

Children's minds are a little less busy than the average adults. Their parents shoulder a lot of the responsibilities, so they can focus on being a child. Learning mindfulness from a young age is beneficial because children's minds are a less busy place. It can make learning mindfulness a little easier for them.

#2: They Learn to Regulate Their Emotions Better

Most parents will tell you that the terrible twos are a real thing. However, they typically roll over into the terrible threes, fours, and so on. This is a coming of age that exists because toddlers are learning their emotions for the first time. They are starting to find their place in the world and when the world does not fall into place the way that they want it to, it causes them to become sad, angry, and upset.

Teaching children mindfulness also teaches them emotional regulation. As they learn about the different emotions, as well as the thoughts and physical feelings that go along with them, they learn how to better manage these emotions. They also learn techniques for handling stress and other negative emotions, such as the Squish and Release technique that will be covered in the second section of this book.

#3: Increased Ability to Focus

Cognitive focus is something that benefits anybody, but it is especially helpful for children. Kids often have high levels of physical energy than adults. Even though they may not have to juggle as many tasks, their minds often race and become easily distracted. By increasing your child's ability to focus by encouraging mindful practice, you are giving them a better chance at academic success. They will be able to calm themselves better and focus on the task at hand.

#4: Improved Self-Esteem

Kids of any age are at a critical point in their lives that can shape their future. One major struggle that some kids have is with their self-esteem. This can cause them to doubt their abilities, struggle in school, or even become victims of bullying.

The way that mindfulness helps is because it teaches children not to listen to the negative thoughts in their head. Often, there is a voice of self-doubt. When we make a mistake, it might say that we are 'stupid' or 'incapable.' This is far from the truth—everyone makes mistakes. Mindfulness gives children the rational thought to overcome this voice, as well as the voice of bullies and other critics that might hold your child back from being all that they can be.

How to Practice Mindfulness

Plot twist: You actually already know how to be mindful! While you read this sentence, notice your awareness of the following: the meaning of the words, the sounds you hear around you, the thoughts in your head, and the rhythm of your breathing. Congratulations—you just practiced mindfulness! Mindfulness meditation just means doing this deliberately.

To break it down further, mindfulness is the practice of paying attention to what's happening right now in your mind and body in a kind, interested, and nonjudgmental way. It allows you to be aware of what's happening as it happens, rather than getting caught up in stories, judgments, or worries about what did, might, could, or should be happening. Once you have that awareness, you can respond to what's going on in a way that you choose rather than reacting on autopilot. Mindfulness trains you to focus on what you want when you want and to ground your attention in your body and senses, so you don't get carried away with thoughts and emotions (if you don't want to).

It's all about that feeling when you want to give up, because your brain is telling you that you're too ugly, too fat, too dumb, or too skinny; when you can't sleep at night because your mind will not settle down; when you actually did something great but feel like you don't deserve any praise or love; or when you start to freak out because someone didn't message you back. If you've experienced those or similar feelings, you know how your automatic reactions aren't always helpful. Mindfulness lets you train your mind to see what's happening in a way that's appreciative rather than judgmental, and accepting rather than resistant or analytical. That perspective lets you be kinder to yourself as you look in the mirror, get more rest because you can let go of worries more easily, feel the pride of your accomplishments or enjoy the love you deserve, and be more patient with yourself and others when you aren't getting the response you wanted.

At its best, your mind is amazing. It lets you learn, solve problems, play sports, try new things, and more. At its worst, your mind can be like an Internet troll—judgmental, mean, quick to argue, and UNRELENTINGLY LOUD. It can also be like an overzealous therapist, analyzing every little thing you do, obsessing about the past or what's coming next or why things ended up this way. Mindfulness is like a friend, teacher, or parent who tells you that you're doing great, this too shall pass, and you don't have to listen to that shouting jerk or the nattering worrier. Mindfulness trains you to be here now, just as you are, and know that that's okay. As cheesy as it sounds, it's about being a friend to yourself and your experiences rather than needing to change them, get rid of them, or believe the voice that says you're not good enough.

How It Can Help You

This is not about "fixing" yourself or getting rid of who you are. It's about relating to yourself and the world around you in a way that promotes your own happiness and well-being. It doesn't mean that life will suddenly be perfect, but rather that you can be kinder to yourself when everything feels wrong. It's actually really empowering, because you get to be in charge of your mind rather than it being in charge of you.

Sadly, the superpowers of mindfulness are limited. It won't make exams, curfews, demanding bosses, mean people, or unrealistic body standards go away. It can't do much about racism, homophobia, or sexism on a broad scale. But it can help you deal with all of that in a way that makes your life easier, letting you find more compassion for yourself and other people. Instead of hating the exam, calling yourself dumb, or being sure you're going to fail, mindfulness lets you just take the exam. It lets you see what's happening for what it is (nerves, mistakes, pain, discomfort, frustration, distracting thoughts) without adding extra stress. The goal isn't to make those pains or discomforts go away (which is usually out of your control, anyway), but to see that they are actually just uncomfortable feelings that won't last forever. You might still be stressed, but you won't be stressed out.

You can't change a lot of what happens to you. You can't change the past, mistakes you've made, much of what you look like, where you're born, etc. But, if you can see and acknowledge those experiences, then you can decide how you want to relate to them. With practice, you can live your life in a way that lets you accept what you can't change and have the strength and compassion to be the person you want to be.

Neuroscientists are discovering more and more about how our brains can grow and change based on our experiences and habits. Basically, your brain gets good at what it practices. This concept, called neuroplasticity, is what meditation is all about. You probably weren't very good the first time you picked up a violin, hopped on a skateboard, or attempted a three-pointer—but the more you practiced, the better you got. Your brain works the same way. The more you engage in self-criticism, catastrophizing, and judging yourself and others, the better you'll become at those reactions; they'll become more automatic and will be easier to access whether you like them or not. The good news is that every time you pause before reacting, take a breath, are kind to yourself, focus on your good qualities more than the bad, or forgive yourself for making a mistake, the more those habits will become a part of who you are. By reading this book and completing these exercises, you are choosing how you will train your brain and what kind of person you will be.

What to Know before You Start

Reading about mindfulness is like reading about music—you can't get the full experience only through books. To get what mindfulness is all about, you have to try it.

These can be applied to almost every part of your life. They cover everything from using your breathing to focus your attention, to dealing with emotions and thoughts skillfully, to cultivating gratitude and self-compassion. The rest of the book addresses specific scenarios. Each practice includes one of four tips:

- Buddy Up: how to do the practice with a friend, family member, or partner

- Change It Up: ways to vary the practice

- Take It Further: how to dive deeper and explore the practice further

- Am I Doing This Right?: helpful hints and suggestions, or common obstacles

Responding Vs. Reacting And Expectations Vs. Intentions

These meditations build the basic skills for mindfulness. You're training yourself to respond rather than react. Mindfulness teacher Sam Himelstein describes the difference: "Responding is when you think before you act. Reacting is when you act before you think."

When I started meditating, I noticed that I had lots of automatic reactions about meditation itself. It was a combination of "this is amazing, it's going to solve all my problems," "this is a huge waste of time," and "why am I the only one who can't do It?"—none of which was all that helpful for simply being in the present moment.

The ability to respond rather than react can have life-changing, real-world implications. I've worked with teens who use these tools to stay focused while being taunted by competitors at major sporting competitions. Others were able to walk away from a fight rather than get sucked in. One student told me about a time she was able to pause and change her mind before hurting herself. In a society where you're judged and targeted for things you can't control, like your sexuality, the color of your skin, or your body or gender identity, being able to choose how you respond can be the difference between well-being and stress—or even safety and danger.

Having said that, it's important to let go of expectations. Of course, you wouldn't be reading this book if you didn't want to get something from it. But the somewhat annoying and totally paradoxical thing about meditation is that the more expectations you have and the more you try to make something happen, the less likely it is to happen.

It's like when you tell yourself to calm down or someone tells you, "Cheer up, stop being so stressed." Does it work? Almost never. The best way to actually calm down or stop stressing is to respond rather than react, to have intentions rather than expectations. Instead of fighting the stress or expecting to feel something different, you can acknowledge it with kindness. The stress might not go away, but you aren't beating yourself up for something you can't control or getting mad because it doesn't fit with how your brain thinks things should be. The best way to approach meditation is to be with what's happening rather than trying to get somewhere else.

Key Things To Remember

1. You Can't Do It Wrong. The whole point is to notice what's happening as it's happening. Even if the thing you notice is the thought "this is stupid," that still counts.

2. If You Think Of It As Homework, It Feels As Crappy As Homework. Try to think of it as a break or a rest instead. It's a time to chill out rather than another thing to do or get right.

3. The Goal Is Not To Make Everything Happy Or Calm. That means that whatever you feel is okay. Mindfulness isn't about making yourself feel any particular way, and it's not about stopping how you currently are. It's just seeing (and hearing, smelling, tasting, touching, thinking, and feeling) what's happening as it happens.

4. Mindfulness Isn't Asking You To Sit Back And Let The World Walk All Over You. If you want to change something, you still get to change it. Ultimately, you can't change anything without seeing it first. Mindfulness helps you do that.

5. You Definitely Won't Stop Thinking When You Meditate! It's not about making your mind go blank or getting rid of thoughts. It's just noticing what's happening and choosing how much and what kind of attention to give it. Everyone's mind wanders.

6. If You Ever Feel Overwhelmed By What You Experience While Meditating (Or Otherwise), Try To Remember That Even If It Feels Scary Or Really Intense, You Are Okay. You aren't doing it wrong (meditation, or just living in general). If you do get overwhelmed, you might want to open your eyes if they're closed, take a few deep breaths, and use your senses to connect to your environment. (See here and here for more.)

7. People Call It The Practice Of Mindfulness Or Meditation For A Reason. Like any skill, it takes practice. If it feels weird or awkward at first, don't worry. The more

you do it, the more natural it becomes.

Tips for Success

Mindfulness is actually easy. The challenge is remembering to do it. Use these tips as a way to support the habit you are trying to build.

Posture Matters. You can meditate in any posture that feels comfortable. It can help to sit with a straight spine, a bit more upright and energized than you normally would. This posture is probably different from how you usually sit, and it can promote clarity and concentration. It's better to practice on a straight-backed chair or on a cushion on the floor rather than on a couch or in bed (you're less likely to fall asleep). Your eyes can be either closed or open with a soft gaze such that you aren't really looking at anything (unless you are doing a practice that asks you to look around your environment).

Make It A Habit. The best way to make mindfulness, compassion, and nonjudgment a more permanent part of who you are is to practice regularly. Try to find a regular time when you can practice these meditations (maybe between school and work, between classes, or right before bedtime). At the same time, experiment with practicing informally throughout your day. Anytime you can stop and take a breath is an opportunity to train your brain.

Use A Timer. It's really helpful to choose how long you will meditate for and set a timer (it can even be your phone) for that length of time in advance. Then hide the timer behind you, so you won't be tempted to peek at it. There are lots of free timer apps you can use.

Keep A Journal. A meditation journal is another helpful tool. It can be a fancy notebook or just notes on your phone. Make it as detailed or as brief as you like—for example, "Practiced for five minutes, noticed my mind felt crazy and felt my breath in my nose." The journal helps support the habit and keeps you accountable.

Find Support. Having a friend who knows what you're doing and who can support you is one of the best ways to promote a regular mindfulness practice. You might text each other once a day with a brief reminder like "Breathe" or "Pause," to share what you noticed when you meditated, or even just send a thumbs-up emoji after you've practiced. Some people really like meditating with others; others prefer to do it alone. Do what works for you.

Also, while this book is a great way to start your mindfulness journey, it's especially helpful to have someone who can guide you in your practice. There are lots of free resources online, including guided meditations. Check out the resources at the end of the book and/or look up teachers or meditation groups in your area. Lots of teachers offer stuff online, too.

Don't Give Up. Some of the meditations will feel like a great fit for you. Others might not. For example, if you have asthma or experience anxiety, paying attention to your breath might be unhelpful. Try to trust yourself, but also don't give up too easily. If it feels challenging, that's totally normal. If it feels overwhelming or painful, trust yourself and choose a different practice or take a break and come back when it feels right.

You Know Yourself Best. Ask yourself what you need to do to make this commitment or to bring yourself back when you lose track. Maybe you need to set reminders on your phone or download an app for this. Maybe you need to write a note for your mirror or schedule it into your calendar. It's like exercise—sometimes you know you should do it even if you don't feel like it. Once you start, chances are you'll keep going.

Chapter 2. How to Teach Mindfulness Meditation to Children

Mind meditation is the practical cleansing of the mind, of witnessing and transcending the mind. Examples of this type of meditation are Buddhist meditation and TM meditation. Focused meditation is the practice of using the mind as a tool for self-healing and internal transplantation. You practice this type of meditation when you are involved in creative visualization, guided images and breathing exercises. Mindfulness-centered meditation is best for children because it allows the child to practice mindfulness through focused and physical relaxation.

As parents, we can start practicing meditation with our children, usually from 4 years old. This constant practice allows your little one to transform meditation into an integral and natural part of his daily life, even during adulthood.

Teaching children is different from teaching adults. Children have less patience, less distance and less ability to sit. On the other hand, they have a more amazing imagination, a feeling of joy and learn, for example.

Why is meditation so important in our lives? Meditation is an important practice to maintain children's balance and ability to cope with stress. As they slowly and slowly find themselves there, children feed themselves with a healthy sense of themselves and, therefore, improve their self-esteem.

Children in each situation will feel a sense of personal power and the ability to defend themselves. You can experience the world apart from a chaotic and winding world of needs and needs. Creating this space for our children to experience relaxation and self-esteem improves the feeling of happiness and the inner understanding that they can really do what they have in mind.

As a result, to teach children meditation effectively, keep the following six principles in mind.

Make it Attractive and Fun

The most important thing when teaching children to meditate is to present forms in a more attractive, fun and attractive way. Never let them get bored. I love that it is a fun activity like a game) and children have to try again.

The principle of "making it fun" means that you should choose techniques that are naturally appealing to children, such as working with their senses and imagination. It also means that you have to adjust the meditation guidelines to make them more attractive.

For example, instead of asking children to "watch you breathe," you can ask them to put a small toy in their belly and drag it up and down. Have them try to move the toy as slowly as possible.

You go there, you just give them a deep breath and don't even notice it! Of course, this approach depends on age. Is your "student" a child 6-9), between 14-14) or a teenager 14-17)? The way you teach a 5-year-old is different from the way you portray an 11-year-old. This meditation training for children needs to apply these principles and techniques to the child's age and personality.

Appeal to Their Imagination

It is difficult for most children to understand abstract concepts. Instead, children enjoy activities that allow them to use their imagination and creativity. So, make sure you involve your imagination in action.

One way to do this is to frame meditation as a challenge. You have to communicate with your creativity and imagination, and that depends a lot on the child. For example: physical rest is a strong door to meditation.

If your child loves action movies, he can create a metaphor like this: "Your soul is like a secret stealthy agent that sometimes wants to disappear. Your mission is to protect him, so follow him in a careful and silent manner. However, be so careful because he could take to his heels in blink of an eye.

Create an Atmosphere of "Lovely Meditation"

Another way is to create an atmosphere of "lovely meditation" at home or at school. Children like to move to another world with different experiences and strange objects. You can say something like: a sacred space, a magical space, and when you enter and follow the meditation, all your things disappear and you feel very relaxed and happy.

Keep It Short

Children do not have to wait 20 minutes on the floor. Therefore, keep the exercise short, especially for children under 10 years. You should never get tired of exercise, but leave the feeling that you want to "want more."

A general guideline is to hold meetings until the child's age, plus one. So, if your child is 8 years old, do the session for a maximum of 9 minutes. To make it more fun, you can use a ring timer program.

Lead for Example

Children learn more by following the instructions below. They like to imitate adults and feel old. Therefore, the best way to teach a child to meditate is to meditate! All areas are striking, so be sure to give a solid example of how to integrate meditation into your daily life.

Let your child feel still while meditating. Finally, he will ask you what you did and then it will be time to teach them. Otherwise, he will increase his curiosity by saying something like: "This is a special exercise that only adults can do, but if you have a good week, I can teach you on Saturday."

Do you want your children to meditate? Be an example.

It also means that you have to meditate with them. Do you want them to be regular in their training? You need to regulate yourself and make meditation a family practice.

Be Flexible and Supportive

At the end of the exercise together, ask them how their experience was. This would be a good plan to draw them what their meditation session is, the experience they have experienced or the "before and after" drawing. This encourages children to express themselves.

Then, confirm what they share. Accept what the child says, even if it is exaggerated, because we leave room for imagination.

Start with Five Minutes of Relaxation at Bedtime

With five minutes to rest at bedtime is easy. The stories presented in the following chapters will help you get started. Create a short break in bed using your imagination and genius to ask your child to imagine a sun just above their head, eliminating stress or worry. This will make your body very calm and relaxed.

Continue with the details of the relaxation waves above and above the body to touch and relax any muscle and body. Children find this very relaxing.

Bring an animal friend to your stage or a lovely cloud where your child can enter. Help your child relieve stress one by one by pressing stress on a nearby balloon and observing the stress and worry of POPs. There are no infinite possibilities for your stories. Your own living imagination makes these possibilities unlimited.

This focused approach helps children in a variety of ways. Children can concentrate better, feel more balanced in their daily lives, are calmer and more comfortable. If we do not teach our children meditation and tranquility, they become a collection of nervous and unhappy energy. Children desperately need a way out of their stress. 69% of children under 10 have trouble sleeping and 76% of school-age children are worried. As responsible parents, we can provide such tools to our children to help them fully realize their life potential.

Tips for Teaching Your Child Mindfulness: Before You Get Started

- 1: Try Mindfulness Yourself

We are our children's role models. If you are constantly yelling when you are upset or you shut down when emotions become overwhelming, your child will see that and mindfulness will be more difficult for them. You will also have a harder time encouraging them to practice mindfulness since it can be hard to do at first and you are not practicing with them.

To practice mindfulness on your own, start by scheduling 5-10 minutes for meditation each day. Find a quiet place where you can close your eyes and relax. Focus on your breathing, inhaling for a count of five and then exhaling for a count of five. Pay attention to how the breath makes your stomach inflate and deflate. If you find yourself distracted, release the thought without judgment and return your focus to your breathing. As time goes on, you will be able to focus for longer periods without your mind wandering. You can even extend the time beyond 10 minutes once you are comfortable.

- 2: Be Mindful During Daily Activities

Over the course of a lifetime, the activities that you do on a day-to-day basis become second nature. For most people, this means that they start to carry out their daily responsibilities in a robotic-like fashion, sometimes letting their mind wander without giving what they are doing a second thought. Have you ever pulled into the driveway of your house and realized you don't remember coming down the last few streets? This is from driving the same way over and over again. The mind goes on autopilot—this is the reason that many accidents happen within three miles of someone's home.

Being mindful during the day simply means being present. It means that instead of letting your mind go on autopilot while driving to work or doing the dishes, you take the time to realize all that is around you. You notice the flower bushes by the park and hear the sounds of the dogs playing there, instead of tuning them out. You feel the way your muscles move while doing the dishes, paying attention to how the way you move your hand removes dirty spots from the dishes.

- 3: Be Sure Your Expectations are Realistic

People who are familiar with mindfulness often associate it with feelings of calmness and relaxation. The idea of a quiet home is enough for any parent to consider practicing mindfulness with their children. You should keep in mind, however, that teaching your child mindfulness does not mean they will be quiet all the time. While you might notice a difference in the number of tantrums and there will be periods of peace, keeping your child quiet should not be the ultimate goal of mindfulness. The goal is to teach your child the skills that will help them become more aware of their experience, both internally and externally. It will help them learn that their thoughts are only thoughts—not something that they must listen to or judge. Though mindfulness can help, your child is likely to still exhibit what could be considered normal kid behavior—tantrums, whining, arguing, and loudness—from time to time.

Overcoming Common Obstacles to Mindfulness

- 1: Your Child Does Not Understand Mindfulness

Not only is mindfulness a big word, it can be a big concept to explain to a child. You cannot explain mindfulness to your child in the way that it has been described in these first couple chapters. Explaining it in a way that makes it seem complex will make your child feel as if they are unable to understand the idea. Without understanding it, they will not be able to find the motivation to practice it.

Keep things simple by explaining mindfulness as awareness. You are teaching your child to be aware. Awareness is feeling things and understanding thoughts as they come, in the present moment. It is knowing what is happening inside of our bodies and minds right now.

- 2: Your Child is Not Interested

Mindfulness is not something that you can just do. Even though mindful practice is meant to induce a state of relaxation, it can be difficult to get your child to be mindful when they are in the middle of a temper tantrum. It can also be hard to get them interested if they have had a long day at school or have been cooped up because they will have an excess of energy that will make it hard for them to become aware of their present moment.

If your child is not interested in mindfulness or seems to wound up, do not force it on them. It is important that mindful practice is related to positive emotions if you want your child to be motivated enough to do it. If they seem to be too energized, try practicing mindfulness after playing or other physical activity. If you do become frustrated, remember to keep your expectations in check. You should be practicing mindfulness for the benefits—not to achieve a specific outcome.

- 3: You Are in the Habit of Tuning Them Out

Parents lead busy lives, but that does not excuse us from interacting with our child. When your child is talking about something that excites them, give them your full attention. Avoid checking the ping on your phone. If you do need to take a phone call, excuse yourself and then find them when you are done. Encourage them to share with you.

This does not mean that you should allow your child to be rude. There are appropriate and inappropriate times to talk. Teach them the habit of saying 'excuse me' to interrupt other people's conversations. It is okay to ask them to wait before you attend to them, but do not neglect to pay attention to them.

If interruptions are a problem, then get in the habit of setting aside time for your little one to share about their day with you. It does take more than five to ten minutes. Try to avoid doing this right after school, unless they initiate it. Some kids are excited to share after school, while others prefer to keep to themselves for a while and relax before sharing.

Chapter 3. Techniques And Trips To Relieve Stress And Promote Peacefulness

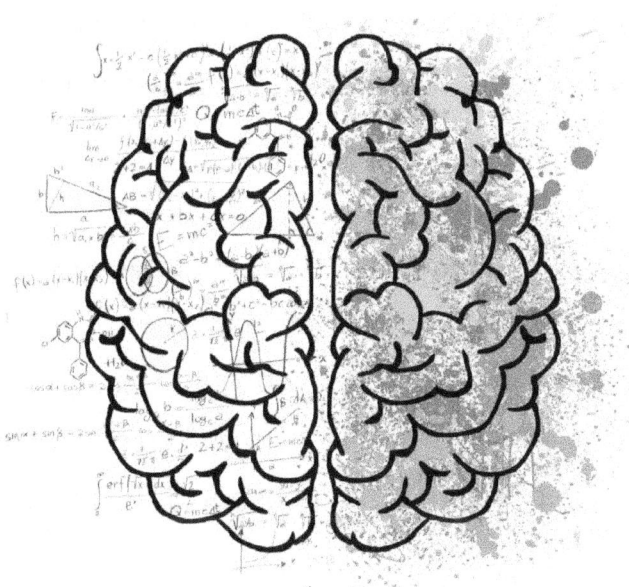

The first 3 steps of practicing mindfulness meditation are the same as the ones you practiced in concentration meditation to relieve stress and promote peacefulness. These steps are: choose a calm place, relax and set a timer. You also need to be seated in a position that respects your spine. Thus, if you are on a hard chair, sit up straight so that energy can pass down to your energy points. Place your feet flat on the floor. If you want to feel even more grounded, kick your shoes off and feel your naked feet on the floor.

Since I have mentioned each step in detail previously, I am not repeating them again. Here are the additional steps you need to perform to become mindful at all times.

It is also a good idea to write down what you want to gain from your meditation and writing in your journal before you start meditation will help to guide your meditation and help you to solve problems that relate to your self-esteem or the problems that present themselves in your life.

- Settle Your Mind: Once you sit comfortably feeling relaxed, detach your mind from all the thoughts of the things going on in your life. It might take a while for you to completely forget everything going around especially if you had a stressful day.

If such is the case, you will notice that your mind is dancing from one thought to another. Don't force it to calm down; just let the thoughts be. Let it dance for a while and once it settles down, bring your focus to meditation, which at the start may feel a strange concept to you but it's okay if you feel this way. Again, if you filled out your thoughts in your meditation book, don't let them go further by continuing to think of them. Just acknowledge that they are there but give them no more credence than that. They are just thoughts.

- Use Your Breath to Become Focused: Once your mind is settled down and your focus is totally on meditation, bring your awareness to your breath as you take it.

Focus on the inhalations and exhalations of each breath. Feel how the air enters your nostrils and then flows through your windpipe into your lungs and then comes back from your lungs to your windpipe then nose and then gets out of your body. Remember the counting that you did when you did the breathing exercises in this book? These will help you because you need to develop a deep breathing rhythm that is steady and if you need to use counting at the beginning, of course, you can do this until you feel comfortable that the amount of breath is just right.

Your mind may come up with a thought to distract you. If that happens, ignore it and bring back your focus to your breath. Keep in mind that focusing on the actions you are doing right now is itself a practice to become mindful.

Whenever a thought pops up in your mind, instead of fighting with it, just let it flow. Bring in this alternate thought, "Oh! I need to focus on my breath" and then replace it with the action of focusing on your breath. The thing that you need to learn is to acknowledge a thought rather than pretending it isn't there, and simply tell it to go away because you are busy at this time. When you do that, don't attach any emotions to the thought and view it just like it's a scene that is passing you while you are sitting on a train. Judgment is human failure and when you are able to let go of this in your life, you will find that it's much easier to meditate.

- **Explore One Thought At A Time:** Once you feel more focused and calm, let yourself a little loose and don't shun away any thought that enters your mind. Now your job is to explore them and know yourself better. If you feel any sensation, emotion or feeling, hold on to it and try to understand it better. Ask yourself questions like 'Why do I feel that way?', 'What exactly happened that made me feel this way?' and similar questions. By asking such questions, you try to identify the reason behind that emotion and thought. Make sure not to label any emotion or thought as good or bad, negative or positive; accept it wholeheartedly. Be very patient with it and use it to know yourself better. After doing it for a few minutes, you'll find something new about yourself and the way you think. For instance, you may discover that you feel you're a failure because you don't work hard and this makes you realize the importance of working hard on your goal. This makes you realize your problem and gives you a fix for it too. When your mind is quiet and thoughts arrive, you can explore them and do this very logically instead of involving your emotions and judgment which is when thoughts go haywire.

Repeat this exercise of mindfulness meditation twice a day for 5-10 minutes per session at the start and increase the timing of each session as you progress. Explore new thoughts daily and understand them better to get a true insight into your mind.

As you do that, try to bring mindfulness meditation into each and every aspect of your life as well. What does that mean? Why am I feeling this way? You are perfectly entitled to acknowledge thoughts but not to let them take over your mind to the extent that they impose emotions upon you. When you find that you have had enough of thoughts, go back to being in the moment, in the breath and concentrate on the breath instead of thinking, shunning the thoughts that you really do not wish to deal with at this time or which you know will make you emotional. You are in control of this moment. You can go back to concentrating on the breath at any time. Just think to yourself that this kind of meditation helps to make you aware of your thoughts and the reasons that they occur. However, try to carry on this line of thinking even after you have meditated, because it helps you to accept thoughts, to process them without emotions and to move on to the next thought in your everyday life.

You will see from the next section that you can bring mindfulness meditation into everyday actions and this helps you as a continuance of your mindfulness meditation sessions to accept life as it is, rather than wishing it was different. We cannot change who we are. All that we can change is our approach to life and mindfulness brings you back into the moment, so you don't miss anything along the way.

Bringing Mindfulness Meditation into Every Aspect of Your Life

This means that you have to be fully involved in everything you do without thinking of anything else or jumping to another task. If you are reading a book, focus on it completely and don't let your mind wander off in thought to something else. Tell yourself 'I have to focus on the book right now' and try to enjoy each word of it. The more you focus on it, the more you become involved in it. This helps you stay in the present and live each moment of it fully.

Similarly, if you are doing laundry, be fully involved in it, so you do or think of nothing else but the act you're involved in right now. It will take you a little time to be mindful of each moment all the time, but practice will help you get there for sure; and when that happens, you'll unlock a beautiful, happy life that will keep you stress-free at all times.

We were never intended to multi task. It really goes against the natural workings of the brain and when you learn to concentrate totally on everything that you do, it takes a whole load of strain off the mind. You also get more done and can work out your goals and really make an effort to reach them, one step at a time. You can make all kinds of tasks meaningful by paying attention to what it is you are doing. I remember one day cleaning the tiles in the shower and thinking how much they sparkle and shine when in the past I would never really have noticed the fruits of my own labor. It was a moment that I enjoyed as I could see my smiling face in the reflection and had used mindfulness to get me through everything that I had to do before folks dropped in to stay at my house.

While you work on this, do introduce body scan meditation into your routine too. It is an excellent technique to get rid of the stress stuck in your body and become fully relaxed.

Chapter 4.   Daily Exercises

You get a million messages about the person you should be: what you're supposed to look like (big lips, flat abs, perfect eyebrows, and more); how you're supposed to act (tough, smart, funny, not too loud or quiet); and how you're supposed to express your sexual or gender identity. And somehow, amid all of that, you're also supposed to "be yourself." These practices are all about taking care of yourself just as you are. Then you can be in the best frame of mind to decide who you want to be.

Silencing Self-Criticism

Very few of us would talk to others the way we talk to ourselves. We'd never be so harsh or mean. Would you ever call your best friend the names you call yourself? Yet it seems to come naturally to be super self-critical.

Mindfulness helps you see that not only are those thoughts not true, they only have as much power as you give them. This practice lets you see your automatic thoughts without needing to believe them, and then choose a different response.

1. Take a moment to pause and notice what's going on right now. Use your senses to bring yourself into the present moment.

2. Notice any sensations in your body right now, particularly your feet on the floor. Remind yourself that it's okay to feel however you feel. Then keep coming back to the feeling of your breath and your feet. (You might also try the postures in the Self-Soothing Practices.)

3. Instead of focusing on the content of the thought, keep returning to how this moment feels in your body.

4. When you're ready, consider if there are any other ways of seeing this situation. Look for counterevidence. How would your best friend interpret this? How would you talk to your closest friend or family member if they were going through this?

5. Next, try to find a more balanced thought. Your automatic reaction might be, "I'm a loser. I always fail." A balanced response might be, "I made a mistake" or

recognizing that you thought you'd fail last time but didn't.

6. The critical thought might not go away, but you don't need to fuel it. Remind yourself that the judgments in your head aren't true, no matter how convincing they are.

7. Keep your attention on your breathing and your body. You might choose to focus on something you're grateful for or even the tiniest thing that went well this week.

TAKE IT FURTHER

Almost everyone has this bully (or monster, demon, or troll) in their brain. However you picture it, it's very convincing, very persuasive, and quite charming. It tells you that it knows how to make you feel or be better, if only you'd listen to it. And it thrives on attention. The more you listen to it, the louder it gets. But here's the truth: It's wrong. It's totally wrong. You don't get better by making yourself feel worse. And while you might never be able to make it go away completely, if you know it's there, if you expect it, then it can't surprise you and knock you off balance as much. Use this practice to really see it. Even give it a name or decide what it looks like. Then the next time it shows up, it's not some immovable force. Instead, it's more like that smelly uncle at Thanksgiving. It's inevitably unpleasant, but you don't need to let it get to you.

Mindful Eating and Moving Mindfully

Have you ever eaten lunch and then forgotten that you did it? Ever walked home from school and didn't remember the walk at all? Or finished a bag of chips without even realizing you were eating? Most of us have had the experience of eating mindlessly or even going to the wrong place because we were distracted by something else. Mindfulness helps us be more present because we are attentive to what's happening as it's happening.

1. Whatever you are doing, take a moment to pause and set the intention to do it mindfully—just that one thing, right now.

2.Take a few deep breaths and notice how your body feels in this moment.

3.Then explore the task at hand with all of your senses.

4.If you're eating, notice what the food looks like, how the light hits it, how it smells, how it feels in your mouth as you chew and swallow. Really take your time with it. Put your fork down between bites. Notice any habits you might have, such as reaching for the next piece before finishing the first one. What is it like to just eat, rather than eating while looking at your phone or even listening to music?

5.If you're walking, notice how your feet feel touching the ground. Hear any sounds that are around or within you. Try to place all of your attention on the feeling of walking. Notice how your muscles and joints propel you forward. It's actually amazing how much goes into keeping you upright and moving.

6.You can try this with any activity. Just use your senses to feel what's happening as it's happening. Whatever you are doing, try to do only that one thing.

7. When your mind wanders, bring your attention back to your senses in this moment.

AM I DOING THIS RIGHT?

This might feel weird at first. Who really pays attention to what walking or eating feels like? But the more you do it, the more you'll likely appreciate those chances to stop and just be. You don't even have to do it for the entire walk or meal. Try it with just a few bites or steps. See what happens when you commit to doing just one thing at a time.

Waking Up Mindfully

Ever wake up and immediately feel like it's going to be a terrible day? Or you grab your phone before you're even fully awake? Those first few moments can help you set the tone for the rest of the day. This practice asks you to take just two minutes before picking up your phone or planning your day to be in your body and orient to your environment, so you can make a choice about how you're going to relate to yourself today.

1.You've just woken up. Notice how your body feels. Enjoy the feeling of not needing to do anything before your day starts. You might also check out the light in the room or the sounds you hear.

2.Take a few deep breaths. You can place your hands on your abdomen to feel your body breathing even more fully. Notice what it feels like to breathe.

3.Let your breathing be natural. Notice any stories or thoughts going through your mind. Send yourself kind thoughts (here) or set an intention for how you are going to be today. You might choose to be kind or compassionate or make someone else feel good. This isn't about ignoring anything negative; it's about choosing what you want to focus on.

4.Take a few more moments to connect to your senses. Notice anything you can hear, smell, see, taste, or touch.

5.When you're ready or it's time to get up, renew your intention for how you want to be today. See if there's even one small thing you can look forward to or appreciate in this moment. Rest your attention on that kindness as you get up and go about your morning.

TAKE IT FURTHER

Each moment is an opportunity to start again. If you wake up feeling grouchy, let yourself feel that, name it, and notice that it moves and changes. Then come back to your body and to deciding how you want to be in this moment. You get to be in charge here.

It's important to know that this isn't about being super-optimistic or ignoring any problems you have. Rather, you're seeing that you get to decide, in every moment, how you are with whatever's happening. Consider how you really want to feel when you get back in bed at the end of the day.

Loving Your Body

Most of us have body-image issues, because we have this idea that our bodies don't look like they should. We believe we look wrong: wrong skin, height, legs, hair, everything. The amazing thing is that it doesn't matter what hair, skin, or height we have—someone will always say it should be different. It's like it is in elementary school, when no matter what your name is, someone will find a way to make fun of it. You can always choose to find something that isn't good enough.

Loving your body isn't about having the perfect arms, abs, or butt. And it doesn't mean you can't work out or eat healthy. It's about seeing that being kind to yourself makes you feel a lot better than treating yourself like crap and that you can choose which messages you take to heart.

1.Take a few deep breaths. Notice how you feel.

2.Let your breath be natural and turn your attention to what your body feels like.

3.Take some time to feel yourself breathing and try to marvel at the ability of your body to breathe and keep you alive.

4.Notice that your senses are working all the time, giving you information and connecting you to the world. You don't even have to tell them to do anything; they just do it.

5. If you feel down or critical, take some time to notice how that feels inside. Let yourself feel that discomfort as sensations in your body rather than focusing on the thoughts or judgments themselves.

6. Try to avoid making major decisions right now. If your mind is saying, "I hate my body" or "I have the ugliest nose ever," try to notice that, right now, your mind is upset. Right now, you feel angry or sad. Right now, frustration feels this way. And it won't last forever even if it feels like it.

7. Remind yourself that you can't change your body by hating it. That only makes you feel worse. Remember that no one is perfect and pictures only tell part of a story. Imagine you could inhale peace and strength and exhale negativity and anger.

8. Take a few more deep breaths and notice how you feel now. Remind yourself that you are enough, just as you are. You might even say it in your head or out loud: "I am beautiful. I am enough. I am strong." Even if it feels

strange or forced, the more you do this, the more you'll build kindness instead of judgment.

CHANGE IT UP

As you're noticing how you relate to your own body, notice if you're stuck in a pattern of checking out or critiquing other people. Observe how that makes you feel. You might try to send a silent compliment instead of a critique. Those kinder thoughts can actually have a very significant impact on your own mood and your relationship to others.

Making Choices about Technology

Did you know that tech companies deliberately make apps as addictive as possible? They spend billions of dollars researching ways to turn our phone use into a habit, something we can't live without even for five minutes. Some people call it "brain hacking." Phones aren't bad inherently, but they do become a problem when we check them without realizing it.

This meditation isn't about getting rid of the phone or

social media. It's about recognizing how technology makes you feel and then deciding to use it only because you choose to, not because someone wants you to be addicted.

1. Pause. Take a few deep breaths. Notice how you feel as you breathe deeply.

2. Let your breathing be normal.

3. Take a moment to check in with how you feel as you go on social media or use your phone. What happens to your body and mind when you see someone else's photo or image of a perfect vacation? What thoughts automatically run through your mind? What happens in your body? Notice your jaw, your stomach, and your throat. What sensations can you feel?

4. As you notice how this feels, you might also ask yourself, "How does this post or picture make me feel?" Let the answer come to you.

5. As you keep looking or keep checking your feed, notice if you're always wanting more, comparing yourself, or

perhaps telling yourself, "I'll be happy when I look like that . . ." Explore how these truly make you feel inside.

6. Let yourself be interested in this experience. It's not black and white. Observe all the nuances of what happens. Then you can decide how you want to proceed.

CHANGE IT UP

It seems ironic to suggest using an app to see how much you use other apps, but it can be really informative. Find an app that tracks your phone or social media use, and make the commitment to use it for three days. Notice what happens when you see the results. Did you know you were checking your phone that often? Then, you might try an experiment to you limit your phone use for a few days and see what happens. Notice how it feels. (Let your family and friends know what you're doing in advance, so they don't freak out.)

Taking Care of Yourself

Have you ever noticed that you can't focus when you're hungry? Or that your mood totally changes after you've gone for a walk or had a shower? How it's so much easier to get annoyed on an empty stomach? (That's why someone invented the word "hangry"!) It might seem rudimentary, but taking care of your own basic needs can change your mind-set, feelings, moods, emotions, and even levels of pain for an entire day. Use this practice as a way to check in with your basic needs before making judgments of yourself or your life.

1.If you find yourself starting to lose it, getting frustrated, wanting to run away, or getting really down on yourself, try to pause where you are and take a few deep breaths.

2.Let your breathing be natural and notice what you can feel with your senses. Feel your feet on the floor and the air on your skin. Notice what you hear and any tastes in your mouth.

3.Then check in with yourself. Before you judge yourself or give up, try to explore some of these questions:

Have I eaten enough today?

Have I drunk water in the last hour?

Could I use more sleep?

Have I gotten dressed today?

Have I showered?

Have I gone outside? Could I go for a walk?

Do I need a hug or connection with a friend?

Have I had any physical exercise at all today?

4. Whatever you need, make the decision to take care of yourself. If you can't do it right now, make a plan to do so when you are able. Remind yourself that whatever's going through your mind right now, you don't have to take it personally or give it too much focus. It's not you; it's hunger or fatigue or some other part of your system needing attention.

5. Once you tend to what you needed, notice how you

feel. Take the time to really enjoy the shower or the glass of water. Explore how the air outside feels or what happens when you do put your phone down and take a nap.

TAKE IT FURTHER

Write yourself a reminder for what you need when you get down. Do you need to wait a few days after starting something new before you make a judgment of it? Do you need to go for a walk when you feel depressed? You might make a playlist of songs that bring your mood up when you need them. Then, next time you're feeling down, you have your own tailor-made prescription for what to do.

What to Do If You Feel Overwhelmed

There is nothing wrong with you if you feel like you can't meditate, you're losing it, or you can't think straight! Sometimes your nervous system overreacts or gets triggered, which makes you feel overwhelmed or out of control. Whether this happens while you're meditating or during the rest of your day, you can use these techniques to rebalance yourself. Find one or two that feel right to you.

BREATHE: It's annoying, but there's a reason everyone tells you to breathe when you're anxious. A deep breath is a signal to your nervous system that there aren't any threats around.

LONGER EXHALATION: This is the ultimate body hack. If you can lengthen your exhalation, you cue your nervous system to tell your body to chill out. It calls for the release of hormones that relax the whole system. Try to breathe in for a count of three or four and breathe out for a count of six to eight. Find the rhythm that works for you.

ASK YOURSELF: "What's the kindest thing I can do for myself right now? What do I need right now that will be helpful?" Focus on things that are healthy and nonaddictive, like going for a walk, resting, or exercising, rather than turning to something that might feel good in the short term but is actually harmful in the long term (like using technology or social media or mind-altering substances).

FOCUS ON OTHER PEOPLE: Sometimes the best thing you can do is to consider what kindness you could show for someone else right now. It's amazing how focusing on others' happiness gets us out of our own ruts. It doesn't have to be big. Write a note of kindness—saying you're doing great or you got this—and leave it on someone's locker or car. Give a random person a compliment. Even pick up a few pieces of garbage.

FOCUS ON THE MOST NEUTRAL THING IN YOUR BODY: This is usually your feet on the ground. Really put all of your energy and focus into feeling your feet. Notice how many toes you can feel without wiggling them. You might walk slowly to really emphasize the sensations.

FOCUS ON SOMETHING PLEASANT: Find a spot outside a window or in the sky that looks pleasing. Focus on a flower. Or notice the sound of the wind or the sun on your face. Let yourself really soak in those feelings and linger on what is pleasant to your system. See the Soaking in the Good practice.

ORIENT TO YOUR ENVIRONMENT: That means looking around you, specifically moving your head and neck to see in front, to the sides, and behind you. Notice anything that catches your eye.

If overwhelming feelings arise while meditating and you feel fine to keep going, try to be with the feelings for a bit and then come back out again, like dipping your toe in the water before swimming. Try the Self-Soothing Practices.

TYPES OF TOOLS AND ACTIVITIES FOR SENSITIVE KIDS

Meditation Activities:

Here are several exercises and practices you can teach your ADHD child to help bring the body to relaxation – one of which is breathing. These include traditional meditation and the Chinese martial art of tai chi. Simply put, meditation is training a mind to relax so that it can focus on other things afterward. Many self-help books and business books recommend meditation to reduce stress and to prepare the mind for challenging tasks that might bring stress. The type of meditation you should teach your ADHD child should have its focus on helping your child loosen up, mellow out, and calm down.

Here's how to go about it:

• Move the body into a posture that opens the lungs, as well as stretch and relax the muscles.

• Close the eyes and envision certain images in the mind, with the objective of stopping the mind from racing or wandering so utmost concentration can be placed on controlled breathing.

Breathing In and Out Activities

The quickest way to change an AHD patient's mood is to change the breathing. Simply by focusing on your breathing, you can halt a cascade of inner events that cause anxiety and stress, both of which reduce your capacity to pay attention.

How to do it

• Focus your attention on your breath. Notice if it is quick or slow, shallow or deep.

- Continue breathing in and count to three.

- Exhale for a count of three. Continue to practice this conscious breathing for two minutes.

Sensory Activities

Poor working memory and forgetfulness are characteristic of children and teens with ADHD. In addition, if their attention was not engaged throughout the instruction, they may not remember a lot of what the teacher presented. Many people with ADHD also have coexisting learning disabilities in auditory or visual sequentiality is an excellent means of helping memorize and recall information. Teach and encourage children to create first- letter mnemonics (acronyms and acrostics), which are very helpful in remembering steps in a process or procedure, a sequence of any kind, or other information.

Pair unfamiliar new vocabulary with similar-

sounding familiar words

This is called the keyword mnemonic technique, which involves looking for ways items go together (perhaps they sound alike or look alike) to help remember.

Gratitude Activities

Sometimes it feels like walking on pins and needles. You think you've got it figured out. No tags or tight clothing. You know the lists of foods that wig them out.

Relish in Their Successes

It doesn't matter how small. This not only shows them that you care, but it's a great way to remind them that they can achieve and improve. It's also a good way to remind yourself of the good they do and the progress they make even if they still have a long way to go.

Chapter 5. Tips and Tricks to Improve the Effectiveness of Meditation

Meditation helps you relieve stress regardless of the technique you use to practice it. However, there are some tips and tricks that you can apply to enhance the results and increase its effectiveness. Follow the tips mentioned below to get enhanced results.

1: Meditate Twice a Day

If you want to see great results in a short period, then you need to make meditation a regular practice. The best time to meditate is at sunrise and sunset or 6am and 6pm. At these times, there are hardly any distractions and interruptions around you, which allows you to meditate easily and effectively.

In addition, you need to at least meditate twice a day. The effects of one small session of less than 30 minutes don't last for more than 12 hours. Therefore, to feel peaceful and relaxed at all times, it is best to meditate at least twice daily. If you meditate for around an hour and have quite a hectic routine, it's alright to meditate once a day too. However, make sure to stick to this practice and make it a routine. You can also use meditation during your working day in the manner I have suggested helping to calm you and to help you to concentrate on things that are important to you. Meditation awakens the mind and that can be very useful to you in your lunch break, but be sure to do it before you eat rather than trying to do so afterwards.

Secondly, always meditate at the exact same time. If you meditate at 5pm on the first two days, ensure to meditate at the exact time daily. This practice cultivates consistency and punctuality making you regular with meditation. What you may not realize is that habits are formed by repetition. This is true of any habit and adding the habit of meditation to another daily habit will help. This form of habit stacking has been proven to be very effective. What this means is listing things that you do every day at set times. For example, you get up at a set time – so you can meditate on it. You get home from work at a set time and probably sit down and have a coffee or a tea. You can choose this moment to meditate. The point is that with repetition each day of the habit of meditation it will become second nature and part of your daily routine.

In fact, with practice, you will easily get into meditation without trying too much since your body will know 'it is time to meditate' when that time comes. You should also turn off all distractions during your meditation time so that you can concentrate on just being instead of worrying about whether the phone will go off or someone will knock at the door. By choosing a meditation time, you also get those who live with you accustomed to respecting this time that you put to one side for meditation.

2: Eat something but don't be too full

Try to meditate on an empty stomach to easily focus on the practice. When you have just had a meal, your stomach is full, which often makes you lethargic. If you meditate at this time, you're likely to lose focus on the practice and drift off to sleep instead. You may also find that your digestive system makes it too difficult to sit still in the same position and concentrate on just being. Your stomach may be making noises and uncomfortable in an upright position.

However, if you feel really hungry at the time of your meditation session, then eat something light such as a fruit or a piece of chocolate so you can stay alert and concentrate on your meditation and don't become distracted during the practice due to an empty stomach. I always take a glass of water into the room with me as well as this may help to stave off any hunger or stop you from craving food during your practice.

3: Meditate at the Same Place

Try to dedicate one place to your meditation spot and don't do anything else there. By practicing meditation at the same spot every day and not doing anything else on that spot, you will naturally feel like meditating whenever you go to that spot. As a result, it will be a lot easier to build a habit of meditating when you have a dedicated spot that makes it very easy for you to get into meditation. As we have already mentioned, having a space set aside for meditation will make you more serious about the practice because you will have devoted the space to something you are trying to incorporate into your life and it will be wasted if you do not use it for that purpose. You may have to make adjustments if you find that you are getting sidetracked by noise or by too much light. You will find that perfect spot and when you do, will see the sense in having one particular place in which to meditate. It helps to reinforce the habit.

4: Minimize Interruptions

Put on a "do-not-disturb" sign on the door of your room before you start meditating. Also, switch off your cell phone to remain focused; if you can't do that, just put it on the silent mode so there is nothing that holds you back and you can completely focus on your practice. Minimizing interruptions will increase your concentration in your practice resulting in better performance. Let people know that this is a time when you need to be alone and need silence. Most people who are aware that you are doing this for your health will respect that you need to be alone. You can also put your phone on answering machine and place a sign on the door of your house to not disturb you for the next twenty minutes or so.

5: Write your Thoughts before Practicing Meditation

One thing that you are likely to struggle with as a beginner is experiencing distracting thoughts while meditating. You can escape this problem with a simple solution. Before starting the session, write down all the thoughts that cross your mind. By doing this, you tell yourself that you have this thought on record, which you will deal with later when the time is right. For instance, if you wrote everything that came to your mind including the thought of ironing your clothes as you won't get the time tomorrow as you have to leave for office early, it will be easy for you to focus. In fact, if this thought disturbs you, you can relax your mind by telling yourself that you have it on your notice and you will do it when the time is right. This comforts you and helps you return your attention to meditation.

Follow this writing of thoughts with an additional note of why you are meditating, to try and reinforce the idea. You can also add thoughts of things that you are grateful for before you meditate as this puts you in a positive state of mind.

Moreover, also create your meditation journal. Write down your feelings in it before and after meditating every day to understand how you felt after each session. A meditation journal also helps you to understand your weaknesses, which you can work for the next time. Do go through this journal once every week to track your performance and feel good about yourself. If you feel you're doing a great job, treat yourself to something nice to encourage yourself to meditate regularly and develop a habit of it.

Many people write an introductory prayer for their meditation which reminds them of the purpose of meditation and betterment of their approach. This is useful if you are finding it hard to find the incentive to concentrate over a period of time and feel that your efforts are not paying off. You may not feel the benefits straight away. It takes time and persistence, but once you make this a habit, it is certain that you will enjoy your meditation sessions and use them as a better way to get to know who you are and what you want out of life.

6: Use Mudras to get Enhanced Results

Mudras are hand or body positions that influence your

energy, mood and feelings. Mostly, the fingers and hands are held in some position, but your entire body can be used to form a mudra too. Here we will discuss some hand mudras to relieve stress and become happy, as it is believed your fingers have nerve connections that connect to different parts of your brain to produce different emotions. Here are some amazing mudras to let go of stress and become happy and peaceful.

1. Tse Mudra to relieve stress

Tse Mudra is well known and is considered as one of the best mudras to combat anxiety and depression. According to Chinese tradition, this mudra is practiced to drive away stress, sadness, fear and brings good luck. It is said that this mudra also increases your intuitive ability. Given below are images followed by the instructions on how to practice this mudra in your meditation.

- When you're sitting or lying in your comfortable position for meditation, place your thumbs on your thighs.

- Now put your thumb between your little and ring finger as you can see in the first picture. Do this with both hands.

- Now encircle your thumb with your other four fingers as you can see it in the second picture.

- Hold this position in your hands throughout your meditation session.

When you incorporate this mudra, you will notice that your stress levels drop more than when you meditate without this mudra.

2. Ksepana Mudra

It is also a very helpful mudra to improve the effectiveness of meditation as well as to increase your inner peace and happiness. This mudra is known for its magical powers to release all the negativity that is being ingested within your soul. You can use this mudra in your meditation especially in those cases where you had a very bad day and you are flooding with negative emotions. Given below is an image that shows the

Ksepana mudra along with instructions on how to incorporate this mudra into your meditation.

- When you start your session and get a comfortable posture, clasp both hands: all the fingers crossing each other.

- Then take out both index fingers and join their tips as you can see in the picture above.

- Now drop your hands pointing to the ground. Hold this position for at least 2 minutes, or you can hold it to the entire length of the session.

You will notice great effects after your session ends as the negative thoughts that were flowing through your mind before the session will have greatly reduced.

3. Prana Mudra

Practicing Prana mudra is a good way to collect energy from the universe. Therefore, you can use this mudra to get energized, brighten up your mood and reduce your stress levels. Use this mudra on days when you feel drained out and you don't feel like doing anything because of the energy deficiency. See the picture and instructions below to learn how to practice this mudra.

- When you get settled for meditation in your comfortable position, join your thumb little and ring finger together as you can see in the picture above and extend your index and middle finger outwards as shown in the picture.

- Then hold your hands either in a horizontal or vertical position.

- Keep holding the posture for at least 5 minutes or for the entire duration of your meditation session. Once you complete your session, you will notice that you feel energy running through your body that was not there when you started your session.

4. Lotus Mudra

Lotus mudra is a symbol of purity. In Buddhism, lotus position of hands is reserved to represent the opening of the heart. When you face rejection; you close your heart by slouching your shoulders and collapsing your chest. In other words, you make yourself unavailable to others when you're in stress which raises the tension between your peers and others close to you. As a result, you feel more stressed out when others neglect you because of your behavior.

By incorporating lotus mudra in your meditation, you open your heart to others and in return others return the favor and show gratitude to you, which ultimately reduces your stress levels and makes you happier than ever.

Use this mudra in cases where you find yourself in stressful situations because others are being rude to you. Given below are the instructions along with an image on how to perform this mudra.

- When you start your meditation session, join both hands in a way that your thumb meets your other thumb and your baby finger meets your other baby finger and both palms meet each other at the bottom. It will make a position of a flower in bloom.

- Hold this position throughout your session. You will feel a considerable change in the behavior of your peers and others close to you. When everybody is showing your gratitude, your mood will automatically lighten up and your stress levels go down.

Practice all the mentioned tips and tricks to enhance the effectiveness of your meditation sessions. Whichever route you take to fight your stress and anxiety, just remember one thing- change occurs with time but staying persistent is the key to accomplish and enjoy those changes and turn those temporary changes into everlasting ones. Therefore, keep fighting your stress through practicing meditation regularly and you will ultimately defeat your stress to live a happy and peaceful life.

Chapter 6. Guided Mindfulness Meditations for Deep Sleep

Guide Meditation to Improve Insomnia

Sleep has been a significant issue in the whole world. Many people have insomnia, and this affects their average productive level. Insomnia is a condition feared by many. People who practice mindfulness meditation can fight off this condition. They can fall asleep sooner and stay for long in bed.

Meditation can also reduce pain. It has the power to control any discomfort, be it emotional or psychological. People have perceptions connected to their state of mind. Attitudes like these elevate in the presence of stressful conditions. When you meditate, you will have more activities going on in the part of the brain that controls pain. You will also have less pain sensitivity.

Lastly, meditation is essential in weight loss since it directly involves the mind. The mind will then form perceptions to a particular food as well as start releasing positive thought to healthy food since a healthy mind means a healthy body and soul. Through guided meditation, you can change your eating habits, lifestyle, and even healthy health choices like exercise.

Deciding to stop your bad eating habits is not a onetime thing but can be done gradually by incorporating healthy foods in the diet. The brain triggers the mind to eat, and food cravings also come from the mind. If the mind can accept that there is a need to eat healthily and live positive, so will the brain be triggered towards healthy eating. Weight loss is necessary for healthy living and can keep you away from the many lifestyle diseases, many of which are not curable.

There is a lot of patience involved since it is not the easiest and fastest step towards weight loss but workable none the less. Meditation will help you clear your mind and reduce dependence on food that makes you feel beautiful yet not healthy. This is because the mind is cleared of negative emotions that can be an element of distraction or stress. It is like a painless stress reliever without medication or therapy. It brings weight loss naturally over the long term and creates a very positive and acceptable self-image and self-view.

Guided meditations are not all the same: it depends on the purpose you want to achieve through this practice. Do you just want to relax? Fight insomnia? Become more resilient? Accept a major change? Lose weight?

In most guided meditations, it's essential to try to use as many senses as you can: the smells, the lights, the sounds, the textures. Usually guided meditations have a musical background that invites the mind and body to relax: sounds of nature such as rain, rainforest, sea waves or the sound of a waterfall; or more traditional music like that of the Native American characterized by the sound of flutes, tubes and rattles.

Choose the musical background you prefer, what is important is to create the best condition to relax. To start, you can do a very quick guided meditation for beginners. The basic principle is to pay attention to what you do, always keep it in mind from the beginning to the end of the practice. Close your eyes and start taking three deep breaths, inhaling through your nose and exhaling from your mouth.

When you breathe in you are full of positive energy and when you exhale all kinds of negative energies, such as stress, tension and worries, abandon you. Find your breath and feel your body. Simply observe it (Headspace, n. d.).

Guide Meditation for Depression, Anxiety Relief

Everyone probably experiences stress at some level in their lives. Nearly half of the adult population suffers from its adverse effects. Among these effects include anxiety, depression, arthritis, asthma, high blood pressure, skin conditions, heart problems, and headaches. 75 to 90 percent of doctor visits are because of stress-related issues. When chronic stress is untreated, it can lead to emotional disorder.

Life could really get so stressful, and these days, it's important to find ways to relieve stress without using too much money, or creating more hassle.

One of these ways is hypnotherapy. Research has it that hypnotherapy is one of the best ways of relieving stress, especially for children and teens dealing with anxiety issues. It is said that with the help of hypnosis, feelings of helplessness are lessened and that it's proven to be even greater than that of other traditional relaxation techniques.

It is actually common for kids aged 11 to 15 to develop

and experience signs of panic attacks and anxiety. If one wants these experiences to be lessened, he has to learn how to target them right away, then one should at least try going through hypnosis.

A person who has been in a serious automobile accident may have no recollection of it. They may be perfectly fine with no memory loss or impairment. Yet, they are simply unable to recall anything about the accident.

In this case, the conscious mind has taken the memories of a traumatic event, an automobile accident, and archived them in the subconscious mind. By doing this, the mind is protecting the individual from having to relive the traumatic experience over and over.

Nevertheless, archiving the memories does not mean that they don't exist. The fact that they have been put on the shelf does not mean that they are not there, festering beneath the surface. So, while you are going about your day to day life, you may not experience any ill feelings. Yet, there are moments when certain triggers bring up such emotions. When this happens, your body's stress levels may begin to rise, along with other symptoms such as anxiety. Underlying, subconscious causes may also lead to depression.

A qualified hypnotist is unable to use hypnotic techniques in order to access your subconscious. When this happens, you are able to express your feelings and reveal what is truly affecting you. The way that a hypnotherapist gets you into a "trance" is through the use of a combination of relaxation and suggestion. There are no gimmicks or tricks like in the movies.

In essence, hypnosis is a state of deep relaxation in which your conscious mind shuts off. This enables the subconscious mind to emerge. At this point, the hypnotherapist would be able to determine what issues may be affecting you. At that point, you can begin addressing them through the conscious mind.

However, there is a caveat: when buried feelings begin to emerge, you must have proper counseling and support. The reason for this is that you may not be able to cope with these feelings on your own. As such, you will need to count with professional help so you can process such feelings and learn to manage them.

The biggest benefit of this course of action is that you will be able to identify what is affecting you. Therefore, you will be able to deal with these feelings and the corresponding physical symptoms which may be leading you to struggle with your weight. Most importantly, you will be able to heal emotional blockages which may have been lodged there for years.

Frequently taken medications for treating migraines, blood pressure, seizures, and depression, when used in excessive amounts—more than prescribed by your doctor—can lead to weight loss in addition to various other physical and mental health issues.

Stress is an emotion alters our body chemistry, and this changes our eating habits. When our bodies are under stress, more hormones are produced. These hormones depend on the degree of stress you have. In acute stress, your body releases epinephrine, whereas, in chronic stress, it releases corticotrophin.

Acute stress can be experienced in situations that are very dangerous, while chronic stress may occur in situations like separation, mourning, or anxiety. Stress can as well stop the body from releasing important hormones and at the same time, stimulate it to release others. When our bodies release cortisol and epinephrine in excess, it is a signal for preparing the body for action. These hormones push our system to get ready to handle a difficult situation or to run away from it as it is beyond our capability. Either of the above reactions could keep you alive or diminish the threat. Our emotions are affected by our brain and body, and at the same time, our brain and body affect our emotions.

For instance, when cortisol is released in excess, it affects metabolism. Energy is directed to our major parts of the body to prepare them for action. I know we have all been in a do or die situation, and we can all remember the energy we felt in our bodies; your heartbeat also increased, but the adrenaline did not last.

Our systems have a feedback cycle such that when the emergency is handled, the body starts releasing cortisol at its normal rate. This system is also influential to cortisol itself as it self-shuts itself. When cortisol goes to the brain, it gives it a command to stop the body from producing more of it. In the case of chronic stress, the system runs throughout, and it does not shut.

You find the production of cortisol keeps continuing and this makes us feel anxious or depressed. In periods when we are stressed, the brain gives instructions to the body to release some chemicals to handle the stress.

These chemicals affect our emotion center of the brain. Other than the influences of the brain chemicals on our emotions, other physiological influences alter our emotions.

These influences are the nutrients we get from food and access to fat deposits by the body. It is made possible by the location of the liver making it get abdominal fat and break it down to produce energy.

Nevertheless, when you have chronic stress, it is not easy to break down those fats quickly and at the same time, replace what is being used.

Therefore, the body tends to look for a quick replacement in fatty and sugary foods.

They replace the exhausted energy reserves and also comfort our emotions because of their high palatability.

These fatty foods may reduce stress in some of us, but when we over-consume them, we become obese. The psychological characteristics that help you to choose the comfort food of your choice are depression, neuroticism, premenstrual dysphoria, and sufferers of emotional eating. We can also note that the size of our meals and the content in it depend on the consumer's needs, expectations, and habits.

In regards to our discussion above, we have noted that what we eat is determined by neurotransmitters and hormones.

We can get different habits, depending on the degree of stress.

We eat food to replace the exhausted energy reserves due to chronic stress. Different individuals react differently to stress. For instance, one study by Oliver showed us that stress did not change the food quantity the participants consumed but that the participants with emotional eating disorders ate more of the comfort foods than those without stress or the eating disorder.

If our immediate response to the body demands during stressing periods were food, we would not be having so many cases of obesity. The problem lies in the type of food we run to consume to comfort us. Most obese and overweight people prefer foods that contribute to their conditions.

Therefore, food reduces stress, and it also produces it due to psychological and physiological problems. Different studies have found that some people select food because of their chemical effects, while others choose to meet their emotional needs as a response to stress. Emotional eaters eat more fatty, salty, or sugary foods as opposed to the belief that they eat food in large quantities. Finally, the relation between food and emotion is demonstrated well in a stressful situation. Stress has the power to alter our eating habits.

Just like in the case of weight, stress, and anxiety can induce in you weird eating habits that include overeating and under-eating.

This happens when you do not find an effective way of dealing with stress. Constantly eating because you are stressed has the same effect as alcohol. You will eat all you want, but when the food is digested and assimilated, your stress or anxiety will come back, maybe with an even higher intensity.

The food you eat because you think it will reduce stress is not normally healthy and balanced. A careful observation of such eating habits shows the kind of food that is eaten by the individual is mostly junk food, and the eating itself is irregular.

The other aspect of eating habits related to stress is eating less than the recommended amount or starving yourself. This is already a disaster before arrival. This is not only bad for your body health; it can also worsen your stress and anxiety level. Either way, you will always be alternating between a starvation/binge eating and stress.

During the fight/flight response, which is activated by adrenaline in the event of a threat or danger, we tend to get active and fidgety. Anxiety kicks in, and you feel wired-up as adrenaline responds to the threat of stress.

You find that you feel unsettled, and you may begin to run around anxiously, reaching out for a solution. Such anxiety triggers emotional eating. In an attempt to calm down, you find yourself eating or overeating unhealthy foods. This is a prevalent response to stress.

Anxiety makes you eat mindlessly, and you find yourself eating more without getting satisfied. You cannot even tell how much you have eaten because you are busy churning worrisome and stressful thoughts around your head, to the point where you cannot even focus on the taste of your food.

You eat more emotionally, and less mindfully when you are anxious and stressed, and you feel less satisfied, however more you may eat. This emotional and anxious overeating leads to weight gain.

Anxiety and stress can make someone engage in binge eating. One may go through a stressful event like losing a loved one or losing all his/her property and results in binge eating. Eating emotionally is not permanent, and it may, at times, not be binge eating.

A person who is anxious about a particular event or situation may result in binge eating. People who are anxious or stressed about something are more likely to binge eat. Binge eating can be caused by a stressful ordeal or a situation that makes one be anxious.

Relaxation Scripts

The art of relaxation is a state of mind. In other, you need to set your thoughts in such a way that leisure is essential. Even when you are eating, you can`t just keep consuming all the time.

You need to relax and take some break that will help your mind settle and think of other things.

The minds also need to shift from one aspect to the other. In other words, if you keep doing something for long, there are chances that you will get bored and hate it. In the same way, you can`t eat for more than an hour and expect that all is well. Even your jaws, let alone your teeth need to relax and prepare for another meal.

Also, if the snack is so sweet, there are chances that you

can't take all the time and eat everything at a go. You need to relax and allow the process of digestions to swallow, let alone.

Several studies have been carried out to determine the effects of failing to relax while eating. It is worth noting that if you eat without allowing your gut to shallow well, there are chances that you will be choked.

There are other cases where one fails to register in the brain that one is full since they are not relaxing. In other words, if your minds do not have time to relax, there are some complications that one may develop. For instance, people who develop the disorder of binge eating do not improve the condition in a single day.

However, it occurs gradually such that the minds fail to register that one is full. The desire to keep eating develops, and one thinks of eating rather than deducing anything else. They are the kind of people who will prefer eating at night, during the day and at any time. The art of eating in such a manner is not right as the mind does not relax.

One of the primary reasons that cause the brain or rather the body to develop the urge of relaxation is the fact that when one relaxes, there are several cells that rejuvenate, and one gains more energy from the tasks ahead of them.

One of the best methods that individuals prefer relaxing with is sleeping. After toiling for several hours, preferably after eating, a lot of people prefer sleeping so as they can relax. In other cases, it may lie down on a mat and reflect on what has been going on.

The art of relaxing is essential in the sense that it allows one to have some more time to think of the things that can be done for life or rather the eating habits. Relaxation is essential as one will have some ample time to analyze whether the food is taken or the activities being done were achieved in the right way.

The other aspect that people consider as a means of relaxing exercises. After having a heavy meal, the best means of relaxing is taking a ball or any other item that will help you do some exercise. It is worth noting that when you exercise, the body graves for more energy. In other words, your body will require more energy to sustain the exercises.

Thus, the food taken will be broken down quickly, and you will have more reasons for eating again after a period of six to eight hours.

Scholars have identified that people who can exercise from time to time have some of the nest digestion processes. In other words, there are not affected by issues of digestion or rather complications that develop from improper digestion. The food they take is well broken down and converted into energy that is required in the exercises.

Mind games are the best means of relaxing after a heavy meal. Although some snacks encourage one to sleep, a mind game plays a critical role in ensuring that all the food is broken down quickly.

It is worth noting that the brain uses a lot of energy to deliberate in a task.

For instance, when you are playing a game such as chess,

you will be required to think and think well. It is worth noting that when you are considering as such, the energy consumed is more than the power you would use to lift a certain weight deliberately. Therefore, a mind game will play a critical role in allowing your mind or rather your body to relax and regain the strength of doing other activities. In other words, even after eating, the body requires some time to relax. Relaxation helps the cell as well as the tissues of an individual to regain some aspects of healing for the future.

For instance, if one has been eating, there are chances that there were some cells destroyed in the mouth, let alone the alimentary canal. One may require some more time to heal and regain the strength of eating again.

Relaxation is essential.

The how and the, when to relax, depends on the type of food taken or the activity that one was engaged with previously. For instance, if you have been doing some hard labor, there are cases where you might feel that you need to lie down and relax.

In addition, if you have been sitting down for long, there are chances that you will need some exercises to help you relax. The aspect is linked to the fact that when you stretch, you allow your cells to relax and prepare for the next activity or instead of the other session. Also, if you have been sitting in a class for long, there are chances that your body needs some time to relax. In such a situation, after eating, the best method of relaxing is engaging in one exercise.

The aspect is critical in the sense that you will have time to stretch and regain some of the energy loss when you are sited. He minds to regain its strength, and you will be in a good position to grasp more of what your teacher is saying.

People react differently to hypnosis. Some are able to continue a conversation while hypnotized. Some people feel a complete sense of detachment from their surroundings. Others experience a heightened sense of relaxation which removes all stress. Whereas, other people have described their state of mind as feeling outside their conscious choice, giving them a feeling of complete control from their hypnotist.

Only 10% of adults are difficult to hypnotize and if you are a person who loves to fantasize and have a vivid imagination, you will do well.

Hilgard is a well-known theory. Hilgard's neodissociation theory suggests that people in a hypnotic state experience a split consciousness. One mental stream of activity focuses on suggestion and the other gathers information outside of your conscious awareness.

There are common myths about hypnotism I would like to discredit, these are simply untrue. The first myth is the one that is most common. The myth claims that you will have no memory of your hypnotized state. This myth blows things out of proportion because amnesia only occurs in rare cases. Then there is posthypnotic amnesia which is a temporary state. Posthypnotic amnesia can make you forget things that happened just before or after hypnosis.

Your memory will come back. Don't allow this to deter you. Another common myth says that you can be hypnotized against your will. This is a blatant lie. An untruth that was made famous by movies and fiction. The myth where people lose control is another myth I would like to tell you about. Remember there is a difference between hypnosis and mentalism. Hypnotism requires you to participate willingly.

You are in constant control during a hypnosis session. So please don't believe any of these myths (Cherry, 2019).

I would like to focus on using combined techniques for hypnosis for this audio guide. One of these techniques is solution-focused hypnotherapy (SFH). This form of hypnotherapy is a combined effort between the hypnotist and yourself. I find it easier to work toward a solution rather than running away from a problem.

Set yourself a goal and take small steps forward. Don't crucify yourself for being a smoker. Instead, use hypnosis to become a non-smoker with time and effort. Another technique is behavioral hypnotherapy. This form of hypnosis is used to modify future behavior and habits. Hypnosis bypasses your conscious mind and allows you to speak to your subconscious mind directly.

Changing behavior is like planting a seed.

The deeper the inception goes, the more likely it is to stick and grow. And last but not least, I will use inspiration from cognitive hypnotherapy as well. Cognitive hypnotherapy focuses on the thoughts and emotions attached to certain behavior.

I will approach hypnosis using a combination of these three techniques. Behavioral hypnotherapy will focus on your behavior but you will benefit from understanding the emotion attached to that behavior through cognitive hypnotherapy. Using these two techniques combined with solution-focused hypnotherapy allow you to see your end goal and strive for it (Fulcher, 2018).

Now that you understand hypnosis better, I want you to understand the benefits of hypnosis. Let's look at a few examples of how hypnosis can help you.

Fear or phobia has a debilitating effect on your mind and body and hypnosis can help you overcome your fear. Fear plays a major role in your approach to social experiences or trying something new. Your fear affects your confidence when approaching a new person or when you have to get up on stage. Stage fright is definitely a form of fear. Fear also holds you back from skydiving for the first time because you over-analyze the possible outcomes. Thinking about everything that can go wrong before you jump. Being afraid of public speaking can affect your chances of acing your job interview too.

Another great advantage of hypnotism is to quit an addiction. People who want to quit smoking are the most frequent newcomers to the world of hypnotism. Add hypnotherapy to your current methods of trying to quit. As a matter of fact, it is advised by the National Center for Complementary and Integrative Health.

Hypnosis is also a great approach to anxiety and stress. Stress and anxiety can affect you physically and mentally. They can break you down and weaken your mind. A weakened mind is vulnerable to future stress and anxiety. Being anxious will prevent you from living the life you want to. Let's help you live the life you deserve (Russel, 2018).

Another key benefit of hypnosis is deep sleep. Deep sleep is essential to your mind's well-being. Without enough deep sleep, your brain struggles to function. Insomnia is not only defined as the loss of sleep but it's also defined as the loss of sleep quality. Millions of people are affected by insomnia worldwide. To combat this problem through hypnosis, we need to understand what deep sleep is.

There are two main categories of sleep. One is called rapid eye movement (REM), the other is called non-REM sleep. Your body and mind cycles through both stages in a regular pattern when you sleep. You will cycle through these stages a few times in a single night. Hypnosis will teach you to regulate this pattern so you can achieve more deep sleep. Deep sleep helps your brain recover from thinking and is essential to your mind's health. Deep sleep encourages your pituitary glands to secrete human growth hormones to help tissues in your body grow and regenerate. This leaves you feeling refreshed when you wake up.

A mind that doesn't gain enough deep sleep in one day, will compensate the next day by cycling through your sleep pattern rapidly. This will deprive your brain of the stable pattern your mind needs. Your brain will find it difficult to store memories and retain information. Hypnosis can increase the amount of time you spend in deep sleep by 80%. Deep sleep is also called slow-wave sleep (Mozes, 2014).

You feel another gentle, warm touch on your skin. Trust my voice and don't be afraid. Keep breathing deeply in through your nose and slowly out through your pursed lips. Blow the air out gently each time. Listen to your heart beating. One, two three, four, and five. Feel yourself soaking up the sunlight. Each ray touching your skin is more gentle, more calm. Each ray, a perfect amount of warm.

Notice how calm you are. No wind is blowing, only your breath. The soft, gentle sand kissing your skin from beneath. The warm, refreshing water tickling your toes from the sea. The sun dancing warmly off your skin from above. Count with me in your mind. One, two, three, four, and five. Every number is two heartbeats. Breathe in deeply with every two beats and breathe out slowly with another two beats. Feel your mind transcend further into relaxation. You are so comfortable, more comfortable than you have ever been before.

Keep your focus on my voice. Remember to feel every

beat of your heart pumping relaxation through your veins. Breathe in through your nose and out through your mouth, slowly. You can see something now but you are unsure what you see.

Notice how your heart keeps the gentle rhythm as you look closer at this unknown image you see. Every word is spoken, transcends you deeper. You are so comfortable and calm. Fear has no place anymore.

This unknown image beckons you, closer and closer. You feel drawn to the unknown image in a welcoming way. Listen to your heartbeat. One, two, three, four, and five. Breathe deeply through your nose and hold your breath for a moment. Count to three and release your breath slowly.

Remember to purse your lips lightly as you do so.

Sleep Scripts

In order to properly set yourself up for a meditation

experience, you need to make sure that you have a quiet space where you can engage in your meditation. You want to be as uninterrupted as possible so that you do not stir awake from your meditation session. Aside from having a quiet space, you should also make sure that you are comfortable in the space that you will be in.

For some of the meditations, I will share, you can be lying down or doing this meditation before bed so that the information sinks in as you sleep. For others, you are going to want to be sitting upright, ideally with your legs crossed on the floor, or with your feet planted on the floor as you sit in a chair.

Staying in a sitting position, especially during morning meditations, will help you stay awake and increase your motivation. Laying down during these meditations earlier in the day may result in you draining your energy and feeling completely exhausted, rather than motivated. As a result, you may actually work against what you are trying to achieve.

Each of these meditations is going to involve a visualization practice; however, if you find that visualization is generally difficult for you, you can simply listen. The key here is to make sure that you keep as open of a mind as possible so that you can stay receptive to the information coming through these guided meditations.

Aside from all of the above, listening to low music, using a pillow or a small blanket, and dressing in comfortable loose clothing will all help you have better meditations. You want to make sure that you make these experiences the best possible so that you look forward to them and regularly engage in them. As well, the more relaxed and comfortable you are, the more receptive you will be to the information being provided to you within each meditation.

This is a great meditation to engage in during the day anywhere from one to three times per week, or at bedtime.

They say that meditating right before you fall asleep can be particularly potent, as you are meditating during a time where your subconscious mind is particularly active, and your conscious mind is already beginning to fall asleep. During this time, you are most likely to experience the level of relaxation and receptivity that is needed for your subconscious mind to really digest the changes that you are seeking to make within it.

"You'll fall into a deep sleep soon". I am sure you have heard this famous phrase. Well, Bonnie has. She considered hypnosis something mysterious or half-serious and a half-spiritual ritual that she had absolutely no intention of trying. She hadn't even believed that her problem had roots in her subconscious.

It was Evelin who convinced her about the benefits of this practice after an incredible change in her. One day she met one of her ex-dates from the past before her marriage, George who had become a famous therapist and offered some free sessions to her for old times' sake.

Evelin talked about her marriage, her divorce and how she let herself go. George proposed hypnotherapy to reveal the underlying problems and ultimately induce her subconscious toward wanting to be beautiful again and losing weight. After some months of hard work, Evelin started to change. She became braver and more confident. She became wonderful. It was about her radiance in the beginning.

It was like she started knowing who was she in reality and it gave her spirit. After a short time, she began experiencing another benefit as well: she lost weight (and gained love). She lost a lot of weight. She returned to her pre-divorce shape.

As a good mother, she wanted the same happy results for her daughter, but first, she had to overcome Bonnie's skepticism about hypnosis. That's why it was necessary to make some notes about the material, as we will do in this part of the book.

When we are asleep, the brain waves slow down and produce the so-called delta frequency waves. When it reveals relatively higher frequency vigilance, this is called beta frequency waves. Research has shown that brain waves are at theta frequency during hypnosis. In the theta frequency, there is both a level of subconscious awareness as well as a high concentration in sleep.

It has been noticed that theta frequency occurs more

frequently in the brains of people who are more susceptible to hypnosis. Besides, some researchers claim that hypnotizability is inherited and strongly conditioned by the presence of specific genes (Adachi, Jensen, Lee, Miró, Osman, Tomé-Pires, 2016).

Sleep induction isn't a truth serum in the real world. Even though during subliminal therapy, you are progressively open to a recommendation, regardless, you have through and through freedom and good judgment. Nobody can make you state anything you would prefer not to say — lie or not.

In a word, the genuine brains behind the strategy are your subliminal personality—it does the greater part of your reasoning, and it settles on a ton of choices about what you are doing. Your cognizant personality works when you're conscious of evaluating a great deal of these considerations, settling on decisions, and setting a few thoughts in motion. It likewise procedures and transfers crisp information to the subliminal personality. In any case, the cognizant personality escapes the way when you're sleeping, and your subliminal has a free rule.

Specialists pose that sleep induction's significant unwinding and focusing activities capacity to quiet and quell the cognizant personality to take a less dynamic part in your procedure of reasoning. You are as yet mindful of what is happening in this state. However, your cognizant personality takes your intuitive personality rearward sitting arrangement. This empowers you and the subliminal specialist to work with the intuitive legitimately. It seems as though the technique for trancelike influence is opening up a control board inside your mind.

Insomnia can result from stress, poor eating habits, and bad sleeping habits. When it occurs, you might have difficulties sleeping at night, waking up in the middle of the night, feeling sleepy during the day, or lack of concentration.

You find that the main reason an individual lacks sleep is due to some mental and emotional issues that they are going through. When it occurs, it results in a lot of anxiety, depression, or stress. All these are mental issues that can be controlled by having a change of mindset. As you meditate, you analyze the various challenges that you are going through.

In that process, you realize the causes of the challenges and the effects that they have on your mental wellbeing. At the same time, you can come up with some possible solutions to the problem at hand.

When you adopt a routine of regularly meditating, you will realize a lot of change in your sleep life. You will find it easier to rest since your mind is at peace, and it helps you in overcoming stress.

Chapter 7. Bedtime Meditations For Kids

The following are sample meditation scripts that you can teach your kids.

The Relaxing Warm Water

Start by finding a position that you are comfortable in, and of course, your favorite couch or chair in your house.

Make sure that your chair or couch is big enough to allow you to sit down with your legs crossed and that it has a soft and fluffy cushion so you will not feel any discomfort later.

Take three long breaths and as you are breathing, imagine that relaxation and comfort is slowly flowing towards you, like warm water slowly hugging your body and then entering you so you feel warm and comfortable inside too. Begin with your eyelids, try to feel the pleasant warm water pressing against it, and imagine that it is slowly climbing up to your forehead. Now, it flows up into your head and covers your hair, then, it falls at the back of your neck and as it touches it, your neck begins to start relaxing.

The relaxing warm water is now flowing down your face, making your cheeks a bit warm and loosening your jaw. Your teeth are unclenched, and all of the muscles in your head and neck are relaxed. If you find the water to be a bit heavy on top of your head, imagine moving it further down to your shoulders or wherever you want it to be so long as you feel comfortable. Let the warm, relaxing water flow down from your shoulders and in to your arms. As it touches your shoulders and arms, the muscles start to loosen up and you feel as if your arms are floating in water. They are light and do not drag down your shoulders.

The water flows all the way down, hugging your elbows, and then your hands. It reaches your fingers and wraps your fingertips in its warmth and comfort. Each of your fingers are feeling warm, and the water is slipping in between. Your fingers become submerged in it, and the warmth embraces each one of them.

Any tension that you feel in your arms, your shoulder, your neck, head, and fingers start melting away. The melting tension turns into mist and floats away from your body. The muscles in your back, your spine, and your tailbone, start to unclench as the warm water embraces them. The warm water flows along both sides of your spine like a stream and makes a warm puddle at your tailbone. Your body can now sink a little bit more into the chair, into the puddle of warm water that has covered you in a warm, relaxing hug.

Your chest and stomach area are loosening up, and your

breathing starts slowing down as you feel the warmth creep inside your chest. You begin to feel very comfortable as the warmth travels down to your stomach and rests there, like your favorite hot drink. After it settles in your stomach, it then flows further down, wrapping your thighs, your knees, and then your lower legs and feet. The warmth creeps in between your toes. You begin to feel that even the smallest muscles in your feet are slowly relaxing, as if the water was massaging your soles.

Your feet feel as if you have worn a pair of very tight shoes all day long, and you have just removed those shoes and dipped your feet into warm water. Every breath you slowly take, in, out, in, out, makes you feel more and more relaxed. All the tension in your legs are being pushed down to the soles of your feet every time you inhale, and every time you exhale, the remaining tension comes out of your mouth or nose as warm mist.

After freeing your entire body from all the tension that it had, imagine that you are slowly standing up from the couch and walking towards your door. You feel very light, as if your entire body has just been thoroughly massaged and you have bathed in a warm bathtub for a long time. As you open the door, instead of seeing the usual place outside your house, you are now transported to a beautiful beach.

The sun is shining brightly but it does not feel hot. You can feel the cool breeze caressing your entire body, the sand under your toes softly embraces them, you can hear the ocean waves or the calls of your favorite birds in the beach, and you can smell the salty smell of the sea in the air. You could be alone in this beach, or if you want, you could also be with your favorite friends, siblings, parents, cousins, or neighbors. You can also add any animal that you want to add and imagine them laying around the sand, enjoying the warm sunlight and the cool sea breeze. The sea can be either wavy or very, very calm, like a sheet of metal reflecting the sun. Today is the most perfect day to be outside in the beach.

Find a place in the beach where you feel most comfortable in and sit down and rest. You can sit or lay down in the sand, and nothing in the world can affect you. You have left your problems behind. No one can disturb you here, and everyone that are present in the beach are people that you love to be around with. Your place in the beach is very peaceful and very comfortable. You feel the sand as you sit or lie down, and the warmth from the sun is hugging you very gently. The sound of the waves and the birds lightly fill your ears as you slowly close your eyes and let the relaxation and comfort embrace you.

Inside you, the warmth from the sun starts to glow out, and you feel that your skin is slowly warming up from the inside. Your chest, your stomach, your legs, and your back are slowly coated in warm sunlight both inside and outside, and your head is light, as if it is a cloud floating the sky. The warmth from inside slowly spreads out to your arms, legs fingertips, toes, and even to the tips of your ears and hair. You notice that the palms of your hands are becoming warmer, like you have just been holding a warm bowl with your favorite soup in it. Allow this warmth to stay and flow throughout your body as you listen to the pleasant ocean waves and feel the cool sea breeze lightly touching your skin.

After a moment, we start traveling back home. Imagine yourself slowly standing u p and opening your eyes, then following the path that you walked before to get to your house's door. As you open the door, imagine yourself smiling and returning to your couch where you were sitting or lying down, and very gently, open your eyes. Count slowly from 1 to 10 as you look at the room and take a deep breath and exhale.

An Adventure in Ice Cream World

Find somewhere you can sit comfortably in. Slowly close your eyes and take a deep breath and exhale very slowly. Do these five times with your eyes still closed. Today, you will be going to a palace made of your favorite delicious ice cream, chocolates, cakes, and candies.

Imagine standing up and walking outside your house. Outside, you see a lot of hills, but instead of grass, the hills are coated with your favorite flavor of ice cream. The hills are like giant scoops of that ice cream, and you rush towards them. You take off your shoes or slippers and you feel the ground. It is fluffy and a bit cold but the cold does not hurt your feet. The smell of your favorite ice cream flavor covers the air, and the sunlight is very bright but not hot at all.

You dig your hands in the ice cream ground, and you take a bite, tasting that very delicious and cool flavor. After one bite however, you hear the sound of a stream. When you look down form where you are standing, you see that the stream is made up of warm melted chocolate. You take a deep breath, you close your eyes, and you slide down the ice cream hill.

At the stream, you smell the rich chocolatey air and you dip one finger into the stream. The melted chocolate is warm, and it tastes like your favorite chocolate in the entire world. You see your favorite cup beside your feet, and you pick it up, then dip it into the chocolate river. You close your eyes and take in the rich smell of the chocolate. You breathe in and out and relax yourself, before taking a sip of the drink. A cold wind blows under you and your feet are suddenly feeling cold. You dip them into the warm melted chocolate stream and you instantly feel much better. You leave your feet in the stream, relaxing in the warmth, and lay back while closing your eyes, enjoying the feel of gentle sunlight and a cool breeze touching your skin. The smell of your favorite ice cream flavor and your favorite chocolate fill the air, and you smile while laying back and warming up your feet in the stream.

After taking five deep breaths, slowly inhaling the pleasant-smelling air and very gently exhaling it from your mouth, imagine that you are now standing up. The warm chocolate is slowly melting away from your feet, and every time you take a step, you leave behind a chocolate footprint on the ice cream ground. After you walk for a bit, you see your favorite snow pants hanging on a tree, but the tree does not have leaves. Instead, it is covered with all of the candies that you like most in the world. You take the snow pants and wear it. It feels very warm and you feel the muscles in your legs relax when they touch the fabric of the pants.

Up another hill, you see a banana boat, and a gentle slope. You feel excited, as you run towards the boat and find a comfortable seat. As you sit inside the boat, you notice that the boat inside is very pleasantly warm and comfortable, and your lower body slowly relaxes as if you were sitting in a bathtub filled halfway with warm water.

You gently close your eyes, breathe in through your nose, and out again in your nose. You do this very slowly five more times. You then imagine opening your eyes and seeing the thrilling slope that will surely give you a fantastic ride. At the bottom where you will land, the ground is made up of giant soft fluffy marshmallows.

You put your hands at each side of your hips, and very slowly, you begin to push towards the boat towards the slope. You whoosh past everything, making all the ice cream hills and candy trees disappear in a blur, and you laugh as the cool air hits your face and sends your hair back. The bottom is still a bit far so you close your eyes and you smile a very wide smile. You feel the air going into your mouth and you try to inhale it. The air mixes with the butterflies in your stomach and you feel giddy and very happy. When you open your eyes, you see that the giant marshmallows are already coming closer and closer. When the boat hit the marshmallow, you get thrown off and you bounce in the marshmallow. You feel exhilarated. That was such an exciting slide.

You smile widely and you take in slow breaths as you lie down on the soft fluffy marshmallows. You close your eyes and you feel your back and your shoulders sink a bit into the marshmallow like they would when you lie down in a very fluffy bed. The marshmallows begin to massage your shoulder and back and you feel the muscles in there just untangling. All the tension in your muscles are slowly disappearing as your back and shoulders are being massaged by the marshmallows. You feel very comfortable and relaxed.

After a while, you open your eyes and stand up. You walk past the soft marshmallows and you head towards a field made of very powdery snow. When you come near, you realize that the snow smells like your favorite cereal, so you taste a little bit and are very surprised. The snow looks like snow but it is very tasty. You smile and you lie down in order to make a snow angel. You close your eyes and take a refreshing breath through your nose. The air smells like your favorite cereal, and you breathe out through your nose. You do these five more times, and each time you do this, you flap your arms and legs to slowly make a snow angel.

Afterwards, you start to feel a bit cold, so you stand up and see a coat made of waffles in the ground. When you wear it, it instantly warms your entire body, and you feel a warm, calming sensation in your chest, shoulders, and arms. After feeling the warmth slowly spread throughout your body, you hear a laughter at the distance. You run towards the sound and find a laughing child and your favorite animal tossing snowballs at each other. They call you to come play with them, and you quickly run towards them. You form a very big snowball and you hit the child, but after the child trips down, you then get hit by a snowball made by your favorite animal and all of you laugh.

Afterwards, you look up to the sky and see snowflakes made of different gems and metal. Some were golden in color, others were made of diamonds, and some were all sorts of colors that you could think of. All three of you decide to pick your favorite color among the falling snowflakes. After a while, you notice that the sun is already setting, and that it was slowly getting colder. Your neck feels especially cold, so your friends quickly knit up a scarf made from your favorite snowflakes and it warms up your neck very well. You close your eyes and breathe slowly, feeling the warmth hugging your neck and spreading upwards to your head and to the tip of your ears. Your friends also made themselves their own scarves and you all stand in comfortable warmth.

Later, you notice a bright orange glow not far from where you are standing. You go there and find a fire that was warm but never hot. You try to come closer to see if it would get hot, but it never did. It was just a pleasant orange warmth. You slowly poked a finger to the fire and was surprised to notice that the fire did not burn at all. All three of you decided to sit down around the fire and place your hands inside it. It was very warm and very relaxing, and the fire changed color depending on what you wanted it to be. The fire slowly creeps up your clothes, but it never burned. It just felt very warm, and it slowly covered you in a very cool looking bright fire that never burned your skin or your clothes. The fire also smelled like your favorite shampoo. You close your eyes and inhale the smell, and when you opened them, you found the door to your bedroom in front of you.

You slowly opened the door and you found yourself inside your bedroom. The bed felt very inviting as you had such a long and fun day. You laid down your bed. Slowly, you take in five breaths and you very gently open your eyes to find yourself back in the real world. You feel every part of your body relax and you take one last deep breath before standing up with a smile from all the fun you experienced.

A Script for Exams

Find a place in your house or anywhere else where you can freely be alone. The place should ideally be quiet and free from as much clutter as possible. Find a spot where you can sit down with your legs crossed. Try to bring a cushion so you will be more comfortable as you sit. If you are doing this in your room, try to clean your room first by putting everything in place. Your goal should be to have as much space and as few distractions as possible.

As you sit down, slowly close your eyes and try to imagine that all your weight is concentrated in a ball somewhere inside your abdomen. Imagine that the weight of your head is slowly melting down to your shoulders, and that in turn melts down to your chest until all these collects and forms a heavy ball at the center of your abdomen. Focus your mind on that particular center. As you imagine this, breathe slowly and allow your hands to gently fall in place on top of your lap. Try to imagine that all the weight from your shoulder, arms, and head have all been transferred to that center, and all that is left is lightness.

Take a moment to pat yourself in the back. You are doing this because you are dedicated, you have a goal, and you are committed to do whatever it takes to reach that. Thank yourself for being strong enough to not turn away from the stress that you are feeling. Congratulate yourself that you are trying your best to face that. It might be that you are struggling to concentrate for your studies, or you are simply overwhelmed by everything that you have to memorize and learn for your exam. It might be that you are feeling pressured to get a high score, or to simply not fail. Whatever your reason maybe, do not worry. You are here, you are doing something to help you achieve your goal, and that is all that matters.

Through your nose, inhale very slowly, hold your breath for five seconds, and slowly exhale though your mouth. Do these five more times as you repeat these words inside your head: "I will succeed. This stress will soon go away". Feel each breath as the air passes through you. Every breath that you take places you more firmly into the floor. You are becoming more stable. You are becoming safer. Nothing can harm you. Nothing can scare you. You will succeed.

Acknowledge your own presence. Feel the air that is passing through you. You are making the air pass through you. You are here. You are being committed. You are being strong. You are not the problem. The problem is the way you look at your studying, at the way you look at your exam. But you can change this. You will change this.

Imagine a cactus in front of you. Try to visualize what a cactus looks like for you. How big is it? Does it have a flower? What is its color? How spiky is it? Are the spikes thin or thick? Try to fill in as much details as you can on the cactus. Engage all of your senses in recreating it inside your head. When you put your nose close to it, does it smell nice? Think of all these sensations and relate it to the cactus. Visualize your own interactions with it. Imagine touching it. How does it feel? It hurts, right?

Now, gently shift your focus from the cactus to yourself. Imagine that the cactus is slowly floating away, and in front of you, you see yourself. What do you look like? Recreate your entire body inside your mind with as much details as you can. What is the color of your hair? What about your eyes? Can you try counting how many teeth you can see when you smile? How do you think do you smell like? Do you have any scars or birthmarks on your body? Try looking at them intently.

Imagine that you can see your eyes are projecting all of y our thoughts and worries like a movie. Can you see yourself stressing over the exam? Now try to look at the background of that movie. You see other people, right? You see classmates, you see other students, you even see your teachers and your parents. You are not alone in this movie, right?

Blur out yourself from the movie and slowly focus on the people at the background. What do you think is your seatmate thinking about? Try to picture him/her out inside your head and see whether or not he/she is feeling stressed about the exam too. What can you possible say to him/her to lessen that stress?

Continue breathing, taking in air very slowly and exhaling it through your mouth. You see, you are not alone in the movie. You are not alone in this exam, and you are not the only student in the world that is feeling stressed right now because of it.

Breathe in through your nose. Hold your breath for eight seconds. Exhale through your mouth very slowly. Imagine that every breath you take adds confidence to yourself. Now, imagine that every breath you exhale adds confidence to others: to your classmates, friends, and all the other students in the world that are feeling stressed right now for the exam. Imagine that every time you breathe, your body becomes lighter and lighter. The heavy ball at the center of your stomach is slowly melting through your skin and evaporating like mist. You are not alone in this. You will succeed.

Now visualize that you are back inside your classroom and your test paper is already in your desk. Take a deep breath, exhale, and slowly run your hands over the sheet of paper. This exam is just a sheet of paper. Imagine picking it up and letting a strong breeze carry it away. A light, sheet of paper. You are not alone. You are safe. You can succeed in this.

Gently open your eyes. Take a deep breath, and slowly stand up.

A Flower in the Mud

Imagine that you are a flower. Try to visualize your favorite type of flower. What color is it? How does it smell like? Imagine that you are this flower. Your feet are slowly growing roots. You are stuck firmly in the ground, and nothing can pull you out. Imagine the feeling of mud as it slowly rises up, first up to your knees, and later up to your neck. When you look up, you see the sky.

The sun is shining very brightly, but it is not hot. You feel the cool breeze gently touching your face. But your body cannot move. You are stuck inside this pool of mud. You want to rise above this mud. You want your body and not just your face to feel the cool breeze, to feel the warmth of the bright sun. You want to grow up, up above all this mud, and bask under the warmth and the breeze.

Slowly, imagine that your roots are spreading outwards, digging even deeper into the earth. Take a deep breath. Slowly take in air through your nose and exhale it through your mouth. Every time you inhale, imagine that your roots are taking in nutrients from the earth. The nutrients flow from the base of your feet up towards your head. It feels like being dipped in a warm bath. The nutrients relax your muscles as it covers them with comfortable warmth.

Every time you exhale, imagine that your body, your stem, is slowly growing up. Your roots take in the nutrients as you inhale, and your body stretches past the mud as you exhale. Your stem grows taller and taller. The mud is now at your waist. Imagine waving your arms to the cool breeze. They are green leave. Your head is the flower. The warm sunlight is embracing the flower and its leaves. You breathe in and out again, each time you become taller and taller. Now, the mud is only up to your knees. Your waist feels the cool breeze and the warm sun, and you gently smile as every breath bring in more nutrient for you to grow taller.

Now, you are standing above the mud. Your roots re still keeping you in place, but your entire body is already above ground. You sway with the gentle breeze and you tilt your head upwards, so your petals can catch the warmth of the sun. You are beautiful, colorful, fragrant, and free.

Imagine that people are passing by you, and every time they see you, they stop and marvel at how beautiful your petals are. Your determination to grow out of the mud made you free, made you experience the sun and the breeze, made everyone smile as they pass by you because they could not help it. You are standing tall. You are beautiful. You are determined. You have succeeded.

Very gently, you smile, then open your eyes.

General Muscle Relaxation Script

In this exercise, you will be tensing and relaxing the different muscle groups in your body in a systematic manner as you meditate. Try to find a place where you can be comfortable in, preferably somewhere quiet. With this exercise, you may choose to either open or close your eyes. Before doing this, try to tense up some of your muscles throughout your body. It can be your hands, or your arms, or the muscles in your stomach. Try to tense them and be aware of how it feels when they are fully tensed. Alternatively, you may also try to tense muscles but only very gently, just enough that you are feeling a slight tugging in them.

Start by taking deep, slow breaths. Pay attention to your breath as it flows from your nose down to your chest and finally in your abdomen. Let it sit there for five seconds, then very slowly, exhale through your mouth. As you do this, check-up on your current thoughts and emotional state. What is it that you are thinking most about today? What have you been feeling these past few days? Pay close attention to these things. Acknowledge that you are indeed thinking about them. Now, very gently, imagine that each time you exhale, one of these thoughts or emotions is being flushed out from your body. Do this until you can feel a comfortable silence in your mind. Your goal should be to only think about your breathing.

Next, slowly tense the muscles in your right forearm while making a fist with your right hand. Allow the rest of the arm to stay relaxed. Try doing this over and over until you can reach this balance. Feel the sensation of tensing your forearm and hand. Compare this feeling with the feeling of relaxation in your other arm, and throughout your body. Imagine that you are isolating all the tension in your body into just these muscles, leaving the rest of your body free and relaxed. When you feel that you are ready, inhale slowly through your nose, and exhale very gently through your mouth. As you exhale, imagine that the tension you built up in your right arm is slowly being released. Imagine the tension as water, and that every time you exhale, your arm is slowly leaking out this water until it is empty and relaxed. Pay attention to your now relaxed right arm. How does it feel now that it is free from so much tension? Repeat this entire process with your left forearm and fist. Do this again on any part of your body until you feel calm and relaxed.

Chapter 8. Traits You Will Pick Up from Practicing Mindfulness Meditation

In addition to the numerous benefits of mindfulness meditation for your body and mind, there are various positive personality traits that you will pick up as your practice regularly and diligently. Let us look at some of these traits:

Living in the Moment

Living in the moment and fully immersed in the experience of life is the most wonderful trait you will develop with mindfulness meditation. The benefits of living in the moment are many including:

Having a rich life experience - Most of us are scared to let go of our thoughts and regrets from our past or our dreams for the future because there is a misconception that by doing so, we will become unemotional and, perhaps, an automaton instead of being human. The irony is this; when we live in the past or in the future, we leave a large part of our life experience in an unreal environment.

The only reality is the present moment and if we can put our entire body and mind in this present moment, then the emotional, spiritual, physical, and other human experiences become more powerful and richer than before. We end up leading a fuller life with mindfulness meditation than without it.

Focusing on the most important thing – By living in the moment, our energies are used in the most optimal way so that we can give our best and focus on the most important thing in our life; the present moment. What we do in the present decides our future. So, instead of living in a nebulous future, create a robust one by living fully in the tangible present.

Building better rapport – Living in the moment means you are completely connected with the people who are with you right now and right here. Your body and mind are focused on them which enhances the connection and rapport; the bedrock of any successful relationship. Being present in the moment means you are with your partner in mind and spirit, and paying attention to his or her every nuance of communication. Therefore, living in the moment helps you build strong and powerful relationships.

Mindfulness meditation helps you build and develop this crucial trait of living in the moment and leveraging its varied benefits that affect all aspects of your life positively.

Non-Judging

Being judgmental about everything and everyone around you results in plenty of needless hatred. Every time you feel, touch, see, hear, or sense anything, you are so habituated into deciding whether you like the sensation or not, that you are driven to form a judgment which, in turn, creates stress and anxiety. It is liberating to simply feel and sense life around you without judgment. Mindfulness meditation facilitates the building of a non-judgmental personality. The benefits are huge including:

It opens your body and mind to new experiences – Look back at your life and ask yourself how many times you have chosen to say no to things because you have formed a predetermined idea that you are 'not going to like it.' If you leave out judgment, you will see a rise in the number of new experiences that promise to bring you joy, pleasure, and happiness if you can avoid being foolishly blind.

Improved relationships with people – When you choose not to judge and just be there for your friends and loved ones, the quality of your relationships and friendships will improve. People will open up with you knowing that you are not going to judge them, and they will confide in you without feeling guilty about their actions.

Your friends will be willing to share their deepest thoughts with you safe in the knowledge that you will not ridicule them. All this openness with people in your life will result in improved quality of relationships with enhanced intimacy, love, and affection.

Improved sense of spirituality – Being free of judgments liberates you and helps you become more spiritual and open to giving and receiving love from the divine and also from people around you. Your sense of compassion improves significantly and you will be able to forgive yourself and other people more easily than before resulting in your spirituality rising up a few notches.

Happy person – The liberation from the stress of having to label everything and everyone around as good, bad, average, right, wrong, or in any other way is so powerful that you become a happier person than when you were a judgmental individual. The complexities and complications of putting people and things in various predetermined places does not weigh you down anymore making you feel light, happy, and joyous.

Additionally, your ability to remain non-judgmental will free you of the burden associated with the worries of what other people think of you. You become resilient to criticism and take them constructively without getting emotionally attached. Instead, you use those criticisms wisely to improve yourself.

Understanding the Nature of Thought

Our thoughts flow like the wheel of an endlessly moving mill. Sometimes, we feel we can control our thoughts and sometimes, it seems impossible to control them. Sometimes, you seem to be able to discern between one thought and another, and sometimes, the thoughts seem to be like a big baggage of complexities thrown together with no order or rhythm.

Simply put, thoughts are like little conversations that go on endlessly in our heads. They are opinions, understandings, ideas, emotions, and everything else that keeps taking place in our heads with or without our knowledge. As we keep focusing on the flow of our thoughts during mindfulness meditation, we will slowly but surely develop the power to understand the true nature of our thoughts. We will be able to see how easy it is for our thoughts to control the way we behave because we will notice that our thoughts drive our emotions which, in turn, drive our actions.

As we progress in the intensity of our meditation, we will understand the true nature of thoughts and emotions. We will realize that our mind which forms these thoughts can be manipulated to form different thoughts for the same situation.

For example, if you have failed in an endeavor, the first instinctive thought would be related to emotions of sadness and regret for having failed. Your behavior will reflect these emotions, and you will begin to look for reasons to fail including finding people and things to blame.

However, if you paused for a little while, and took a couple of deep breaths, and directed your mind to think of the learning and knowledge you received from the failed endeavor or then the emotions will be quite different despite the situation not changing. This is only a small example of how powerful the mind is when it comes to directing our thoughts in the way we want it to.

Mindfulness meditation helps you manage your thoughts without succumbing to the associated emotions. It empowers you to teach your mind to think differently so that your behavior is not negatively impacted. With continuous practice of mindfulness meditation, you will discern the true nature of thought empowering you to manage, control, and transform them for your advantage rather than your disadvantage.

Developing Focus & Discipline

Mindfulness meditation helps you develop focus and discipline. The reality is that all of us are capable of focus and discipline because the modern-day life calls for these elements willingly or unwillingly.

We have to get to work on time. We have to get to the station on time to catch the train. We have to reach the airport on time to ensure we don't miss the flight for an important meeting. We have to get the kids to reach school on time. And, many, many more instances of contemporary modern life make us stay focused and disciplined whether we like it or not.

With mindfulness meditation, focus and discipline can almost become second nature to you, and then, there will be no situation where you will not like to be focused and disciplined. So, how does mindfulness meditation sharpen your focus and discipline?

For every meditation session, you rely on your discipline to sit at the allocated place in the allocated time to prepare yourself for the session. You use focus and discipline to remain as still as possible as you focus on your breath or any other chosen anchor.

Each time your mind wanders, you employ the powers of your focus to bring it back to the present moment. Each time a judgment forms in your mind about a particular thought, you use your focus and discipline to ignore it, and compel yourself to remain a witness to the thought.

Mindfulness meditation helps to clear the clutter from your mind freeing it of wasteful thoughts so that your power to focus on productive work improves. Mindfulness meditation requires tremendous focus and discipline to practice consistently, and as you keep practicing, these elements become more powerful just as the strength of your muscles increases as you keep exercising.

Self-Awareness

Self-awareness is the ability to delve deep within yourself to connect with your true self. It goes beyond knowing your likes and dislikes, understanding what kind of skin you have or what kind of personality you have.

Self-awareness is knowing our core emotional, spiritual, and physical self. Why is self-awareness so important? Because it helps us understand what our body, mind, and spirit truly want to live a completely fulfilling and meaningful life. Self-awareness is also a complete acceptance of who and how we are without judgment. It helps us understand how and why we behave in a particular way in any given situation and also gives us insights into how we can change ourselves for the better.

Meditation is the perfect solution to increase self-awareness. As you focus on your thoughts, emotions, and feelings, and peel them layer by layer, you will be able to see yourself for what you truly are – with absolute zero judgment.

For example, suppose you are at a loud party, and you appear to be enjoying yourself with dance, drink, and food. The external atmosphere could be driving you to enjoy the party. Move away from the noise, people, and the electrifying atmosphere of the party, and ask yourself, "Are you really happy in this place?" The answer you get in the silence without the effects of the external atmosphere and from the depths of your heart will be as close to the truth as possible.

Mindfulness meditation in a quiet and peaceful place will help you truly understand what your heart and mind want. Being happy or sad is easy for everyone. Knowing exactly what gave you happiness or sadness requires self-awareness. As your self-awareness increases, you can navigate our behaviors and actions more towards what is good for you and less towards what is not.

During mindfulness meditation, you learn to observe and track your strengths and weaknesses in an objective way which increases your self-awareness significantly. Other benefits of self-awareness include:

Being at peace with ourselves – When you observe and accept yourselves for what you truly are, you are at peace with yourselves. You clearly understand the reasons for your sadness, happiness, and other emotions, and find ways to align your body and mind to the situation.

Improved clarity in communication - As your self-awareness increases and you understand yourself better, you will able to articulate your thoughts in a much better way than otherwise. Your own clarity is passed on via the power of communication and speech.

Improved decision-making capabilities – Knowing your true self will help you make the right kind of choices that are aligned with your core values and principles. You will find it easy to quickly decide whether something or someone is suitable for you or not.

Clarity of your life purpose – When you become self-aware, you know the exact direction you need to take to achieve your life purpose. Increased self-awareness clears up the pathway and shows you exactly where you want to be and what you want to achieve.

Mindfulness meditation is a fabulous way to improve self-awareness and take advantage of all the benefits of knowing yourself truly well.

In this chapter, you learned crucial personality traits that you will develop through the continued practice of mindfulness meditation. You learned about how mindfulness meditation helps you:

- To live in the moment for an enriching, immersive, and fulfilling life

- To become non-judgmental so that you can learn from all kinds of experiences in your life

- To understanding and interpret the true nature of your thoughts so that you can transform them for your benefit

- To develop focus & discipline resulting in increased efficiency and productivity

- To be self-aware so that you can follow your dreams and life purposes in a way that suits you best.

Chapter 9. How to Increase Focus with Mindfulness Meditation

Let's start by trying to understand what focus actually is. Focus can be generally defined as the act of paying attention to what is necessary (important) while avoiding what is unnecessary (unimportant). In this chapter, we will look at focus in the context of our day-to-day mental activities (more commonly known as "work"). We will get a glance of what it feels like to have complete focus, how it can improve our lives, some of the common reasons people lose focus and finally, how mindfulness can help improve our focus levels.

What a focused mind feels like

Have you ever seen a laser in real life? A proper laser can emit light so focused that it can cut through solid steel! On the other hand, a bulb also emits light but can hardly burn anything, much less cut through steel. This is the difference between a focused mind and a distracted mind.

A focused mind has the ability to process information, filter out unnecessary options and get to the goal in the fastest route possible. It is very similar to the phenomenon of "flow" or "tunnel vision" or "being in the zone".

Benefits of Having Focus

I don't think you need to be sold on the importance of having focus. If you are already convinced about this, I suggest you skip to the next section. However, if you're curious about what practical benefits focus can bring to your life, here are a few you can get by building a ninja-like focus.

Benefit #1: You will get things done faster. Obviously, we're referring to the mental tasks and activities that you need to finish with your brain. Improving focus might not increase your deadlift capacity. But if you put in the time and effort to develop focus, you will slowly start noticing something strange. Other people tend to take much longer time to finish the same tasks than you. Also, what seems easy to you will appear like a mammoth task to them.

Benefit #2: You will get better at problem solving. Human progress is measured by the scale of problems we are able to solve. The ancient man was able to solve the problem of food and staying warm. In the modern age, we have solved the problem of gravity i.e., going to the moon and beyond. All of this happened because we honed our problem-solving skills. With increased focus, you will be able to objectively define the problem, identify the issue and filter out irrelevant fixes to end up at the right solution. This process involves a lot of critical analysis and paying attention to what is required and ignoring what's not. Notice how this is precisely what focus is about, according to our stated definition.

Benefit #3: You will feel more positive. Getting more work done and possessing the ability to control your attention will make you happier. Nobody likes being distracted. Even more so when we know that we're supposed to be working on our tasks. By developing focus, not only can you finish your tasks faster, but you will also feel better for being able to evade and avoid distractions like a pro. This creates a positive feedback loop where you feel good for staying focused which develops your ability to stay focused which in turn makes you feel even better.

Why we lose focus

Attention is a depleting mental resource. There can be a lot of reasons for losing focus depending on your psychology and circumstances. Listed below are 2 of the most common reasons for losing focus in our day-to-day life.

Reason #1: Distractions

Studies have shown that will power and focus are actually finite resources. This means that the more distracted you are, the tougher it is to get your focus back. This is especially true in the current age of internet and social media. This goes to show that being exposed to distractions and social media in particular can be detrimental to our brain's performance when it comes to cognitively demanding tasks.

In his book Deep Work, author Cal Newport writes that the ability to focus on hard tasks is becoming increasingly rare and valuable at the same time. This means that the people who can figure out how to develop and maintain focus amidst the distractions will thrive in our economy.

Reason #2: Lack of energy

We have all experienced this. You can rarely focus on work when you're exhausted physically and/or mentally. Your brain needs high levels of oxygen and fuel to get the energy it needs to function properly. Although you can develop and maintain focus while being unhealthy, the best results are obtained when your body is physically fit. They don't say "A sound mind in a sound body" for nothing. A healthy body will produce the right levels of hormones to balance the stress of mental wear out. From personal experience, I can say that being physically fit by doing regular exercise has given me a natural boost in productivity and my ability to focus. In the book The Power of Full Engagement, authors Jim and Tony point out that the key to peak performance (both physical and mental) is energy management. High achievers balance energy expenditure with intermittent energy renewal through optimal relaxation. It pays to learn how to invest your energy well.

So, if you are able to spike your energy levels and avoid distractions, you will find that the intensity and duration of your focus increase rapidly.

How exactly Mindfulness can build your Focus

We have already understood that being distracted is one of the biggest reasons for losing focus. If you can eliminate distractions to your brain, you have effectively won half the battle. Here is how mindfulness can help you avoid and deal with distractions.

Think of your attention as a muscle. The more you train it, the better it gets. When you're being mindful, you practice living in the present moment. That means you're training your brain's neural network to prioritize paying attention to the current moment over the past or future(distractions). By repeatedly bringing your attention back to the present moment, you get good at avoiding distractions. The more mindful you are, the more focused you are on the present moment. This is in line with the definition of focus which is paying attention to the important and avoiding the unimportant.

Once you get good at mindfulness, you can translate that developed focus into any field. This is because you are still paying attention to the present moment but just different forms of it. Instead of paying attention to your breath, you will be paying attention to the object of work like a book or a presentation or a software.

A paper published in Psychiatry Research Neuroimaging Journal has shown that practicing mindfulness meditation leads to increase in the brain's gray matter density. For the unaware, gray matter is the part of the brain that handles various functions such as sensory perception, self-control, decision making etc. People with denser gray matter can learn better, memorize faster and most importantly, maintain focus on important tasks for much longer duration.

Bonus tips to increase Focus

Bonus Tip #1: Chew gum. Seriously. As mentioned on a podcast by Scientific American, chewing gum increases oxygen flow to your brain and also injects some insulin into your blood resulting in higher focus.

Bonus Tip #2: Find a line of work that is both interesting and important to you. This has to be genuinely passionate for you and demand your undivided attention. Otherwise, your brain activates a default network that switches your attention to other stimuli.

Bonus Tip #3: No more multi-tasking. One task at a time, fellas. In reality, our brain cannot pay attention to more than one thing at a time. So, people who think they are multi-tasking are actually switching their attention between different tasks rapidly. This has been shown to fray your brain out and reduce productivity levels.

Bonus Tip #4: Observe your body's natural energy rhythm and align your work accordingly. Your brain is usually very active just after breakfast and at dusk. So, schedule your heavy-lifting tasks during those times and maybe take a power-nap or go for a walk during the afternoon. Also, don't forget to take breaks in between work sessions, get ample sleep, eat nutritious food and exercise regularly for best results.

Chapter 10. Meditations for Everyday Life

Your brain is always rehearsing something. The more you say, "I hate my body" or "I'm dumb," the better your brain gets at believing that. The more you get angry in traffic or judge other people who look or sound different, the stronger that neural pathway gets. Your mind is like your social media feed. You get to decide what to block and what to follow. Whatever you follow will affect you (consciously or unconsciously) and influence how you see yourself and the world. Mindfulness lets you see and decide which habits you want to build and which you want to eliminate.

Finding Your Passion

One of the greatest joys in life is finding your own passion. It also happens to be a huge stressor, because you don't always know what you want to do, and you get a million messages about what you should or shouldn't do. Meditation can help you find some clarity about what you really love. It can also help with creativity, because you can let go of fixed ways of thinking and explore the world as it appears in that moment.

1. Find a comfortable posture and take a few deep breaths. Notice how it feels to breathe and be in your body.

2. Let your breathing be natural and focus on how you feel. Use your breath or sound as your anchor and rest your attention there.

3. When you're ready, let go of the anchor and allow your attention to be with whatever is predominant in your awareness.

4. If whatever you're noticing lasts for only a moment or two, just notice it and then let it go. But if it sticks around, try to pay attention to it as you would your breath, sound, or body sensations. See if you can be interested and curious about this experience just as it is. Notice it with all of your senses. What can you see, hear, smell, taste, and touch? What happens as you explore this stimulus?

5. When that sensation or stimulus disappears, come back to your anchor until another prominent experience arises for you to explore.

6. Once you've practiced this for a bit, you might gently ask yourself, "What do I really love to do? How does x or y make me feel? Is this something I want to work at no matter what anyone else says?" You don't have to try to answer these questions—let them be there and notice what happens as you bring them to mind. You can let them percolate for hours, days, or even weeks. See what arises when you don't need to force an answer.

7. As you finish, take a few more deep breaths and notice how you feel now.

AM I DOING THIS RIGHT?

Both finding your passion and meditation require a degree of letting go and trusting yourself. You don't have to know everything or have all the answers. It doesn't have to make sense. And it won't always feel all that nice. The idea is that you'll want to work at it because it makes a difference overall.

The Everyday Stuff Practice

You almost certainly have stuff in your life you'd rather not deal with. Doing chores, helping out with siblings, or working late—necessary tasks you'd prefer not to do. The key is to just do the activity, notice what your body feels like as you do it, and see if you can find something to be curious about, without adding resistance or commentary to it.

1. Wherever you are, take a moment to pause and recognize; then recognize and let go of any stories, judgments, or critiques.

2. Take a few deep breaths and let your body settle as much as possible.

3. Letting your breath be natural, place your attention in your body, particularly in your feet. Notice what it feels like to stand, even bending your knees a bit to feel more grounded.

4. As you engage in this everyday task at hand, try to keep your attention in your body, finding something to

hold your interest. It might be how the steering wheel feels beneath your fingers or how the lawn mower vibrates in your hands while you cut the grass.

5. Your mind will likely keep wanting to make a story out of this task ("Why do I have to do this? No one else is working this hard."). Try to let those thoughts come and go, then come back to the feeling of your body in this place.

6. If you start to get annoyed or frustrated with the people around you, you might try sending them some kind thoughts (here). Send yourself some, too, if you feel particularly stuck in negative thinking.

7. As you finish, take a few deep breaths and notice what it feels like to be free of your usual frustrations with this activity.

TAKE IT FURTHER

If you start doing this practice regularly, you'll notice the same stories or judgments come up a lot. So when you're standing in line somewhere, instead of getting caught up in the whole "Why is this taking so long? I always pick the wrong line" story, you can just notice that thought as a thought, and then come back to this present moment where all you are really doing is standing, feeling your feet on the ground, and breathing. This frees you from the unhelpful habits you didn't even know you were building.

Seeing Past Differences

No one sees the world the same way you do. Everyone gets their unique perspectives from their own beliefs, backgrounds, experiences, values, parents, education, and more, which is pretty incredible when you think about it. Your perspective is completely unique to you. And while most people do their best to be nonjudgmental about others, it can be hard to identify with people who have different backgrounds, look unfamiliar, or have different values.

This practice helps you recognize your own perspective. It helps you see some of the judgments you might not even know you're making about other people and lets you focus on the things that you have in common with people who seem different, rather than the things that divide you.

1. Find a posture that feels comfortable and take a few deep breaths, feeling the breath go in and out of your body.

2. Let the breath be natural.

3. Check out how your body and mind feel right now.

4. When you're ready, bring someone to mind who feels different from you. That might be based on how they look, act, or sound; a group they belong to at school; or simply what you think of them.

5. Try to let go of your thoughts about this person or interactions you've had. Instead, simply picture this person and consider what you both have in common as people. What makes you both human? Just like you, this person gets scared and lost, feels wonderful, doubts herself, wants to be happy, etc.

6. Say to yourself:

This person has feelings, thoughts, a body, and a mind . . . just like me.

This person is doing their best . . . just like me.

This person makes mistakes . . . just like me.

This person wants to be happy . . . just like me.

You can make up your own words or phrases that feel right for you. Focus on what you share with this person. What makes you both vulnerable human beings trying your best?

7. Notice if this person feels more real after making these connections. Perhaps instead of being "a bad guy," you now see someone who is a fallible human, just like you.

8. Explore how this feels in your mind and body as you take a few more deep breaths.

TAKE IT FURTHER

You can pair this practice with the next one to help you deal with difficult or challenging people in your life—for instance, that kid in your class or person at work who drives you wild. Or when your siblings or parents just don't get it. It helps you recognize some of your automatic judgments or reactions about others, so you can have more say in how you relate to people who are both similar to and different from you.

Dealing with Difficult People

Whether it's at school, at work, on the bus, or in your own household, there will always be difficult people: people who don't like how you look, how you talk, or what you're doing—regardless of anything you do or who you are. Maybe this is because they're unhappy. Maybe it's because it's a full moon. The truth is, it's about them, not about you. As RuPaul says, "What other people think of me is none of my business."

We want to protect ourselves from difficult people, yet it helps to see that they're also struggling, just like us. This creates compassion and connection.

1.Pause. Breathe. Notice how it feels to be in your body.

2.Explore all of your senses in this moment without needing to change or solve anything.

3.When you're ready, bring someone to mind who is a difficult person in your life right now, noticing what happens in your mind and body. Try to be gentle and compassionate with whatever occurs.

4.Pairing this practice with the previous one, Seeing Past Differences, notice what it's like to see this person as just another human being. Just like you, they feel lost, want love, and get confused.

5.Take a moment to recognize that, no matter what they are doing, it isn't about you. Even say aloud, "What they think of me is none of my business." That doesn't excuse pain they cause you, but it lets you get perspective. Their (wrong or hurtful) view of you doesn't diminish who you are.

6.Remind yourself that you can't control their actions, only your own response. You can notice what hurt feels like and then decide what you let affect you. (Feeling the hurt gently isn't the same as reacting to it or feeding it with angry thoughts.)

7. As you do this, come back to your body sensations and breath. Let those be your focus.

8. As you finish, take a few more breaths and notice how you feel.

9. When you're done, take a moment to either write down or consider aloud these questions: What do I need to do to care for myself? How does being with this person truly make me feel? Am I letting them dictate my emotions by reacting? What could I do when they start to really get to me?

BUDDY UP

At times, the healthiest thing is to protect yourself. A friend or family member can help with this. Talk to someone you trust in order to come up with a plan. Maybe you need to set boundaries or avoid the troublesome person. Maybe you choose to pause and feel your feet when a person you can't avoid gets to you. Sharing this with someone else helps you be compassionate with yourself and know you aren't alone.

Receiving Feedback

Getting feedback is a necessary part of your life. You get grades and test results at school, and evaluations at work, not to mention likes on social media. Yet it's likely no one has ever told you how to actually do this well. You're just supposed to be okay with whatever people tell you. Often, that's not easy at all.

The idea here is to take what's useful, discard what's not, and respond rather than react. A compliment becomes a gift. You can receive it and enjoy it without needing to keep getting more or basing who you are on what other people think of you. And a critique is an opportunity to use what's helpful and then reject any part that makes it a personal comment on who you are.

1. Take a few deep breaths. If you've received a compliment or critique, this helps you pause, break with your automatic reaction, and choose a different

response.

2.Let your breathing be natural. Feel your feet on the ground and the temperature of your skin.

3.If you've received a compliment, notice how it feels in your body. Experience what it's like to have something positive happen. Let yourself receive this compliment. If some part of you thinks you didn't deserve it, try to see that as only a thought and focus on—and feel—the good in your body with your senses. Soak it in as much as possible. You deserve it.

4.If you've received a critique, again pause and feel your feet on the ground. Concentrate on what's happening in your body, rather than any reaction in your mind. If it feels uncomfortable, can you notice how that discomfort feels without automatically reacting?

5.As you focus on your body, remind yourself that this isn't personal. It's not about you. Take in what's helpful in the feedback and then come back to your body. Ask yourself, "What can I learn from this? Can any of this help me once I've calmed down a bit?"

6. Explore any judgments about yourself or the other person as just thoughts coming and going.

7. If someone criticizes you personally, acknowledge that it isn't a helpful critique, but a verbal slap. Feel that discomfort in your body without reacting to it. Explore the Dealing with Difficult People practice to find a balanced response.

TAKE IT FURTHER

Sometimes, your brain needs to vent or share how it's reacting. There's a lot of momentum that comes up when you feel wronged. You don't have to ignore it. You can go for a run or write an angry letter, but don't send it—at least not until a day when you've cooled down to see if that's how you really want to respond.

Know Your Brain: Positive Neuroplasticity

With all the talk of stress and difficult emotions, it can seem like mindfulness focuses only on the negative. In fact, it's just as powerful to practice with the good stuff. Remember, the more your brain does a task, the stronger and more efficient the neural pathway for that task becomes. Whenever you notice contentedness, calm, peacefulness, delight, happiness, safety, comfort, or satisfaction, your brain gets better at recognizing them and making them a permanent fixture in your life.

Take time to focus on what you're good at, what you're capable of, and what you dream of doing. The more attention you pay to those moments, the more you'll notice them in the future. Every time you laugh with a friend, hear a good song, or eat something delicious, notice and savor those moments. Instead of focusing on how things could be different or what other people have that you don't, be mindful of what is working (you passed a test, assisted a goal, or helped a friend) and how you really are doing your best. Practice enjoying your achievements, even tiny ones like finishing a chapter in a book. You get to be in charge of growing your brain the way you want. Rather than thinking about meditation like medicine you take when you're sick, think of it like food that feeds your mind rather than your body.

Conclusion

Parents who take the time to teach their children mindfulness will notice benefits in their child's life, as well as their own. It teaches the ability to regulate emotions and form healthy social relationships. It can give them the self-esteem that they need to fight against mental bullies and the ability to understand their experience as it happens.

With all these things, your child will develop skills that can carry them through their entire lifetime. You might not be able to curb temper tantrums or emotional outbursts completely, but you will notice positive changes in your child.

Remember that mindfulness should be practiced regularly so that your child sees the most benefits from it. Only by practicing with you will your child have the instincts and skills to apply these exercises in difficult moments by themselves. Simply look forward to the wonderful development benefits that your child will see as they grow up. I hope your child enjoys these mindfulness exercises as much as my little girl. I do them with her all the time, and if I start to get too busy in my day, she reminds me!

Mindfulness is a great tool – all you have to do is use it. So what are you waiting for? Compile the exercises you want to use with your child and get to it! Mindfulness may not be able to solve all your problems, but it will sure put a dent in them!

Daily meditation practice can make you healthier, happier, and more successful than ever. Only a few minutes of meditation practice daily can help you lower stress, improve your mental and physical health, boost your focus and increase work productivity.

If you heard about meditation but don't know how to begin – or you have practiced meditation in the past, but need help to get started again, this beginner's meditation guidebook is for you.

Whether this is your first experience with meditation practice, or you have practiced before, this book will transform your relationship with yourself and the world around you. This book opens the door to a life lived in the freedom of your innermost being. We hope that this book is going to help you to find best method for mindfulness meditation, useful exercises and practices, good music suggestions for relaxation, stress relief and better sleep. We encourage you to try implementing meditation to your everyday life because we live in stressful time and our mental and physical health could depend on it.

www.ingramcontent.com/pod-product-compliance
Lightning Source LLC
Chambersburg PA
CBHW071552080526
44588CB00010B/878